THE INTERNET WEATHER

Balancing Continuous Change and Constant Truths

JAMES W. MOORE

John Wiley & Sons, Inc.

Published by John Wiley & Sons, Inc., New York.
Published simultaneously in Canada.

ISBN 0-471-06408-4

Printed in the United States of America.

10 9 8 7 6 5 4 3 2 1

Contents

Foreword

Like the weather, the Internet has become an integral part of our daily lives. Our physical atmosphere sustains life by providing water to drink and grow crops, but that same water in an atmosphere of a storm can reap great destruction. In just two decades, humans have created another atmosphere—the pervasive atmosphere of the Internet, which, for most of us, has become as much a part of our daily lives as the weather. It, too, has its storms, in the form of software glitches, disc crashes, and viruses that can put our business networks into a state of chaos.

But there's a critical difference between the physical and Internet atmospheres. The physical atmosphere operates on time and space scales that are comparable to the rates at which humans function. The Internet, on the other hand, operates at light speed, transferring data faster than humans can effectively process and manage it. Moore brings to light the myriad and complex ways that this accelerated pace has transformed our business and personal lives, and the values that have become increasingly precious to us.

Much like a meteorologist, Jim Moore has courageously predicted the future of Internet commerce and what it will take to be successful in this environment. He also offers insight as to how enlightened individuals will regain some of their lost time and privacy, create trust, and discern truth. *The Internet Weather* is essential reading for everyone living and working in the atmosphere of modern information technology.

Bob Serafin, Director Emeritus,
National Center for Atmospheric Research

Preface

What will work be like in the future?

I began asking myself this question in the early 1990s, when the Internet was still the domain of geeks and gadgeteers. Given who was using the Internet—graduate students, the "network" guy, and other high-tech researchers—I could not imagine the impact the Internet would soon have. Only recently, however, did I conceive a framework for understanding what will continue to be important, and what will always be ephemeral. I was surprised and intrigued, and then motivated to think about those things that will always be important.

Although futurists often try to predict the future of worklife by looking at how the Internet and technology have changed our lives, I now realize that it's far more useful—even essential—to view the future by examining those things that *don't* change: the human desires for time, truth, trust, and privacy. Adopting this point of view can help managers retain employees and improve their businesses.

Analogies are helpful in describing the impact of accelerating technology. We are surrounded by technology in the same way we are surrounded by the weather. As you go out in the weather, so you go out into the atmosphere of communication, data, and images. I have coined the term *Internet weather* to describe this phenomenon. It is difficult to chart navigational principles that lead to the future because they are obscured in the atmosphere of the technology surrounding us.

Unlike some other popular books on this subject, the perspective of this book is that we cannot view the future simply by examining all the changes around us. Rather, we need to view the future by *examining those things that do not change*. Time does not change. Nor does our desire for truth, trust, or privacy. Physical laws and the laws of economics do not change. By viewing the verities of time, truth, trust, and privacy through the invariant prism of economic laws, I arrive at some surprising and optimistic conclusions about the future: Corporations will organize themselves according to "principled agility," anonymity will become the ultimate luxury good, and individual sovereignty will become more important than becoming a traditional employee.

Despite considerable print to the contrary, there are no new laws of economics. Value is still defined by the balance of supply and demand. In this book I describe events that are the logical conclusion of these laws. For example, Gresham's law describes the relationship of devaluing currency to sound currencies: "Bad currency drives out good." When government printing presses churn out trillions of rubles or Weimar marks, these currencies flood the street, while gold, silver, and U.S. dollars are hoarded. So, too, the voluminous data surrounding us drive out good, journalistically vetted data. The overwhelming flow of data compromises truth, as described by a journalistic process or a scientific process of uncompromising peer review.

What is new, however, is the arrival of network effects with their peculiar economic alchemy. A network effect occurs when the future sale of product increases the value of product sold in the past. This effect is predominant in the areas of technology, software, and Internet economics, and helps explain the enormous wealth created in such short time frames. *Serial monopolies* are a result of this effect.

A companion of this economic alchemy is a dramatic acceleration of the pace of work. We have become chipmunks in a wheel of time, racing to keep pace, racing to achieve a serial monopoly. Our reward for keeping pace is yet more acceleration of the wheel. This acceleration, combined with the changing content of work from industrial production to knowledge production, places inordinate demands on the use of an essential finite good—the time we have. Many of us sense the increasing value of time. Time is now of such extraordinary value that it is measured in nanoseconds.

The Internet weather also causes a relative scarcity of privacy, trust, and truth. In this book, truth is defined in two ways: journalistically and scientifically. The journalistic process, which involves verification and fact checking, produces more truthful words than those of an Internet chat room. The scientific process requires replication and peer review to produce truth. As the Internet deluges us with words from hundreds of millions of voices, these kinds of truth become scarce. In this environment, the Internet data drives out good data, we hoard vetted and reproducible knowledge from trusted sources.

So, too, with trust. Electronic media, such as digital interfaces, sacrifices the intimacy of business and society that produces trust. Trust is under double assault from diminished truth and distanced interaction. In this environment, trust is becoming scarcer and more valuable.

Privacy has disappeared. We surrendered it before we even realized it was gone. In this environment, anonymity, the ability to move, to buy, to exist without a data trace, is becoming the ultimate luxury good. Because of the incredible value of privacy, anonymity is being produced as a luxury good, soon to become a mass-market product. Many other products, such as cruises, air travel, cars, and consumer electronics, have followed the same trajectory with a launch in the luxury segments that gradually moved to broader markets.

The dynamics of scarcity caused by the imbalance of supply and demand can increase the value of goods. As goods or services become scarce, their prices increase. As time, truth, trust, and privacy become scarce, they increase in value. In this way, new technology reinforces old values. Indeed, the Internet weather—the pervasive atmosphere of technology—exaggerates the value of verities. As their values increase, products will be created to provide more of each. In particular, behaviors that produce more of these scarce goods will be increasingly rewarded. The increasing value of time, of truth, of trust, and of privacy will have a profound impact on our businesses, careers, and relationships within our society.

These trends imply that work will be organized according to *principled agility*, which is a form of work and organization typified by the open sharing of information and the sovereignty of individual work. Principled agility is emerging in the high-tech world because it is the fastest way to work. The emergence has been Darwinian; the surviving companies are trimmed for movement and speed. To bind a weblike organization, overarching principles of trust, truth, and privacy become tantamount. At the same time, by adhering to this organizational style, a firm gains perpetual acceleration.

The X-generation (or the "net generation," to use a term coined by Don Tapscott) is entering the workforce with backgrounds, expectations, and capabilities that are widely different from any generation before it. They are entering a work world of evanescent job descriptions and unprecedented wealth as well as unprecedented insecurity and pace of change. To prosper despite these contradictory forces in the Internet weather, the X-generation must also adopt different behaviors from those of any previous generation.

The Internet Weather explores the impact of the changing and increasing value of time, truth, trust, and privacy on individuals and businesses. Truth, defined as journalistically reviewed text, or scientifically tested information, is compared to the devalued ruble. Each of these concepts is described with a memorable yet simple analogy. The increasing value of time is contrasted by comparing the agrarian life of a Russian peasant with the globe-trotting frenzy of an IPO road show. Trust is demonstrated with the Black Cabs of London, one of the most venerable institutions in the world. The thrust and parry of technology both assaults and assuages privacy. And privacy, in the form of anonymity, is described as a luxury good.

Businesses face the same issues as individuals. The accelerating pace of business cannot be avoided nor can it be controlled. Business, in the Internet weather, must get up and run. This acceleration has profound implications for the way they organize to achieve and sustain speed. The organizational style that is emerging is principled agility. Corporate privacy is a critical issue because a corporation does not have the opportunity for anonymity that an individual enjoys. And the netherworld of the Internet is creating a viral presence of bots—some friend, some foe, some neutral, and some nuisance. As our communication infrastructure becomes interwoven and internetworked, the bot-agents can become soldiers of business technoespionage. In this environment—an arcane environment of game theory, encryption, and digital certification—corporate privacy and corporate identity are set inexorably in conflict.

As with the weather itself, the surrounding atmosphere of technology is neither good nor bad. However, the impetus for the creation of this atmosphere of technology is nearly all good—the desire to communicate, to know, to explore, and to enrich ourselves.

I hope this book provokes thought and assists readers to examine what is important in the future. And I also hope that I have communicated my enthusiasm for evaluating the future in terms of the verities—time, truth, trust, and privacy—and for finding the balance between continuous change and constant truths.

JAMES W. MOORE

CHAPTER 1

Relevance in the Internet Age

The Internet has turned the world upside down: Failure is success; losing money makes money; and students hire their professors. We work like chipmunks in a wheel and are rewarded by an acceleration of the wheel. Why is this occurring? And what will the future hold? Increasingly, we are challenged to remain relevant; to remain current in an exponentially changing business and social climate. To remain relevant, we must project a future that is changing too quickly for easy assimilation.

My goal is to provide a viewpoint for examining these counter-intuitive events by considering those things that do not change, rather than attempting to encompass and comprehend the myriad changes wrought by technology each waking day.

Technology is impacting business, society, and individuals so rapidly that it is extremely difficult to keep up. Technology is changing the way we speak, the way we work, the way we manage our families, the relationship of nations, even the way we think. No one—not Microsoft, not IBM, not AOL—is exempt from the challenge of keeping pace. To be relevant, we need to forecast our roles in the future, yet the pace of technological change prevents predicting those changes.

So, if we cannot predict change, can we succeed by focusing on things that don't change? Our desire for privacy will not change. The amount of time each of us is given will not change. Our need for truth in communication will not change. Our need for trust in relationships will not change. Each of us, however, suspects that time, truth, trust, and privacy are becoming scarcer. Among the white noise of abundance, speed, and wealth, what has become of the face-to-face character of business? What has become of the Organization Man and the concept of a career? What has become of our privacy in our search for convenience? What has become of the vertically integrated firm, as free information dissolves hierarchy?

Given the unchanging law of supply and demand, how will the increasing scarcity of truth, trust, and privacy change their value?

Scarcity creates value, and as these verities become scarce, their value goes up. As we compete for the essential fixed commodity—time—it, too, assumes extraordinary value. It has been the history of humankind that as a good assumes more value, more of it is produced. Is this also true of time, truth, trust, and privacy? I believe the future holds both subtle and dramatic changes of behavior that will produce more of these scarce and fundamentally precious goods. To predict the future, ironically, do not look at the changes; look at the verities. Therein lies the key to finding our role and to remaining relevant.

Keeping faith in these navigational anchors can be difficult, especially when upside-down, counterintuitive, oxymoronic concepts (such as losing money to make money) routinely assault us.

During the dot.com boom, I was working with three very bright interns from Georgia Tech. I asked these college juniors about joining our firm after graduation. The students responded that my asking them was curious because they thought I was pretty sharp, too. *And they were wondering if I wanted to come work for them instead!*

It turns out they had started a dot-com during the summer of their freshman year. It had survived the first round of venture capital financing and had grown substantially during their sophomore year. Now, at the end of their junior year, they were being advised that it was ready to go public. They were going to New York the following week, along with their venture capital firm, to talk with Goldman Sachs about taking their company public in the next 10 to 12 months. The investment bankers at Goldman Sachs had recommended that the students dramatically increase their sales force and had advised them to look within the Big Five consulting firms. The students took the investment bankers literally, and since we were among the first senior people from a Big Five consulting firm they had met, we were, therefore, the objects of scrutiny for a job at the new dot-com.

Having students interview a corporate recruiter with the intent to hire the recruiter is shocking—at least to the recruiter. Our firm was one of the most desirable employers sought by college job placement offices. Our interview days on campuses were oversubscribed by factors of 10, and getting an interview has always been considered a prize. Yet, here we were, being interviewed for jobs by the very students we had wanted to work for us! This is an inversion of the way things are supposed to work. The world was upside down.

> **To view the future, we need to balance continuous change with constant truths.**

Upside-down events like this now occur with disorienting frequency. Fledgling firms went public and were advised to plan on losing money to increase their stock price and market valuation. The traditional wisdom dictates that stocks must be evaluated by multiples of earnings and cannot be valued by projecting losses. Failure in the dot-com world was a form of accomplishment. Individuals who have led a series of start-ups were highly valued in Silicon Valley. The experience of starting and failing was viewed as a sign of intrepid risk taking and even a form of courage—both necessary characteristics of leading a start-up. Losing money to increase stock price, or failure as accomplishment, seem upside down according to our traditional viewpoint. Is that viewpoint irrelevant?

For each of us, as well as for our firms, families, and governments, the future will be a constant search for relevance. To be relevant is to be pertinent, to be important, current, and involved. As change accelerates yet again and again, we all are challenged to keep pace—to understand how losing money can make money, how failing can be accomplishment, and how we must adjust our behaviors to benefit from changes.

Dramatic changes will occur every year for the foreseeable future. The changes are so vast and pervasive that there is a danger they will leapfrog beyond comprehension. The surface of an inflatable globe is a helpful image to comprehend the dimensions and pace of change. Imagine that our society and the technology that weaves it together are stamped on the surface of the globe like a logo. As the globe is inflated, the logo geometrically increases in size. Likewise, changes wrought by technology are inflating our globe faster and faster, with the result that the surface increases geometrically and expands in all directions. As you stand on such a surface, you change position even if you simply stand still because everything moves away from you at an accelerating rate. This analogy indicates only roughly the speed and expanse of the change around us because the changes are occurring, not just in two dimensions over the surface of the globe, but in hundreds of dimensions.

In such an environment, you need navigational anchors to evaluate your position within the multidimensions of change. It is no longer possible to anticipate the direction and scope of change because changes are too rapid and numerous. Navigating this change requires invariant compass points. To discover these compass points, I have returned to the concepts of time, truth, trust, and privacy. These concepts do not change. I have viewed them through the prism of economics, relying on the law of supply and demand, since that law, and the laws of science, also do not change. The questions I have asked myself are: Do I have less time? Does technology drive out truth? Does technology diminish trust? Do I have less privacy? Each of these already precious things—time, truth, trust, and privacy—will become yet more valuable. And, as they grow in value, there will be changes in behavior among us and among our businesses to produce more of these precious things. *Our values do not change, but our behaviors to enhance those values will change dramatically.*

We change jobs and change our residences to gain more time. We cocoon ourselves with caller ID, credit watch services, and rental mailboxes to recapture our privacy. We are more than suspicious of new Internet retailers, and it takes more effort and promotion for us to grant trust to new services.

We are surrounded by an atmosphere of data, images, and communication: the *Internet weather*. The term Internet weather broadly describes not only an electronic communications network, but also its surrounding envelope of technology. *Business-Week* called this envelope an "electronic skin."[1] This atmosphere of technology is being created by the convergence of computers, communications, miniaturization, and micromachines. The manifestations of this envelope are everywhere. *BusinessWeek* (January 17, 2000) reported on iMode from DoCoMo, the Japanese cell phone phenomenon that offers real time, continuous connection to the Internet on DoCoMo cell phones. Currently, anywhere else in the world, continuous connection to the Internet is available only by cable modem or high-speed digital telephony such as DSL. To have cell phones continuously connected to cell phones is a considerable advance in technology. As *BusinessWeek* states:

> Right now, I-Mode lets users perform all kinds of cool tricks. In Silicon Valley or Scandinavia, friends can't swap pictures of their pets on sleek, three-ounce cell phones. Japanese do that every day.

Household appliances provide other examples of information technology permeating our lives. On May 8, 1999, syndicated columnist Joseph Coleman published an article in the *Chicago Tribune* about the Matsushita Home Information Infrastructure.[2] According to the article, this Home Infrastructure converts virtually the entire home into an information appliance. Coleman's third paragraph reads:

> The house burst with little high tech perks. Lights go on by themselves when someone enters the room. The toilet weighs you, monitors body fat and measures the sugar in your urine. . . .

In this home, data servers manage information provided to them by all the appliances of the house, and the entire home is bathed in infrared radiation to monitor movement regardless of lighting conditions. Miniature cameras continually record the events of the house. The cameras are equipped with enough disk storage to record and file a lifetime of activity within the house.

The January 2000 Consumer Electronics Show, held in Las Vegas, demonstrated refrigerators that monitor their own contents, taking continual inventory and notifying the owner of expiring codes on food. Each refrigerator contains a video display terminal and Internet connection that can be hooked to a grocery store to reorder food. There are also microwaves with embedded video display terminals and Internet connections.

The Internet atmosphere does not stop when we leave home. While in our cars, we can now link to the world, send and receive faxes, or stay connected to the broad electronic community via our cell phones and Palm Pilots. Each day, as we move, eat, use the telephone, purchase gas, purchase anything, we leave an electronic trail. This trace of our existence is then used to improve and target services for us.

Even independent, freedom-loving truck drivers are now linked to the world with electronic umbilical cords. Up until the early 1990s, truck drivers were referred to as the "kings of the road." Truck driving was a job uniquely without supervision. There was no real way for a driver and his management to communicate while the truck was on the road. The rules of communication were generally pretty simple: Call when empty, or call dispatch once a day. Otherwise, a truck driver was left alone to drive and to stop wherever he wished, whenever he wished. Then came various satellite technologies that could locate a truck in real time and provide short two-way messages. Using this wireless technology, the management of a truck driver could actually view the progress of the truck in real time on a computerized graphic of U.S. highways. As the 1990s progressed, such messaging technology improved, and there are now several competing wireless technologies that can locate and communicate with a truck as it moves down the highway. Included in these technologies are electronic time clocks that can track time on duty and prepare a record of this time. Formerly, most drivers approximated on-duty time if they had exceeded the number of hours they were allowed behind the wheel because such approximation could mean being able to go home instead of having to stay out for another night. For example, a run that normally consumed nine hours for a round trip and returned a driver home, could sometimes take ten and a quarter hours. A driver would generally round off the quarter hour in order to go home. The electronic device is remorseless and always precise. Now the driver must shut the truck down within 15 minutes of home. The former king of the road, with a great deal of discretion about his work flow, has lost his crown.

Although the term Internet is used to describe this massive envelope of technology, much more is involved. We are experiencing a massive convergence of all technologies—telephony, computing, video, materials science, genetics—indeed, all knowledge, in all dimensions. It is said that knowledge now doubles each year. Things are no longer things, they are becoming information appliances. As demonstrated in Matsushita's Interactive House of the Future, the toilet and the refrigerator are information appliances. The toilet provides blood chemistry, pulse, blood pressure, and other vital medical information, and is to be linked, via the Internet, to the user's doctor. The refrigerator is designed to sense the inventory of food within it, reorder appropriately from the grocer, and hook itself to the power company to report on its power consumption. With such information, the power company can profile the most energy-efficient use of the refrigerator, or partner with an appliance manufacturer to recommend the optimum replacement of the refrigerator. Thus, the information about a thing, or the information that can be derived from a thing is becoming more valuable than the thing itself.

Truthful communication can be drowned by the speed and volume of data and images.

Much good comes with the increasing power of technology. Yet too much communication, too fast, can become confusing. The ease of communication is the first, and most obvious, change wrought by technology. Beginning with the popularity of CNN, and now extending to our homes via Internet streaming video, we can experience instantaneous observations of the world. The increasing power of computers and communications facilitates communication among us, and among the greater world community. The convergence of communications, computers, and data transmission technology makes possible nearly magical capabilities to view, as a spectator, world events at the precise time they are occurring.

The sheer volume of data and images can be overpowering. The startling images of the Patriot missiles used in the 1991 Gulf War provide a dramatic example of watching world events in real time. Hundreds of millions of people watched as CNN showed the missiles arcing into the black night sky. Minutes later, we saw tremendous fireworks as the Patriots destroyed inbound Scud missiles on reentry to the atmosphere. Such reentry occurs about 8 to 9 miles in the air, and the closing velocity of a Scud and a Patriot missile is about 5,000 miles per hour. This virtuoso display of technology continued for several nights during the war and provided a sterling example of American scientific capability. The media gushed over the uncanny and magical accuracy of the Patriot, reported by U.S. Army reports to be more than 80 percent. A General Accounting Office (GAO) investigation of the accuracy of the Patriots a year later, however, discovered that the Patriot's kill rate could have been as low as 40 percent or even as low as 10 percent.[3] It turns out that the Iraqi Scuds were so poorly manufactured that they tended to self-destruct during reentry into the atmosphere.

Furthermore, the events were recorded against the blackness of a desert night, so it was easy to conclude that the Patriots were the cause of the explosion. For each Scud that exploded, there was at least one Patriot in the vicinity. The explosion took place some 7 or 8 miles from observation, and the closing velocity was equivalent to 80 miles in a second. At this speed, it would take only 10 seconds to travel from New York to Chicago. It is easy to see how the military, the media, and every individual who watched CNN concluded that the Patriot was responsible for the kill of the Scud. It was true that the Scuds exploded. It was not true that the Patriots nearly uniformly killed them.

Thus, we can be inundated with data and images that appear to be true. As we witness dramatic and rapidly accelerating development of tools and technology, can we be sure of our observations?

As this proliferating expanse of technology surrounds us, what criteria do we select for relying on some data sources and rejecting others? And, as technologies are spawned like pollen in the wind, how do we predict which of these novelties will last?

CNN viewers watched the Patriots in real time and concluded, with the military and with the press, that the Patriots were highly accurate. This observation and commentary occurred in real-time video. However, the complete analysis to discover a reliable, verified, and peer-reviewed statement of the accuracy took a full year. This event took place in a matter of seconds, beyond the capability of the human eye to judge depth and proximity of a Patriot to a Scud. If you don't believe me, spend some time looking at the lineup of airplanes in a landing pattern at night. There is no way to tell what kind of airplane is coming, even though some of them might be less than one mile away. The Patriot action took place 7 or 8 miles in the air, at night. The action of hitting a Scud missile with a Patriot missile has been compared to firing a needle from a rifle to hit the head of another needle (each moving at several hundred miles per hour), across a football field. To determine the success of the needle hitting another needle, we would need precise measuring devices. So, too, with the Patriots and the Scuds. To actually determine the Patriot kill rate, it was necessary to create a 3-D image by viewing radar images from several directions. The precise 3-D image was necessary because a Patriot could miss a Scud in any direction within a great proximate sphere of space surrounding the target. Then the trajectory of both Scud and Patriot had to be painstakingly determined in precise fractions of seconds to confirm the sequence of Patriot arrival within this killing sphere near the Scud (at 80 miles per second), then the Scud explosion.

If we cannot trust our own eyes, whose can we trust? How can we trust the hundreds of thousands of sources now flooding us with information?

As the sheer volume of data and images surrounds us in real time, we become pressed for the truth. As with the Patriot missiles, we can view images, in real time, on television, only to discover later that those images did not depict a factual event. A rumor can be repeated a million times within a minute as it is electronically distributed to the world. Thus are created "urban legends." In this environment, truth becomes yet scarcer and more valuable.

Throughout history, philosophers have debated the meaning of the word *truth*. In this book, I am focusing on truthful processes, not on trying to define the eternal verity, Truth. As data, images, and words are electronically spawned around us, we will value processes and tools that can help us sort through this volume. These processes must be able to validate an image, a word, an idea, or a fact and make it replicable.

Actually, there are two processes that do just that: journalistic editing and the scientific method. Such newspapers as *The New York Times* or *The Wall Street Journal* use an editorial process that requires checking every fact and double-verifying source material. Before a word or sentence appears in print within those august pages, it is subjected to verification and confirmation. Therefore, the information in these newspapers is more true than that found in an online chat room. Likewise, the scientific method requires replication of results. And scientific words are not published without significant peer review. This process also leads to words that are more true than the words in an online chat room.

Fact checking, verification, and peer review consume considerable time. So the real question becomes how much of one precious commodity—time—are we willing to invest to produce more of another precious commodity—truth? In this sense, truth is valued by the amount of time required to produce it.

> **The amount of time is fixed and constant; the demands for the use of time are exploding. Time, thereby, is becoming much more valuable.**

This valuation process also extends to time. Time is the essential fixed commodity. No matter what you do, you cannot create more time nor can you save more time. We all are pressed for time. Time moves by us, around us, and with us, at the same pace no matter what we do. Yet, today, we are given many more choices for the use of time. The workplace is becoming more flexible, and the character and the content of work is changing drastically. We are often required to add creative content and problem solving to our work product, thus adding to the time spent because *creativity cannot be scheduled.* If you have spent time trying to solve a riddle or a puzzle, you can appreciate the unpredictable arrival of creative insight. I admit that some 10 years after I scrambled it, I still have a jumbled Rubik's Cube on my dresser, awaiting the arrival of creative insight to align the colors. When our work involves debugging software, editing a presentation, planning a product launch, writing advertising, defending a legal action, or other such creative activity, the arrival of insight is unpredictable. Yet, we are usually working within defined deadlines, and the only way to coax the insight from our minds is to apply more time each day to the problem prior to the deadline day. This process usually ramps the hours spent per day dramatically upward as the deadline draws closer. Applying the law of supply and demand outlines the resulting impact on the value of time: the quantity of time is fixed; yet, the demands for using it are rapidly increasing. This relationship ratchets up the value of time, as most of us can innately sense.

As we move from being task workers to being knowledge workers, we increasingly do not report to a place of work having a defined schedule. There is no start time, no end time for our work. Yet, the rewards for being first with a product, with an idea, with a service, are magnified in this technological society. In many technology-intensive markets, the first-mover advantage is so compelling that there is no room for a second-place finisher; eBay is an example of this phenomenon. As this is written (August 2001), eBay commands more than 85 percent of the online consumer-to-consumer auction market. It was first, and, as such, has conquered this market. The success of eBay has produced a market capitalization of over $16 billion (August 2001), while all other competitors merely burned money and ate eBay's exhaust trail. To command markets in this way, speed is paramount. Or, to paraphrase Vince Lombardi, "Speed isn't everything, it is the *only thing.*" Thus, we spend more time working because speed to result is so much more important. Because we spend a few more hours per day creating our product, it arrives in the market first and creates the wealth of

Bill Gates. If we are late by a few weeks, we merely burn through a lot of money. This environment radically increases the demands for time. Work seeps into every free moment. The disturbing unsolved puzzle interrupts your cheering at your son's soccer game. In this environment, time—scarce, fleeting, unassigned time—becomes precious.

It is a paradox that we are surrounded by convenience, and yet are more pressed for time than ever. We have fast food, flex time, fax lines in cars as we commute, and services of every kind to make our lives simpler. As we have freed ourselves from the plow and the field, we have yoked ourselves to an accelerating treadmill of software, services, and creative content. The United States, the current leader in the cybereconomy, has the lengthiest average work year in the world. The average work year for an American is twice that of a Russian peasant of the late nineteenth century.

And what is true for an individual is even more true for a corporation. The cybereconomy crowns the swift; it punishes the good; it destroys the laggards. But, again, the laws of economics apply. Supply and demand still determine price. Economy of scale still provides increasing profit margins. Economy of scale leads to higher margins and potentially lower prices, and such scale for a software company can occur with the speed of light. Contrast, if you will, the manufacture of software and steel. A steel mill has a limited, fixed capacity and is designed to operate at a peak economy that ranges from about 85 to 90 percent utilization of its production. At that level, economy of scale can be considerable, since the production cost is spread over a greater volume of steel. Once the mill approaches 100 percent utilization, however, the costs of production dramatically increase. Overtime, maintenance, congestion, and many other cost elements begin to increase radically if the mill exceeds optimum production tonnage.

Software has no such limit. Once the design and coding of a software product has been completed, producing and distributing it has virtually no additional variable cost, since software can be produced by electronic replication and distributed over the Internet within seconds. With this dramatic time compression, there is no practical limit as to the number of copies, just as there is no practical limit for electronic distribution. Software is manufactured by replicating at the speed of light. It is then distributed anywhere in the world at electronic speed. The limiting factor for the delivery of software is less distance than the size of the electronic pipe being used for delivery. Thus for all practical purposes, software has infinite economy of scale. This leads to economic models of "serial monopoly," such as that enjoyed at one time by IBM, followed by Intel-Microsoft and Lotus, followed by Excel.[4] This kind of market leads to dramatic wealth for the fastest to market. As corporations seek to increase the value of their products using information technology, they cross the line into the world of speed over cost. And in this world, the value of each hour lost is incalculable.

> **The pervasive atmosphere of communication has taken privacy from individuals and businesses.**

As we feel pressed for time, so we are pressed for privacy. From our birth, each of us has initiated an electronic trail that becomes richer, deeper, and more accessible with time. This electronic record determines creditworthiness, entrance to colleges, and access to health care benefits. It is used to secure privilege and helps determine our status in society. This permanent record lays us bare. Our phones ring incessantly with telemarketing pitches provoked by personal data purchased from the credit card companies we use. Our electronic files can be linked to provide information about us without our knowledge or approval. Special cookies track our travels on the Internet and provide surprisingly precise profiles of our behaviors. These profiles have emerged from an accumulation of thousands of bytes of information, which have been merged with increasing technology to become millions, then billions of bytes specifically about us. When these profiles begin to describe our values, we have lost our privacy without knowing how or when. Often, our personal privacy is traded for a social good. For instance, some privacy is traded for the privilege of driving a car. Obtaining a driver's license requires the trading of private information about us, including our Social Security number.

Despite the intimidation of such an electronic skin, I can see several beneficial uses of the Matsushita's Home Information Infrastructure. For example, I could use this capability to watch over my mom. If her house were so wired, I could cue the cameras to watch out for actions indicating she is eating properly. All the electronic sensing devices in the house could allow me to monitor her blood pressure and other vital medical signs. In this case, I would have to negotiate with my mother regarding a trade-off between her privacy and her health.

As our privacy becomes scarcer, it assumes more value. We begin to trade some convenience and to spend money to assure our privacy. In addition to paying for unlisted telephone numbers, many of us have purchased products that prescreen telephone calls and only allow in certain known numbers. Hewlett-Packard has created a product called "DigitalMe," designed to shield a person's privacy while using the Internet.[5] As privacy becomes more and more valuable, the ultimate luxury good is anonymity. Indeed, a start-up company in Montreal, Zero Knowledge, is offering five pseudonyms for use on the Internet, at a fee of $50 per year. These pseudonyms, and all transactions sent or received by them, are completely untraceable. Zero Knowledge uses robust and modern encryption to protect communications on the Internet. In addition, the company uses a series of Internet servers that divide the electronic messages into separate, encrypted digital hash. A single stream of such hash could not be made intelligible, and each stream is protected by strong encryption. The design of this product is such that no one, including the system administrators at Zero Knowledge themselves, can re-create the original messages. The only one who can decode them is the sender. This makes this system impervious to any attempt to break it, even including a judicially ordered search. There is nothing to search except uncrackable digital hash. Imagine the beauty of complete anonymity over the Internet! Immediately, it comes to mind that women could freely use the Internet to meet men with no fear of stalking since it would be impossible to find out the woman's identity without her assent.

Privacy is a concern for individuals, but it is also a critical matter for corporations. A corporation has a special privacy challenge:

it cannot logically use a pseudonym. For many corporations, the value of their good name, their brand equity, is worth more than their physical and financial assets. The Coca-Cola Company is valued at $118 billion (August 2001), yet only has $7.4 billion in traditional book value (August 2001). So, how could Coca-Cola use pseudonyms to cloak its activities on the Internet? And should it? With electronic markets, and networking of information systems, a corporation's activities are becoming more and more transparent. In some markets, it may be possible for a competitor to view your activities in enough detail to construct a daily profit-and-loss statement of your firm.

Our free market in ideas and technology will lead to the creation of privacy products. Privacy will be bought and sold. Unlisted telephone numbers are but a small example of these products. Zero Knowledge is an example of a new product for providing privacy on the Internet. Initially, the cost of privacy will probably be high, due to great demand and limited supply. However, as these products are produced in greater (and networked) volume, the price will begin to fall.

The speed and electronic distance of technology diminishes trust.

As we trade time and, sometimes, money for privacy, so privacy is traded with trust. Most of us cherish our privacy. Some areas of our lives and elements of our thinking are closed to the public. We may share these areas with close friends, but only after we have established trust with them. Trust and privacy, then, are related, and valued in our homes like fine wine and precious gems. We unveil our privacy and trade privacy to develop and enhance trust. The Soviet Union, at the peak of state surveillance during the Stalinist era and during the era of police control of communication, was a stark example of the need for trust and privacy. Dissident writers, artists, and performers were censored and persecuted in public. Because of this, they developed trusted communities of colleagues. In the homes of these artists, ideas and expression were free and open once trust had been established.

Trust cannot be asserted: When we hear the words, "Trust me," our tendency is to do just the opposite. Most often that statement triggers increased wariness and an attitude of cautious wait-and-see. Because trust is founded on truth and actions, its development takes time. The time and contact necessary to establish trust is at odds with the pace and electronic distance of our methods of communication. And thus, the answer to my question, "Does technology diminish trust?" is "Probably so." At the same time, trust, as a trading partner value, is becoming more valuable. This will motivate considerable investment in creating or enhancing trust within products and services that use an Internet channel. Because time must be exchanged to achieve trust, and time is accelerating in value, trust will ride along, also accelerating in value.

Think of venerable institutions that have achieved the public trust. Very few are brand-new. When we think of trusted institutions, we think of the Salvation Army, the Red Cross, the Library of Congress. (I further think of the Black Cabs of London, discussed later in this book. The Black Cabs provide an interesting study because most of the features of the Black Cab service can now be replaced by relatively cheap technology.) These institutions have invested decades of consistency to achieve public trust.

Think of venerable corporations that have achieved the public trust: *The Wall Street Journal,* Lands' End, L.L.Bean, United Parcel Service, Federal Express, Charles Schwab. These firms have earned trust by long and consistent service.

All of these organizations have tradition, brand equity, and long service that protect their trusted position in our society. But what if you are E*TRADE, a brand-new stockbroker? How do you establish the trust that has accumulated over time for Merrill Lynch, Morgan Stanley, and other long-established firms? The challenge in today's market is to execute very quickly. The establishment of trust is inimical to speed. Individuals will be more challenged to find trustworthy services and sources in the future as services, sources, and products proliferate. In this context, trust will appreciate greatly in value. So these core goods—time, truth, trust, and privacy—will increase in value in the Internet weather, and products and services will be created to produce or own more of them.

In the Internet weather, what are we willing to exchange for our privacy? for more idle time? for more trust of our Internet trading partners? What are we willing to exchange for trusting someone?

The key navigational anchors of time, truth, trust, and privacy are used to express the character of people and firms and to establish the worth of someone or something. As we brave the Internet weather, we will make choices about the use of our time, according to those things we value most. If we value our privacy, we are willing to invest time to achieve more privacy or to protect the privacy we have. The example of the Patriot missiles in the Gulf War demonstrates that truth in communication often requires the investment of time. The Soviet dissidents who hoarded privacy and trust within the home, yet invested time with each other to create trust, demonstrate the investment and relationship of time and trust. It takes time to become trusted; it takes time to assure accuracy and truthfulness; it takes time to assure privacy. There are trade-offs here, and these trade-offs establish value.

Value is determined by what you are willing to trade. How much convenience in today's society are we willing to trade to achieve privacy? As our anchors of time, truth, trust, and privacy become more valuable, we will change our behaviors to own more of them. Very few of us will become hermits to protect our privacy. We will, however, change our behaviors to produce more of these anchoring values. This change in behavior can be subtle and at first unnoticeable, but over time, produces dramatic societal changes. The use of the Internet itself is a good example. In 1995, very few knowledge workers could easily work at home. Within a short span of six to seven years, it has become common for knowledge workers to have home offices. The small, subtle difference was the free provision of data and communication. The dramatic change is the numbers—millions—of persons who have been freed from place of work.

An interesting example of changing behavior caused by changing technology is the role of human memory. Prodigious feats of memory were required from time immemorial up to the invention of the printing press. Prior to Gutenberg's press, the transfer of knowledge by the written word was laborious, slow, and monopolized by the few who could both read and write. Thus, the preservation and propagation of knowledge relied on people's memory. Any businessperson, any lawyer, any doctor in the Medici court of Florence relied on memory to execute daily business. A Medici lawyer committed the code and the law to memory. A doctor would have memorized the medical scholarship and practice of the day. A businessperson would recall all transactions with a firm, and would have committed to memory all the law and practice necessary to execute daily business. Since the invention of the printing press, such feats of memory have experienced a long decline, and are now extremely rare, as noted in *The Discoverers* by Daniel Boorstin:

> Before the printed book, Memory ruled daily life and the occult learning, and fully deserved the name later applied to printing, the "art preservative of all arts." . . . For millennia personal Memory reigned over entertainment and information, over the perpetuation and perfection of crafts, the practice of commerce, the conduct of professions. By Memory and in Memory the fruits of education were garnered, preserved, and stored. Memory was an awesome faculty, which everyone had to cultivate, in ways, and for reasons we have long since forgotten. In the last five hundred years we see only pitiful relics of the empire and the power of Memory.[6]

While there remains a demand for information retrieval, there is little demand today for retrieving information from the memory of an individual. The printing press marked the decline of individual feats of memory and reduced the need for such feats. With mass-printed books, the supply of memory was overwhelming and more easily accessible to all. In addition, a printed book was not subject to the failings of memory and survived beyond an individual lifetime. All in all, the printing press created exponential increases in memory and dramatically improved the quality of this stored record. The demand for individuals to commit long texts to memory rapidly decreased. Today, how many of us can actually remember any text at all from either high school days or college?

In the case of memory, a new technology, the printing press, radically changed the behavior of people. We no longer memorialize our literature, our professions, our religion, and our commerce in the memories of individuals. We changed our behavior because the reward for feats of memory diminished. Eventually, no one (or very few) could claim a reward for feats of memory. Demand for this attribute withered in the face of exponential supply of superior printed material. Now we can access information from libraries, from online data warehouses, from the Internet, from books, from video and sound recordings, and myriad other sources. This access can be instantaneous and voluminous.

If the printing press changed the way we remember things, will the revolutionary technologies that brought us the Internet and its attendant Internet weather change other aspects of our behavior? How will the convergence of computers, communications, and video change the way we think, interact, and form communities?

As these products become available, we also will change our behaviors. We gave up our reliance on memory, a key characteristic of being human, because it decreased in value and was replaced by the superior goods of the printed word and electronic data storage and retrieval. We have always changed our behavior to acquire more value, and we will continue to do so. We will change, strangely enough, because our *fundamental way of valuing behavior has not changed*. We will change our behavior in startling and delightful ways to use time better, to have more privacy, to have easier access to truth, and to achieve trusted sources faster. This change in behavior as individuals and as a society will have profound and positive impact. Scarcity creates value, and we will behave more truthfully, more trustingly, and more openly because such behavior will have greater rewards.

The first generation to experience the full force of the Internet weather is currently in high school and college. For these young people, the abundance of wealth and opportunity has created new ways to behave. The anchoring values and new tools will change behavior also, by offering profoundly different careers and ways of organizing work.

> **The phenomenon of communication, data, and computing becoming free, and the verities' increasing value, will profoundly affect the way we organize our work.**

For the future, the extraordinary value of time itself, whether in our lives, or in our productive processes, will demand different behaviors. Foremost will be openness and candor. Firms will organize themselves according to what I call "principled agility." Principled agility will be created to increase the execution speed of firms. This organizational style will be characterized by candor, openness, trust, and individual sovereignty. Openness will be a standard feature, with firmwide information broadly shared among all, as it is produced. Candor in dealing with each other saves time in execution, and trust will be necessary in an increasingly interwoven world of shared production. The granting of individual sovereignty to members of the workforce—the ability to make decisions and take action based on current information—increases the speed of execution. This organization will look like a massive web of communication links with humans at the nodes of the web. This form of organization is by far faster than any hierarchical arrangement. Indeed, some organizations, such as Cisco, are beginning to look like a web of interactions. In this web, each individual is a node in a greater network of information and action. In such a world, the worker-citizens do not create careers; they will refer to their individual portfolios of work. The portfolio will include failures as well as successes, with failures being claimed much more proudly than in the past. The sovereign workers themselves will interact like tribes, moving as cohorts from organization to organization, bound to each other by trust, sharing, and openness. Only organizations that meet the standards of these bands of cohorts will attract and retain a workforce.

As the web of multinational firms and the Internet span the globe, sovereign workers will have more in common with each other than with many of their countrymen.

As these changes of behavior and technology accumulate around the world, we are creating a new, open community in cyberspace. This vast affinity grouping of peoples from all nations will assume some trappings of a cybernation, albeit without barriers to entry or immigration policies. This cyberspace nation will evolve as a medium of free speech, and have profound impacts on land-based nations. Our ability to purchase privacy will lead to our ability to privately enter and exit cyberspace at will. This nation is open to all, without bias. It is open to anyone, from anywhere, regardless of background. It is a nation of sacred privacy and of open, uncensored communication. It is a nation of freedom.

This is a book of discovery, forecasting an age of unlimited creativity and unlimited opportunity. The rapidly increasing technology around us actually confirms old values, in fact, makes these old values yet more important. And in this process, our behavior as societies will change to become more truthful, more trusting, more open, and more productive. But the rapid pace of technological change can, itself, be disorienting. We are pressed for time; we are pressed for privacy; we are pressed for reliable and trusted sources of information. Fundamentally, we are pressed for guidance—for navigation through the Internet weather.

Summary

One of the most daunting challenges of technology is remaining relevant. Is it important to stay abreast of the gadgets and delights of each new technology? Even if it were important, the pace of innovation and change makes such a task impossible. Rather than constantly focusing on those things that are changing, focus instead on those things that do not change. Economic laws do not change. Despite the Internet, there are no new laws of economics. Time, truth, trust, and privacy do not change, but the technological atmosphere greatly enhances their value. Relevance, then, comes from focusing on the increasing value of these verities, and taking action to produce more of them, to acquire more of them, and to share more of them.

People have responded to changing technology before by changing behaviors. One of the most profound changes in history has been the reduced dependence on rote memory that followed the invention of the printing press. As the printing press led to mass-produced books, the need for storytelling and information storage in human memory dramatically decreased. We changed our behavior in a pronounced way as technology provided cheaper, more permanent, and more accurate memory in the form of the printed word. By inference, we will change our behaviors in pronounced ways as technology changes the relative value of those behaviors. And the technology of pervasive communication that now surrounds us is yet more profound than the printing press.

The thesis for this book is that we must view the future in terms of traditional verities: time, truth, trust, and privacy. These verities are becoming increasingly valuable in relation to their increasing scarcity. Because they are growing in value, however, we will change our behaviors to produce more of them. By examining these never-changing values, we can position ourselves for continuing relevance.

Despite dizzying change around us, our human values do not change and will not change. There are no new laws of economics. The law of supply and demand still determines how we evaluate goods, services, and behaviors: The greater the supply, the lower the price, and the lower the supply, the greater the price. The most important corollary to the law of supply and demand is that *scarcity creates value*. As technology surrounds us, time, truth, trust, and privacy are becoming scarcer and thereby more valuable. At the same time, the sheer oversupply of data, telephony, and computing is devaluing these goods to zero.

As time, truth, trust, and privacy increase in value, we will change our behaviors to either own more or produce more of these verities. This book demonstrates how to invest in these increasing and sustaining values. Products, careers, and investment opportunities based on time, truth, trust, and privacy are not just likely to appear; *they must appear.*

The only way to understand and anticipate these changes is to view the future by examining those things that do not change.

CHAPTER 2

Winner Take All

The Economics of the Internet

By what alchemy does the raw intellect of software engineers become the vast fortunes of the Internet? Have we stumbled onto new laws of economics that describe, and prescribe, new relationships of markets? Have we stumbled onto new aspects of human behavior that combine in a magical and bountiful way? The answer is no; the Internet has not uncovered any new aspects of human behavior. Despite many common assertions about the "new economy," there are no new laws of economics. When we hear the words "new economics," we should immediately guard our wallets. We do have new marketing challenges, however: the speed of technology, the coincidence of network effect economics, and practically unlimited economy of scale.

Most historic product markets exhibit economy of scale in which the cost of production decreases per unit as more units are produced. This economy of scale has an upper bound due to such factors as shipping distance from customers, size of plants, and limitations on personnel. At a certain point, increases in these factors cause the marginal cost of production to creep upward. In many information technology markets, there is no effective limit to economy of scale. In particular, software can be reproduced at the speed of light and distributed electronically anywhere in the world for very little cost. This speed, and practically unlimited economy of scale for production are different from the traditional characteristics of steel, automobiles, clothing, and other consumer goods.

Information technology products also exhibit what is called the *network effect*, which is a form of economy of scale for *demand*. A network effect exists when the sale of a new product actually changes the value of products sold in the past. The value for a network effect is related to square of the number of users of the product and therefore increases rapidly. This kind of market—where a network effect exists, where economy of scale has no practical limit, and where distribution can be practically instantaneous—virtually assures a monopoly. These markets become winner take all. There is no reward at all for second place; second place becomes the first loser. To succeed here requires speed. These markets seem to exhibit "new economics" because of the distortion caused by stunning speed, abundance, and rapidly falling prices.

According to Robert Shapiro and Hal Varian, authors of *Information Rules,* information technology exhibits both supply-side economy of scale and demand-side economy of scale.[1] Supply-side economy of scale applies when the total per unit cost of production decreases with increases in scale. Economy of scale for demand occurs when a network effect kicks in, and per unit value increases with increase in scale. As a piece of software is replicated over and over, the marginal cost decreases, and, at the same time, the value of the software increases as more is sold and installed. In both cases, there are nearly unlimited returns for scale. There is virtually no limit on the economy of production since software is replicated at the speed of light and can be distributed at the speed of electronics. And there is virtually no limit on the size of the economy of scale for the demand side. As more users are added, each new user increases value to the installed base of users.

The practically unlimited improvement in marginal cost of many information technology products engenders falling prices. Many products and services are becoming virtually free as they become superabundant. But among this abundance, it is critical to know what quantities are becoming relatively scarce and more valuable. These scarcer quantities can be well analyzed using the machinery of supply-and-demand economic models.

The law of supply and demand remains in effect and helps us discover future value.

Although the economic alchemy of the Internet may be new, the old law of supply and demand still applies. This law states that for a fixed demand for a good, the price of the good will increase as the supply decreases. As the supply increases, in this fixed demand scenario, the price will decrease. We inherently understand this relationship, and all of us have experienced the impacts of variation in supply or demand. There have been numerous changes in the supply of gasoline, resulting in price swings of up to 300 percent in just under two years. During 1999, it was possible to buy gasoline for about $1.00 per gallon. In the spring of 2001, gasoline supplies became tight, and the price in some cities shot up to nearly $3.00 per gallon.

A corollary of the law of supply and demand is that scarcity creates value. In the case of gasoline or Pearl Jam tickets, this value is expressed in terms of increasing price.

But it can also be expressed in terms of barter. What are we willing to trade when given incompatible choices? What of the choice of attending your daughter's soccer game or playing golf? This choice compares your value of each activity to the other. It is a choice of spending time, with time acting as a currency, a pricing mechanism.

This barter of one use of time for another is also determined by supply and demand. The Internet weather surrounding us is about such choices but their number, frequency, and volume are rapidly increasing. The choices assault us so quickly they become white noise. Because many of us are free to work anywhere and the speed of work demands an increasing time commitment during any one week, our free, unassigned time must suffice for the mundane overhead chores of living and for entertainment and pleasure. The pace of work also places additional demands on the time at work and forces us to prioritize choices for each use of time.

We make similar choices about privacy. Only in the past few years has the public in general become aware of the widespread loss of privacy that has already occurred. We are now valuing privacy by making choices about our credit card use and the privacy policies of Internet providers; and many of us are forgoing services if there is a chance of losing yet more privacy. Privacy has become increasingly scarce as communication and computing surround us and can capture an electronic silhouette of our existence.

The coincident arrival of economy of scale for *both* demand and supply is unusual, and accounts for much of the frenzy of the Internet economy. The economy of scale for demand, known as the network effect, accounts for much of the gyrating and rocketing values of the technology stocks.

> **The network effect is important in understanding the unusual economic outcomes we see in the Internet weather.**

A network effect occurs when the purchase of a good impacts the value of goods already purchased. The network effect is demonstrated when the additional purchase of a product changes the value of products *already purchased*.[2] An automobile purchase does not exhibit the network effect, but the purchase of a telephone does. The first Model T Ford provided its owner with great value and utility. The first telephone, on the other hand, had little value. As additional telephones were purchased, however, each new phone added value to the existing ones. The network effect applies likewise to fax machines and, importantly, to software. But if I buy a Ford car, it does not change the value of any other Ford cars that have already been purchased.

While network effects can be both positive and negative, the great technology fortunes of the 1990s were the result of powerful and positive network effects. Robert Metcalfe, a founder of Ethernet, the first desktop networking software, coined "Metcalfe's law," which states: "The value of a network is equal to square of the nodes on the network."[3] This obtains due to the combination of ways that users can communicate with each other within a network. Each user can communicate with every other user, thus the communication links are related to the number of users times the number of users. In part, this network effect accounts for the extraordinary market capitalization of Microsoft. The network effect also is related to "lock-in," wherein a user is locked into the use of a software product due to its extraordinary network effect.[4] This is one of the most important issues behind the Microsoft antitrust trial, and its adjudication is the single most important public policy issue in technology.

Information technologies tend to create networks of use. In the 1970s, IBM dominated mainframe computing, and in the 1980s IBM operating software, such as CICS and DB2 dominated computing. By such domination, IBM's software commanded a powerful network of computers and applications and its compatible software became more valuable. This in turn, created more value for IBM's installed base of application software. Then, as the first personal computers appeared, the network effect occurred with PC software such as word processing. Wordstar, the first word processing software benefited from the network effect. Each copy of Wordstar created an additional user and, as the numbers grew, the value of each Wordstar program already installed increased because of the ease of trading files. The network effect enjoyed first by Wordstar in word-processing software was then enjoyed temporarily by WordPerfect, and is now enjoyed by Microsoft's Word program.

The network effect is not new, and the Internet did not create it. Railroads and long-distance telephony are both subject to network effects. As more rail lines are added to the rail network, with additional stations and spurs, the value of the existing stations and spurs increases. During the late nineteenth century, railroads were the silicon growth stocks of the day. Despite the legendary efforts of such financiers as J. P. Morgan and E. H. Harriman, however, no one railroad was able to own the entire network. Morgan and Harriman competed fiercely, with the entire United States becoming their battleground. At one point, during the 1901 Northern Securities fight, Morgan's and Harriman's forces had consumed the liquidity of the U.S. financial markets in a titanic struggle to gain control of the Northern Pacific railway. Only a large infusion of cash to the U.S. Treasury from John D. Rockefeller and, from Morgan himself, kept the nation from financial panic. In the end, no individual gained control of a continent-spanning rail network, and sparring among competing owners of pieces of the interlocking network compromised their pricing power. The Interstate Commerce Commission also oversaw rate making and other matters to prevent monopoly abuse of the rail system. Long-distance telephony also benefited from a network effect. As additional telephones were added to the Bell System long-distance network, the network itself added more value. In this case, the American Telephone and Telegraph Company owned the network and carefully managed it under the watchful eye of the Federal Communications Commission.

No rail baron was able to command an entire rail network. But Bill Gates's Microsoft owns the network effect accruing to MS Office. Cisco owns the network effect of the ubiquitous Cisco routers. Owning an entire network has a dramatic effect on pricing because the owner will attempt to maximize pricing to increase profits. For example, eBay owns a network of eBay users; the larger that network becomes, the more valuable it is to both existing users and new users. Each new user is a potential additional bidder for some bit of arcana, thus increasing the demand for existing users. At some point, this additional value will be captured through increased transaction or subscription charges. Because eBay enjoys such a network effect, it is valued at $16 billion and 14,500 times 1999 earnings. Ford Motor, on the other hand, with over $8.0 billion of tax earnings in 2000, is valued only at seven times earnings, $50 billion, despite enjoying over $170 billion of revenue and commanding over $200 billion of assets. AOL is subject to network effects, whereas Whirlpool is not. However, to the extent that Whirlpool moves to add intelligence and information technology to its appliances, it is moving into network effect markets.

A network effect market will be dominated by serial monopolies. This winner-take-all attribute of the market causes inordinate demands on the use of time.

The network effect breeds positive feedback with increased demand. With increased market penetration, the value of a networked product—generally a technology, or an information product—increases. At the same time, the marginal cost of producing information technology products is often close to zero. And the zero marginal cost often has no limit in terms of the amount of software produced. Microsoft can produce a million or one hundred million copies of Word at near zero marginal cost because the manufacture of software is nothing more than a very high speed copying operation. Bill Gates, chairman of Microsoft, confirmed this. On March 3, 2000, in testimony before the U.S. Congress, Gates stated, "Any technology company can produce the operating system software for all the world's computers in just one day."

For certain markets that exhibit such economies of both supply and demand, a monopoly is virtually guaranteed. This has been true in the desktop software market. In word processing, first it was Wordstar, then WordPerfect, and now Word. In spreadsheets, it was VisiCalc, then Lotus, and now Excel. These industries create "serial monopolies," as described by Stephen Margolis and Stan Leibowitz in their book, *Winners, Losers and Microsoft.*[5]

A serial monopolist can reap the rewards of Midas himself during the period of monopoly. Given the pace of technological innovation, however, retaining your serial monopoly is akin to riding a unicycle on a wire above a crocodile infested river. Your crocodilian competitors are fiercely brainstorming and fueled by venture capital, stock market frenzy, and exponentially expanding science.

This reward for being first helps explain the brutal pace of technology business. The Internet weather crowns the swift and those who are first; it punishes the swift but second-place finishers; it destroys all laggards. Thus the extraordinary demands on time, and the pressure to work more, complete more, and forsake all except the wheel: We become chipmunks in the wheel of time. Our reward for racing is yet more acceleration of the wheel itself. In a market ruled by network effects, the most likely outcome is a monopoly, and all other pretenders to the crown fall in a trail of debt, falling share prices, and broken dreams. Being first to achieve the power of the network effect for a market is the most important of all considerations in building a new product. You don't necessarily have to be first to market, but you must be first to command the network effect. VisiCalc was first to market, but it did not achieve the extraordinary leverage of the network effect. Lotus 1-2-3 did.

Does anyone remember VisiCalc? I don't. I only know about it from reading about examples of the laggards.

> **Scarcity versus abundance: When data are abundant, truth becomes scarce.**

As with air, so with data in the Internet weather. Electronic data are now available, in virtually any quantity, nearly instantaneously. This increased supply will mean decreasing prices for data. The logical conclusion is that data will become free. Examine the dramatic decline in the price of stock quotes. Hundreds of Web sites now provide free stock market quotes. Formerly, access to real time quote information from the New York Stock Exchange and the NASDAQ was channeled through for-fee services such as Quotron, Reuters, and Bloomberg. Because buying such services was costly—a Bloomberg terminal can cost as much as $10,000 per year—the office lobbies of stock brokerage firms formerly were populated with investors scanning the live quote stream like eagles scanning a salmon run. Now it is easy to log into hundreds of sites and receive quotes on stocks within 20 minutes of their execution. As this information inundated the outlets and began to proliferate across Web sites, its unique value decreased to zero because no one would continue paying for it; data and electronic access are both easily available. Now this kind of information is used to assure traffic at a Web site, and advertisements often pop up in front of you as you scan the stock prices.

The Internet weather is about abundance. It is about free data, provided in any quantity, instantaneously, with the aura of electronic accuracy. There is now a kind of Gresham's law of data: Bad data drives out good. Sir Thomas Gresham was a sixteenth-century financier who studied the impacts of inflation on currency and then formulated his law: "Bad currency drives out good." This is particularly true in cases of hyperinflation, the most cited case being the mark issued by the Weimar Republic of Germany. In 1918, as World War I ended, the value of a German mark was about equal to a dollar. The price of a single egg was about half a mark. In 1929, some 11 years later, the price of an egg was more than 10 million marks! With marks declining in value every day, anyone receiving them wanted to spend them immediately. U.S. dollars, Swiss francs, and British pounds, on the other hand, increased in value each day. So the worthless marks were the only currency on the street, and dollars were hoarded. Thus, the bad currency, the mark, drove out the good currency, the dollar. This phenomenon is now occurring in Russia. Rubles are driving out U.S. dollars.

Gresham's law applied to data would say bad data drives out good. But what exactly is bad data? In this context, free data drives out usable data. Electronic data has an aura of quality, since it arrives in *Sorcerer's Apprentice* quantities, with electronic time stamps certifying its authenticity. The sheer volume of data devalues it. Imagine scanning a gigabyte of raw weather readings. A gigabyte of weather data is nearly worthless; however, the accumulated data presented by a satellite map, in several colors, is freighted with knowledge. The subtlety of Gresham's law is not that it describes the devaluation of currency but that it describes a change in behavior that recurs among all people, in any time, in any nation, during hyperinflation. Hoarding begins, and the good currencies disappear from circulation.

So what occurs with devalued data? What occurs with an oversupply of information? Gresham's law would anticipate a change in behavior. The good information will be hoarded, and the bad, or surplus, information will be flooding the public. Ironically, we will narrow our choices of information and rely on trusted sources. This is particularly true of financial data. Formerly, an astute trader could watch the quote tape, and from movements in price and volume, determine trading strategies. But now, the tape is available to anyone—it is devalued, it has become voluminous and valueless. Thus tips, inside information, and other scarce sources of unique and valuable information are kept close to the vest. High-quality sources of information are hoarded, while the public receives gigabytes of free quote stream. I rely on *The Wall Street Journal* to present me with financial information after its staff has processed vast sums of data and reduced it to relatively compact form. Like a good currency, the columns of words in the newspaper represent trust, verification, and economy of my time. I use this newspaper in lieu of searching numerous Web sites, annual reports, and various government reports. Indeed, I have narrowed my reading selections, and the *Journal* has increased its coverage of such items as travel and real estate since I have started hoarding it and giving away other data sources.

> **When communication and computing are free, privacy is scarce or nonexistent.**

Use of the Internet is virtually free. It is marvelous that we can now communicate with anyone, anywhere in the world, free. Yet, inevitably, free and easy communication compromises privacy.

As we roam the vastness of cyberspace, we leave electronic traces that can be assembled to portray our interests, activities, e-mails, and purchases on the Internet. Hackers can scan the entire Internet, testing the portals of anyone logged on to it for nefarious entry into their computers. The only safe assumption when using the Internet is that there is no privacy during use.

The Internet by itself, however, does not pose the greatest threat to privacy. After all, it is possible to use a stand-alone computer for the Internet, make sure the stand-alone computer has no personal information stored on it, and never make a purchase using Internet sites. The compromise to privacy comes from the Internet's free data transmission, with negligible cost of data storage and processing. Many of the most important databases that concern our privacy do not reside on our personal computers, but are found on the computers of banks, insurance companies, doctor's offices, driver's license bureaus, the Social Security Administration, schools, colleges, and other institutions. With free data transmission and computing, it is now easy to correlate these databases and add each pixel of data to the electronic silhouette of our existence. As just a small example, search the Web site anybirthday.com. It provides the date of birth for anyone who has a driver's license.

The loss of privacy has been inexorable since the beginning of computerized databases. The dramatic increase in computing power has made it cost-effective to accumulate much more data than ever before. The dramatic decrease in communication cost has made it possible to move and sell gigabytes of data that were formerly unavailable. The implication of these two trends is that we have lost our privacy.

The electronic distance and the anonymity of cybermarkets are diminishing trust.

Think about a traditional flea market—the kind that was often established in former drive-in movie theaters. In such a market, a prospective buyer ambled around hundreds of small stands, booths, or open car trunks, examining merchandise, speaking with the seller, and possibly consummating a deal. The potential for fraudulent transactions exists in such a market, but is reduced by the physical presence of goods and the ability to talk to the seller openly. The identity of the seller is known, and competing buyers can be identified.

Now imagine the electronic anonymity of eBay or other Internet auction services. When selling or buying on eBay, buyer and seller never meet. One of the hurdles to success that these electronic flea markets have faced is the issue of trust. The electronic distance and anonymity of these markets diminish trust. Users have reported numerous stories of chicanery including sales of goods that don't exist, sales of fake goods, or bids by a seller against the buyer (the seller uses an alter ego e-mail address). While eBay has been a leader in creating rating systems and experience systems to help build and evaluate trusted sellers and principled buyers, these markets still are distanced, impersonal, and prone to abuse.

The very factors that earmark the speed, novelty, and innovation of technology compromise trust. Trust cannot be asserted, cannot be purchased, and cannot be sold. It is a quality of perception of a person or company by the surrounding community and is earned by principled behavior over time.

A reduction of trust is an inevitable companion to electronic business.

The transformation of a product to an information appliance brings with it the potential rewards and all the risks of a network effect market. Beware of the muse of information technology.

As information technology seeps into all products, it is tempting to contemplate the graduation of a product to the gilded reward of a network effect market. This reward is the domination of a market by monopoly, however precarious, and nearly perpetually increasing margins with increasing volumes. However, another economic theorem must be mentioned; it goes by the acronym "TANSTAAFL." These are the initials of "There ain't no such thing as a free lunch."

Appliance makers are charmed by the potential of their appliances becoming Internet devices. Considerable print is devoted to this phenomenon, such as speculation regarding an intelligent refrigerator's ability to maintain food inventory and reorder perishables automatically. An appliance manufacturer is further charmed with the possibility of the software and protocols developed for his refrigerator to become the standard for all Internet-enabled refrigerators, and thereby gain the value of a network effect market. The chances of this happening are slim, especially when the refrigerator and the software are linked. The chances are slim because the characteristics of the two markets—appliances and software—are so different. Appliances have limited economies of scale for production and none at all for demand. The promotion, fee structure, and costing of these two products are not compatible.

Almost no one has been able to move from a hard good to a network effect market. The Win-Tel monopoly—that of the combined product of Intel processors and Microsoft operating systems—is often used as an example, but the returns and economics of Intel and Microsoft are quite different. Microsoft owns the network effect and exploits it. Intel gains the benefit of near monopoly in personal computer processors, but has traditional physical limits to its economies of scale. The stock market has reflected the difference in these economics throughout the history of the Win-Tel collaboration.

If I were an appliance manufacturer (or any product manufacturer), I would think instead of the inherent compromises that the infusion of technology creates in a product and would ask several questions: Does the addition of technology in my product allow my customer to better husband time? Does this technology provide real knowledge rather than a deluge of precise data? By using this technology, do I increase my customer's trust in my company or the product? Do I in any way compromise my customer's privacy? These questions are not always addressed as the muse of monopoly wealth whispers in our ears, but they are essential to sustaining value.

Summary

Despite considerable print to the contrary, there are no new economics. Price and value are still determined by the relationship of supply and demand. The law of supply and demand is still in effect, and provides the overall framework for analyzing economic events. The network effect, which has a singular impact on information technology markets, has been known for a century and has always affected information technology and communication markets. The effect of economy of scale for *supply* is well known, and dominated industrial development throughout the past two centuries. The effect of economy of scale for *demand*—linked with the network effect—is less well known, but has been studied for nearly a century.

What is new is the arrival of economy of scale for *both supply and demand,* as well as the speed with which scale can be obtained. This combination, of both types of scale economy with speed, has the impact of creating serial monopolies in which the winner takes all in a market. This inordinate reward for winning accelerates work and dramatically increases demand for use of time.

Data, communications, and computing exhibit nearly zero marginal cost of production. With zero marginal cost, supply increases radically and price tends toward zero. As a result, data, communication, and computing are becoming free. As these goods flood the market, it is important to ask, What does free data make valuable? What does free communication make valuable? What does free computing power make valuable? The laws of supply and demand demonstrate that oversupplies of data make quality data more difficult to assemble and thereby more valuable. Free, pervasive communication, combined with free computing, has made privacy relatively scarce or nonexistent, and thereby more valuable.

Trust is achieved through face-to-face contact, consistent action over time, and truthful representation. As information technology markets accelerate the creation of goods, products, services, and companies, our ability to spend the time necessary to develop trust and to provide truthful representation is compromised by the volume of data, communication, and computing around us. These factors diminish trust in distanced, electronic markets.

Information technology is seeping into all products, and as it seeps in, the character of the market for that product changes. Information technology accelerates the network effect. As this transformation occurs, companies must become aware of the exaggerated and chaotic information technology markets. They are typified by abundance, speed, and serial monopolies. In such markets, it is critical to find the scarcities, since scarcity creates value.

The following chapters investigate the relative scarcity of time, truth, trust, and privacy by using analogies and by speculating about products that will emerge to create more of these verities.

CHAPTER 3

Anonymity, the Ultimate Luxury Good

We have lost our privacy. It has simply seeped away as we have lived and breathed. Can we reclaim it once and for all? Can the stunning advance of technology return our privacy and, by extension, our identity to us?

The loss of privacy is a consequence of free communication and free computing. It is a consequence of Internet weather. The dramatic loss of privacy has greatly increased its value (scarcity creates value). This increase will motivate the creation of privacy products whose introduction and use will change markets forever. Privacy, in the form of anonymity, alter ego, and secure personal data vaults, will be bought and sold as freely as word-processing software. These products and services will lead to the sovereign consumer, first among savvy, affluent consumers, then will proliferate to the mass market.

This movement toward privacy products will result in the most desirable consumers—the technoproficient and the affluent—resigning from cyberspace. They will employ a decoy, an alter ego, or an alias to represent them, thereby creating novel customer service challenges.

No one event caused the loss of privacy; it was surrendered over a 50-year period.

Privacy is one of the most cherished values of American society. The Founding Fathers wrote guarantees of privacy into the U.S. Constitution. Privacy has become an implied right in the United States and is addressed as the Fourth Amendment, the right against unreasonable search and seizure:

> The right of people to be secure in their persons, houses, papers, and effects, against unreasonable searches and seizures, shall not be violated. . . .

The stark language of the Fourth Amendment ". . . to be secure in their persons . . . and effects . . . unreasonable searches and seizures . . ." highlights the implications of the loss of privacy. Indeed, the measure and protection of privacy is a barometer of the health of a free society. The history of Western Europe as well as the United States is a history of increasing privacy. From 1791 on, there follows a long tradition of privacy, such that the average U.S. citizen assumes that privacy is the natural order of society instead of having been painfully constructed by centuries of revolt, bloodshed, and political maturation.

Freedom and privacy are inextricably linked. They are interwoven in a free society, like the strands of color in a block of marble. Now, however, privacy is at risk. The threat comes, not from nefarious acts, but from an accumulation of beneficial ones. They include the modest surrender of our "papers and effects" each time we apply for a job, use government services, or accept payments or buy something via the Internet. We embrace the benefit of sacrificing modest slices of our privacy and are unaware that we have, through a long accumulation of these slices, surrendered our privacy. It is dying a death of a million embraces. Ironically, the United States, one of the freest societies in the world, is where privacy is most vulnerable.

As the old adage goes, "You don't know what you got 'til it's gone." Many did not appreciate the full force and beauty of privacy until it was virtually gone. The loss began with the Social Security number system of the 1930s; now technology has raced ahead, dramatically increasing our capability to communicate. The companion advances in the technology intrude into our lives, measure our lives, even watch our lives.

One of the ultimate surrenders of privacy is the achievement of fame. A person who becomes famous is surrounded by recognition that is analogous to the surrounding atmosphere of technology we are all beginning to experience. A celebrity's response to this blanket of recognition provides an instructive example for all of us as our privacy comes under assault.

Celebrities have to seek publicity, yet they hunger for privacy. Once they attain fame, they surrender privacy forever. Thus fame and privacy become a Faustian deal. Dr. Faustus, the fictional scholar created by Christopher Marlowe in the sixteenth century, traded his soul to the Devil in return for all the knowledge in the world. When the Devil arrived to collect his soul, Faustus was broken with remorse and begged to be let out of the deal. He offered to burn his books, to do anything to regain his soul. So it is with fame and privacy: As Faustus would burn his books, so celebrities inconvenience themselves in costly ways to reclaim their privacy. Picture the Robin Leach *Lifestyles* evidence: limousines with blackened glass windows, gated and guarded communities, private aircraft, and "exclusive hideaways in paradise." Privacy begins to be purchased. Once fame is achieved, privacy, now scarce, assumes extraordinary value.

If wealth accompanies fame, the wealth is used to pursue privacy with vigor. A customary feature of hotels and resorts that serve the very rich is "discretion." Do you think that celebrities such as Julia Roberts, Meg Ryan, Leonardo Di Caprio, or Tom Hanks check into a hotel under their own name? No, they use aliases that afford them some privacy. Part of the plot line of the Julia Roberts movie, *Notting Hill,* was the exquisite discomfort of publicity and fame. Sports teams demonstrate this hazard at play-off time. These teams usually have one or two players whose fame in their home city brings notoriety in their opponent cities. By siting the stars, fans, or opponents know the location of the team. So, during play-offs, sports teams often check in under assumed names to avoid crank calls in the night. These people hunt privacy just to get some rest. The exposure of fame and wealth is like the desiccation of the desert sun.

Now, however, privacy is under assault, not by individual fame, but by merely living. By answering the telephone, by buying gasoline, by registering for work, by using medical benefits—by anything we do that leaves a data trail—we are laid bare. Each of us, from the celebrity to the silent majority, is now subject to public exposure of awesome depth and detail.

For a celebrity, anonymity is a luxury good. The Internet weather will soon cause anonymity to be sold as a mass-market good. The product, anonymity, would be following the market penetration path of such formerly luxury goods as cruises, air travel, wide-screen televisions, and other high-end appliances. All these luxury goods became mass-market goods over a short number of years. This is a provocative, counterintuitive, yet logical outcome of the increasing values of the verities—in this case the increasing value of privacy. Just 10 years ago, who would have thought that we would cloak our identities as a preferred method of moving about in the public places of cyberspace?

> **The convergence of communications and computing technology has created a new milestone: Privacy is now gone as soon as you are born.**

I have three teenage sons, and they are unaware of the rich data file that already exists for each of them. They are unaware that the loss of our privacy is a gradual process that begins at birth. As soon as we are born, we are assigned a Social Security number. With that number as our identity, the files begin accumulating the electronic trail: date of birth, weight, name, place of birth, mother's name, father's name, and name of insurance company if any. The Social Security number will be linked with a unique identifier such as DNA print, iris print, or fingerprints.

When a child enters school, his file fattens: immunizations, medical treatments, prescriptions, accidents, injuries, grades, IQ measurement, and hundreds of seemingly trivial data. This accumulation process is like the ongoing work of an ant farm. Suddenly the database ants have accumulated an enormous fingerprint of the child's existence. Should there be errors in the database, which ant do we blame? Which ant will step up to take responsibility for the vast, disparate accumulation of data, and will take responsibility to clean up the mess?

Consider the example of our neighbor's son, an otherwise healthy teenager who passed out twice within six months. He passed out during a particularly gory movie, and he passed out in a dental chair on seeing the novocaine needle. These two episodes led to a preliminary conclusion by a consulting physician that he was an epileptic, even though no signs of epilepsy were actually detected. The data ants accumulated these medical expenses and the doctor's erroneous diagnosis of epilepsy, and this electronic trail was made available to appropriate agencies. As a result, he was denied a driver's license. Two years and $15,000 of medical expenses finally proved that he was normal.

Often, we willingly surrender a slice of our privacy. Usually these surrenders are small and are framed by a situation wherein we receive something in return.

Characteristically, a borrower will sign agreements that allow searches of our "papers and effects" to win approval of a mortgage. We surrender information about income and assets to borrow money to buy a house.

There are other inadvertent surrenders. We routinely sign agreements when completing job applications that allow searches of our papers and effects. We submit information about our age, weight, height, and Social Security number to drive a car. We give up pieces of our privacy in trade for something. Even the Mitsubishi House of the Future, with the all-seeing camera, though intimidating, does provide goodness.[1] With such a house, you could dial up your house while traveling and assure that your teenage son did not party while you were gone. Or, you could assure that your cat was eating properly, or that your house was not burgled. But, the idea of an inanimate thing—your house—"knowing" everything you are doing, your health, your diet, your preferences in entertainment is daunting.

Among these incursions, what is unreasonable?

Each act, by itself, is not unreasonable. If someone is going to lend you a hundred thousand dollars to buy a house, that someone needs assurance, based on personal financial data, that you have the ability to repay. However, is it necessary to give over personal information to receive a haircut? Recently, I walked into a haircut salon that my sons use. I was asked to provide my telephone number since that was the indexing function used within their customer database. I provided a false number in downtown Chicago. However, one of the girls recognized me and told the cashier that I was Kyle's dad. She entered Kyle, who had surrendered our telephone number and address. Am I a growing curmudgeon just because I do not want to surrender personal information to receive a haircut? Again, it is not that single surrender which is unreasonable. After all, there is some good in it, because the shop will likely send me discount coupons in the mail.

With the advent of data-mining capabilities, and advanced data search and correlation capabilities, each small surrender of data becomes a tile of a mosaic. Each data-tile adds definition, accuracy, and power to the mosaic of a person. This mosaic becomes a twin to that individual. This mosaic shadow is being constructed in evermore permanent fashion with increasing precision and detail. However, for the most part, we are unaware of the accuracy and sweep of this mosaic. As we merely live, we are surrendering vital data-tiles to mirror our identity and existence. The most powerful way to combat this encompassing assembly of data accumulation is to feed the voracious maw precise data that profiles someone else—your alter ego. The mosaic, then, becomes an accurate depiction of a phantom.

As our data server-farms are assembling our lives into data warehouses, privacy is becoming inextricably linked to identity. The first of these links is your Social Security number. When this number was established in the 1930s, the implications of vast computing power and linked databases were unheard of. Now, however, the Social Security number is the penultimate identifier. This number is the key to opening vast troves of information about us, including nearly all our financial information. And, once the Social Security number is in the possession of a database company, the number and its link to you can be freely sold, with or without your permission.

> **Communication is a form of intrusion, and there will be a perpetual leapfrog of communication intrusion technology followed closely by technology of increasing privacy.**

We have lost sight that communication *is* intrusion. Therefore, any advance in communication technology automatically begets an advance of intrusion.

The etiquette of Victorian England memorializes the intrusive aspect of any communication. At that time and place (and all over the Western World), it was assumed that speaking was a breach of privacy. Each person was surrounded by the sanctity of silence, and speech was governed by the tried and true, "Do not speak unless spoken to." Thus prior to speaking, it was necessary to ask permission. From this small politesse grew an elaborate structure of etiquette, exaggerated by the ennoblement of the upper classes.

The etiquette of communication became as complex as any tax code. A cardinal rule was that no gentleman spoke first to a lady. A lady always had the first opportunity to initiate and invite conversation. Among gentlemen, a man with superior position would invite conversation or acknowledge the presence of a social inferior:

> A gentleman is always introduced to a lady—never the other way around. It is presumed to be an honor for the gentleman to meet her. Likewise (and it is the more general rule of which this is only specific example), a social inferior is always introduced to a superior—and only with the latter's acquiescence. . . .
>
> From *What Jane Austen Ate and Charles Dickens Knew*, by Daniel Pool[2]

But among the country homes of England and the vast reaches of nineteenth-century America, it was unlikely for people to speak with anyone outside the family on a daily basis. The rules of communication etiquette preserved the sanctity of privacy. There was no need to breach these rules since social meetings were far sparser than today, and there was time in social interactions to provide for proper etiquette. It was a mannered society, with privacy intact.

The development of the telephone was an undeniable advance in our society. Yet despite the unparalleled advance of communication embodied by the telephone, at its core, it is extremely intrusive. During the 1960s and 1970s, few people would have *dared not answer* the phone. The call might have been urgent; it might even have been long distance! Back then, a long-distance call was an occasional curiosity more than an intrusion. When I was a teenager, it was necessary to dial an operator and ask for long distance, and the call was announced: "Long distance calling James Moore." Today, in my household, the phone is rarely answered, but instead is allowed to roll over to caller ID or to voice mail. My 16-year-old son never leaves messages, never takes them. As soon as he comes home, he scans the caller ID and returns calls to all his friends who called. Why? This behavior is ingrained among his community of friends. So now, rather than answer the phone, we purchase unlisted numbers to shield our privacy. We purchase caller ID to know the identity of the caller and can block calls from unwanted callers. However, if we are the frustrated caller, we then purchase technology that will mask our phone number when calling someone to avoid being automatically blocked when calling in.

The telephone practice within the Moore household is a good example of changing technology and its impact on privacy. We are experiencing, and will, for the foreseeable future, a technological leapfrog of communication advances, accompanied by increased capability to intrude on us and compromise our privacy. The technology of telephone privacy has been thrusting and parrying forward.

We are recapturing the benefits of Victorian etiquette, some hundred years later. The telephone rang its way impolitely into our homes, breaking the rules of etiquette that preserved our privacy.

Now, after a hundred years of communication and its attendant intrusion, we have access to technology, in lieu of social protocol, that returns control to us. We have recaptured the purpose of etiquette, if not the etiquette itself. We have returned to a natural order with the etiquette of technology.

As we gain the capability to communicate in real time, all the time, we also become subject to continual intrusion. The "open channel" that is necessary to experience the world in real time, any time, is also an open channel for surveiling our communication. It is a not a one-way mirror for us to review our world. This is a window through which we can see the world, and the world can view us. What do we mean by "view us"? Although the technology is quickly emerging to do precisely that—view us—in general we are observed by the tracks we leave in the data-snow. Our accumulated communications create a multidimensional shadow of ourselves in databases that never forget, never sleep, and never err.

The ultimate intrusion technology has yet to become commercialized, but it will *literally* create an atmosphere of technology. Ultra Wide Band (UWB) technology has been patented by Time Domain, Inc., whose Web site is www.time-domain.com.[3] UWB is a potent method of sending data using very low power. Its primary commercial application is likely to be in cell phones that never need to have a battery recharged. This revolutionary technology provides more bandwidth, at higher speeds and dramatically lower power than any other communications technology. Clearly a winner! Yet its companion capability is breathtaking intrusion.

UWB transmits using a broad expanse of the spectrum: from very long wavelengths up to very short and energetic wavelengths. As X-rays can penetrate flesh but not metal, so various wavelengths have differing abilities to pass through solid structures. Much of the radio spectrum, such as those wavelengths used by am/fm radio and cell phones are capable of penetrating buildings. There are also very long wavelengths and special wavelengths that can thoroughly penetrate any structure. By spreading its broadcasts across all these spectra, UWB devices can be configured to "see" through buildings. A UWB device transmits bursts of random frequencies, whose composition is recorded by a chip. Some of the radiation passes through the object; some is reflected back. By measuring the time the reflecting electromagnetic radiation consumes going to and from the UWB device, the device can determine location and image of the target. Time Domain lists this capability as "Pulson Radar" and describes it as "personal radar that fits in your pocket." The Web site goes on to list security systems, which are alarming systems for intrusion detection and tracking of movement, as well as "through wall imaging."

Time Domain has targeted the use of its technology at such beneficial applications as locating people trapped in burning or earthquake-damaged buildings. Hundreds of lives could have been saved in the 2000 earthquake disasters in Turkey had this technology been available. It can also let police know who is inside a building and provide a comprehensive image of all the contents of the rooms in the building. Thus, police can know whether a room contains weapons, drug labs, or other dangerous or criminal apparatus. Buildings can be inspected inside out for structural integrity.

Since Time Domain's UWB wireless technology has so much capacity at such low power, real-time video transmission will become more affordable, widespread, and useful. Yet, this is a dramatic advance in the technology of intrusion. A police helicopter (or anyone's helicopter) could scan all buildings in a neighborhood and watch the inhabitants. The privacy formerly afforded by walls and roof will no longer be available. We will be further exposed to desert sunlight of intrusion.

UWB is truly an atmosphere of technology. Because the spectrum used is so broad, and the broadcast used in the technology skitters around a vast array of the spectrum, and the power used is so low, a UWB scan cannot be distinguished from ambient background radiation. The pervasive envelope of technology—the Internet weather—is making privacy scarcer.

We are entering a perverse and perpetual leapfrog of communication, intrusion, and privacy response. Communication technology races ahead, bringing with it newfound capability for intrusion. To combat it and regain the privacy lost in the communication advance, a privacy product is created and sold.

What of the ultimate communication channel, the Internet? Has it become the ultimate technology of intrusion? And will there soon be a leapfrog technology of privacy that equals the power of the intrusion?

Privacy, its loss and recovery, will forevermore by a key consumer issue.

In the Internet weather, anonymity is the only form of sustaining privacy. Since our shadows in cyberspace lay us bare, *the emerging strategy to achieve privacy is to become anonymous.* The preferred method for privacy will be alter egos rather than anonymity per se. Alter egos are already popular. Nearly anyone with a common name who uses AOL has been assigned an alter ego. In my case, James Moore, a very common name, would become jmoore907@aol.com. These e-mail aliases presage the creation of alter ego identities for use in the insecure Internet.

Or, alternatively, we will seal our identity within a privacy vault, and sell small peeks in return for services. Such peeks might include a selected history of purchases of gasoline to help a gas company better plan its marketing campaigns. Or, with prior knowledge, we might allow a grocery company to examine our grocery purchases. In each case, we would receive compensation for this peek. Should we not want to allow peeks to anyone, privacy products that create secure alter egos and privacy vaults are already being commercialized. They will become as common as credit cards, and when we use these forms of privacy product, the massive data warehouses will fill with mystery data that precisely profile people who do not exist.

Because of the extraordinary value of privacy and because of the fertility of privacy tools such as Public Key encryption, privacy products are being produced rapidly.

We will reclaim and protect our privacy using two techniques: alter ego and *identity vaults.* Nearly all of us casually use forms of alter ego when we communicate via e-mail. And the idea of storing our most precious identifying data within a protected storage—a vault—is easy to understand. A personal data vault is an extension of the safe-deposit box. The technology to make these widely available relies on the advanced mathematics of encryption, which can create impregnable codes, that are beyond the power of any government to crack. Thus the technology of privacy exists and is getting stronger. It is our behavior that must catch up.

The first line of privacy defense—the use of an alias—is far more common than many realize. For example, read the singles ads in your newspaper. In my suburban newspaper, there is currently an ad placed by "Classy Lassy," a woman seeking a man; and by "Latin Rhythm," a man seeking a woman. Aliases and blind return mailbox numbers are commonplace in the search for a companion. The alias Classy Lassy is a form of "public privacy" in that her description is fairly detailed and available for any reader to see although her identity is cloaked by the alias. Many of the personal ads are encrypted by using aliases or key phrases only understood between reader and writer. Each February 14, the Valentine editions of newspapers are filled with encoded missives between lovers.

Technology has emerged that can guarantee aliases used on the Internet. A service called Zero Knowledge arranges for you to become totally anonymous when using the Internet. As reported by Don Clark, staff reporter of *The Wall Street Journal*:

> Zero Knowledge Systems Inc. today begins limited sales of an unusual service that is designed to protect Internet users' privacy by letting them choose fictitious names for activities such as sending e-mail, visiting web sites, or joining online-discussion forums. The closely held company won't have the ability to link people's real identities with their pseudonyms, even if ordered by a court . . .
>
> The company's service, dubbed Freedom, uses encryption technology that has long been regulated by U.S. agencies to prevent its use by criminals and foreign governments. Users download special software that lets them pick pseudonyms and scrambles their messages and web connections, in a scheme akin to placing a letter in series of envelopes. The packets of data are passed through three independent Internet services, each of which strips off a layer of identifying information to prevent tracing them back to the senders.

Consumers will use various privacy products to resign from cyberspace. This exit will pose novel marketing and selling challenges.

Now, imagine the potential use of anonymity. Imagine, instead of a platinum *credit* card, a platinum *anonymity* card. This card would entitle the user to a handful of encrypted alter egos to be used for whatever purpose the user wanted. Presumably a wealthy or famous user such as Julia Roberts would elect to travel using this alter ego. Using strong public key encryption and digital cash that has been anonymously mailed into the platinum card, a platinum anonymity card user would have two layers of privacy defense. The first layer would be the strong encryption surrounding the transactions of the anonymity card. The second layer would be the alter ego itself. If some group of hackers harnessed enough computing power to grind away at the encryption surrounding the digital money transactions of the anonymity card, they would discover a footprint of someone who does not exist—the alter ego of Julia Roberts. The card becomes a Russian doll of embedded layers of alter ego transactions with encrypted cash.

To be effective, an anonymity card would necessarily link to an encrypted passport of some nation. This may or may not be the United States. Should the United States be unwilling to cooperate with providing an alter ego for travel, I project a competition among nations to work with the anonymity card, since the first users are likely to be persons of considerable wealth. Uruguay, Canada, Luxembourg, the Cayman Islands, New Zealand, and Thailand are nations that may be amenable to providing one or more alter ego passports linked to an encrypted vault that stores the identity of the anonymity holder.

Products from American Express were among the first ones offered. On September 8, 2000, American Express launched an ad campaign in *The Wall Street Journal* (p. B7) featuring a face blurred digitally as if being displayed on a "most wanted" television show. Above the blurred, unidentifiable picture was the tag line, "*Introducing anonymity online from American Express.*"[5] Below the anonymous picture was the text:

> But as we enter a new century, there are places where you may want to reveal less about yourself, such as the Internet. As a company, American Express has a long history of protecting consumer privacy, and we're committed to continuing this tradition online.

The advertisement goes on to describe a service called Private Payments[SM]. This system uses a random number to process payments rather than using the credit card number itself. In addition, the title line above another box of text is the titillating statement "Traveling Incognito." The text indicates:

> And soon American Express will even allow people to choose how much information is available about them when they are simply surfing the Net, from their full identity to anonymity.

To imagine American Express's dream of "Traveling Incognito," picture casual business acquaintances seated next to one another in first class on a transcontinental flight. They are not well acquainted and each is using the anonymity card although they know each other's real name. A conversation could be conducted along the lines of "I know who you are, and *I am not who I am.*" To which, we may hear this kind of surreal response, "You have mistaken me for *who I am not.* Besides, *I know who you are not,* also."

The seeds of such anonymity cards are already in place. Zero Knowledge presents the fundamental capability to conduct anonymous electronic correspondence. IBM has created a method of transmitting that it calls a *Cryptolope,* an envelope of encryption surrounding a message.[6] Various forms of digital cash incubating around the world feature the traceless nature of real cash. Thus there is a suite of products that can allow you to conduct communication without a link to your identity, can layer your communication within uncrackable encryption, and can provide ways to transact commerce with traceless digital cash. Although this suite is not yet integrated, it soon will be. At that point, we face choices, and our actions in cyberspace can be conducted with informed and controlled consent. We can control the use of our data and only impart it with prior consent.

Identity vaults are the next layer of privacy defense. "Digital Me" is among the first of these.[7] In March 1999, Novell announced Digital Me, a product meant to safeguard personal data during transactions over the Internet. As reported by Christa Degnan of *PC Week Online* (March 22, 1999):[8]

> Novell's Digital Me software acts as a digital safe-deposit box for personal information to protect privacy and enable users to sell or barter their data for rebates or discounts.

This product, and others that are sure to follow, will protect your remaining privacy and, over a short period of time, say three to five years, can help you reclaim your privacy. Although you may say this is a long time, is it so long to recover something so dear that has seeped away silently over your lifetime?

That you can reclaim your identity by using an identity vault is due to the peculiar complexity of electronic data storage. Data storage is executed using myriad software. The communication among this Babel of software is not easy, and the expense of customizing data-mining links is only justified for the most promising veins of data. As you opt out of the data warehouses by protecting your interactions, your unprotected legacy data becomes stale or becomes resident on obsolete software. If you regain control of your interactions with the vast cyberworld, you will become less and less of a data vein. More and more of the mosaic of you will be old, and no longer representative of the consumer you really are. As database software is improved and legacy data is ported to new systems, "useless" old, or inactive, data, has a tendency to be purged. Within a few short generations of software (which time is falling dramatically each year) your data becomes inaccessible because your data-tiles were not current. While this cycle of reclamation of your identity and your signature data is not immediate, it is an inexorable result of withdrawing your data behind an identity vault. Things take time. Within a single handful of years, you would likely expire as far as marketing databases are concerned.

The reclamation and protection of privacy is based on encryption, in particular, "public key" cryptography, which is strong encryption for the ordinary person. Public key encryption and its small, elegant machinery pervade the Internet. The machinery of Public Key makes possible such products as digital cash, positive identification using digital certification, digital signatures, and public privacy. It enables the creation of an alter ego that can now exist with total anonymity in cyberspace. Imagine creating digital products for which you receive digital cash, anonymously. Each of us can wrap our identity within the enigma of strong encryption. We will create layers—Russian dolls—of alter ego in an identity vault, whose communication is wrapped within cryptolopes.

So where will this profound leapfrog of communication, intrusion, and privacy lead us?

> **As these privacy products gain market share, the sovereign consumer will emerge—beginning with the savvy and affluent consumers. These are the consumers who are resigning from cyberspace.**

Privacy, once characteristic of our society, has nearly vanished. We are awakening to our exposure and feel naked. We will pay to reclaim and protect our privacy. We will regain control of our name, of our identity. Along the way, we will *establish an indelible property right in our own identity*. As the celebrity receives royalties for the use of his or her identity, so we, the silent majority, will establish a price for the use of ours. Does this seem right? Does it seem right that we have to pay to reclaim our own identity? I don't know, but it is an improvement on the insidious loss that has already occurred. I have faith that the engine of entrepreneurial freedom will create novel, ingenious uses of our identity in ways we cannot now imagine. The sale of our data or the use of our identity may become a considerable income flow for many of us. Celebrities show that although they have lost their privacy, they have established the brand equity of their identity, and many realize considerable income from the use. Picture William Shatner transferring some of his fame to Priceline.com in return for royalties on the use of his name.

The question "Who am I?" will be complicated by technological advances. As we correspond in alias, as we create in alter ego, as we parse our identity among our given name identity and our various cyberidentities, the question is heavy with irony. Am I jmoore907, a cipher on the AOL network? Am I James W. Moore, author and consultant? Am I the embodiment of my data tracks in the data-snow? Have I decided to be someone in cyberspace, and someone different in the wetware world? This is akin to asking,

"Was Shakespeare written by William Shakespeare, or by another person of the same name?" Does MasterCard actually care that they have purchased a profile of jmoore907? Certainly jmoore907 will demonstrate an adequate trail of consumption (as long as I am paid enough to participate in the data). Using this trail, MasterCard could communicate its special promotions to jmoore907 as happily as it could send them to James Moore, especially if jmoore907 actually responds from time to time. In this case, I have consented to the use of my data, but not to the exposure of my identity. This arrangement will have profound utility for individuals and will pose interesting challenges for anyone selling to us.

We can infer that we will have *precise privacy*. Mass-market privacy will soon be here. Although the initial market will be the wealthy, privacy products have broad, universal appeal. Privacy will be rapidly deployed to a mass market, simply because the vast majority of people are members of that market. Precise privacy will exist when we can choose how much of our privacy to barter and when we can exist as privately as our great-grandparents of the nineteenth century.

Technology will create a new capability: *individual sovereignty*. With strong encryption products, with encrypted alter egos, with cybercash, we can, if we so choose, exit our relationship with any company, group, or institution.

Sovereignty creates an active, rather than passive, consumer.

All firms must evaluate the privacy feature of their products and services. Privacy will soon rank among the most important of all features—price, utility, ease of use—and often will be the deciding factor of purchase. It is critical to ask, "Does my product or service enhance privacy? Does it increase privacy?" American Express's anonymity card provides an excellent example of farsighted product development and marketing in this area.

As consumers exit cyberspace and gain sovereignty and privacy, they will not compromise. At the same time, they are more active, informed, and motivated buyers than the general population of consumers. A privacy campaign, then, can produce much higher sales yields than formerly was the case.

These consumers will permit and pursue information and products. At the same time, they will expect to negotiate for the use of data. Because they are decoupled from traditional marketing databases, finding and acquiring their business will require new methods. The difference in marketing is as different as harvesting grain with a combine, and harvesting truffles.

Summary

There has been a universal loss of privacy. It is this acknowledged loss and the entrepreneurial response to this loss that will change markets.

No one event caused the loss of privacy; it was surrendered over a 50-year period. Each small electronic file about an individual, each small electronic transaction, each small agreement to reveal personal data has created an unintended surrender of all privacy. The explosion of the Internet, with its lack of privacy, has heightened awareness of the general and advanced state of diminished privacy. This scarcity has increased the value of privacy and its recapture.

Because of the extraordinary value of privacy and the fertility of privacy tools such as Public Key encryption, privacy products are being produced rapidly. These products are analogous to the products used by the wealthy and famous to capture some privacy: alter egos and anonymity. The ability to travel anonymously and to check into a hotel under an assumed name have always been products of the very privileged. These products will be mimicked technically, mass produced, and available for the price of a cable TV subscription.

As these products gain market share—beginning with the savvy and the affluent—the truly sovereign consumer will emerge. This kind of consumer will negotiate terms of communication with companies and demand value in return for the use of data, identity, or relationship. These consumers will be served by agents of privacy and will present new challenges when companies want to approach and entice them to use products or services. This will create the possibility of mass sovereignty.

Sovereignty creates active consumers. The sovereign consumer permits and pursues, and thereby becomes a much more productive customer. An active consumer is a motivated buyer. It is critical for firms to develop and promote privacy to entice these savvy, affluent customers.

Communication is a form of intrusion, and there will be a perpetual leapfrog of communication intrusion technology followed closely by technology of increasing privacy. The correlation of data will continue and only become faster.

Privacy, its loss and recovery, will forevermore be a key consumer issue. As a feature, privacy will rank with security, reliability, proximity, ease of use, and utility.

CHAPTER 4

Chipmunks in the Wheel of Time

The economics of technology accelerates the pace of work primarily because of the network effect and the race to become the winning serial monopoly. With this acceleration comes greater demand for the use of time, and since time is fixed, its value radically increases. Technology also has allowed us to work anywhere, anytime, further increasing the demands for our time. Work is being decoupled from place and from a schedule.

As time becomes more valuable, novel products are being created to increase its utility. Calendars are changing and becoming a tool for using time in concert with a community. The Palm Pilot and other personal digital assistants are taking roles in managing time, and linking groups of people together. Knowledge work is created by communication—from an individual to many, and from many to an individual. Time products are being created to leverage one individual's ability to communicate efficiently with many others. A greater challenge is to increase an individual's capacity to process the communication from many others.

These products cannot create more time. Although they are meant to make our time more productive, pleasurable, and convenient, they are being created against a background of incessant acceleration of work.

The pace of work has become inhuman.

How have we become chipmunks in the wheel of time? We did not intend for this to happen, and it did not happen overnight. We made this choice because the rewards of working at Internet pace can be so great. At the same time, this is becoming a binary choice: Work at Internet pace, or secede from the Internet world.

Yet, something is awry with our capability to run in the wheel at an accelerating pace. We who travel the globe as part of our activity in the wheel share a common travel malady: amnesia. It is common to have temporary amnesia when awakening on the fifth, sixth, or sixteenth day of an extended road trip. It is not unusual to stare blankly around your hotel room on awakening and slowly reconstruct where you are and what day of the week it is. It seems our minds and bodies have not evolved at the same rate as the work itself. The human body, the mind, and our emotions are being pressed to their limits by the challenge of accelerating knowledge work. We humans have not evolved sufficiently to sustain the inhuman pace of Internet work. Evolution of a species takes thousands of years. Yet, our pace of work quickened in the past century and the past decade, and soon will grow faster every few years.

In May 2001, a study of the long-term impact on airline flight attendants assigned primarily to international travel showed significant declines in cognitive functions for many of these attendants.

In a story published in the *Washington Post* on June 24, 2001, reporter Keith Alexander wrote,

> And now there's some evidence that jet lag doesn't just cause that lethargic feeling as the body adjusts after high-speed travel through time zones—it might also cause brain shrinkage and memory loss.
>
> Earlier this month, researchers from England's University of Bristol used MRI scanners to study two sets of flight attendants. They found the group that had less time to rest between flights has smaller right temporal lobes, where visual recognition and spatial memory are developed.[1]

Our pace of work is indeed becoming inhuman.

Agrarian work evolved over eons, and agrarian workers measured time according to seasons. Now, in the era of knowledge work, we measure time in billionths of a second (nanoseconds).

As a society, we have moved from hunting and gathering, to agrarian work, and now to today's knowledge work. This progression has changed our use of time and accelerated our actions. For hunters, the seasons timed the migration of prey, although the season made no real difference to the hunting itself. The American Plains Indians simply followed the buffalo herds north to south and back with the changing seasons. As we came to rely on agriculture, seasons and the description of time using calendars became much more important. It was critical to recognize the overall cycle of agriculture and manage the sowing, growing, and harvesting of crops. We moved then to the industrial world, which demands a more constant schedule. The production of an automobile is a synchrony of arrival and assembly, with precise coordination required for the smooth operation of the line.

So we evolved from following natural events, traversing continents on foot in search of food, to harnessing ourselves to the numbing rote of the assembly line. Hunters measured time by phases of the moon: for workers positioned beside the assembly line, taylor efficiency divided tasks into seconds. Today's knowledge work has no boundaries of time or place and no scheduled arrival of work. We are left only with commitments to complete on schedule, knowing that being first is the position that pays; there is no payoff for coming in second or third.

The evolution from hunting to agrarian work took place over eons, with no clear demarcation at its arrival. The evolution from agrarian work to industrial work evolved over a century and a half and could be delineated by James Watt's invention of the steam engine in 1765. The evolution from industrial work to knowledge work is really a phenomenon of the past 30 years. Thus, the evolution from industrial work to knowledge work (a work type that has been identified for only decades), is accelerating. And the accelerating pace of work has been a Siamese twin to this evolution.

With the industrial age, we quickened our pace and yoked our-selves to a time clock. Time was measured in minutes. Time is now of such extraordinary value that it is measured in nanoseconds. The cesium atom clocks, which are the world's standard for meas-uring time, subdivide a second into about 9 billion vibrations of a cesium atom, count these vibrations, and then declare the pas-sage of a second. Numerous important technologies require this kind of time precision. In particular, the signals of global position-ing satellites rely on this level of accuracy since the time measured between signals is the measure of distance.

Although we can measure time precisely, we do not experience the passage of time precisely. Einstein's great revelations were born from his innate discomfort with the relative sensation of the pas-sage of time. A manifestation of this relativity is the different expe-rience of an hour using a scythe in the hot sun compared with an hour spent on vacation. Our comprehension of time and assign-ment of value to it are framed by our work, our passage through life, and the pace, complexion, and choices of our activities.

Today, we are assaulted by choices for the use of our time. Sometimes these assaults are not choices, but competing demands that force us to make least-worst decisions about using time for work activities and family activities. As these demands accumu-late, we feel immense pressure to conserve even the smallest slice of time. We have arrived at this state of affairs quickly—in a mat-ter of decades.

The increasing value of time is having profound effects on how we relate to each other and form communities. In particular, in Chapter 9, I describe the importance of time in the organization of business. As individuals, we will purchase products to help us use time with each other and manage the concerted use of time within a broader community. Even the simple calendar will change.

Most importantly, the dividing lines among time spent for work, for family, and for fun are becoming blurred. Given the infinitesi-mal measurement of time, discrete slices of it for any activity can be, and are, marbled throughout a day. Work is now intruding into all other activities, and organizations must appreciate such contri-butions of time. They have real value and represent real compro-mise—family for work or pleasure for work—that have been traditionally traceless. The evaluation and acknowledgment of this "traceless time" will be a key attribute in attracting and retaining talent in the future.

The value of time is a manifestation of a society as a whole. We cannot value time independently of our community.

Contrast the value of time by examining a representative agrarian society of 100 years ago, that of Tsarist Russia.

In Russia at the turn of the twentieth century, some 85 percent of the population consisted of agrarian peasants. The meter of life was sunrise to sunset. In the winter, daylight was precariously short, brilliantly lit by cold slanted sunlight. Daytime was a punctuation of night. Night was deep, frigid, and still. In summer, the reverse occurred, with daytime extending its reach into night.

The day was separated into morning, midday, afternoon, and twilight. Distance was measured in terms of days on foot between points, and gross measures were accepted, such as a half-day's walk, a day's ride. This kind of time measurement was further imprecise because the length of day in Russia varied so widely. A day could be 6 hours during the winter, or 18 hours during the summer.

The vast majority of the peasants were members of the Russian Orthodox Church, which celebrated 180 holy days per year, Sundays among them. On those days, no one was allowed to work, and many of the holy days were observed with feasts. A peasant, then, worked about as many hours as a current-day high school teacher spends in the classroom. Life was measured by days only. Activity was woven into a continuum of time. Events and days were marked by the community, which was centered around the church. Thus, the priest became the personal digital assistant for the community around him, marking the passage of time, and keeping track of Sundays, name days of saints, and the obligations of the community. No one was required to actually know what time it was or even what day it was. The movement of the sun overhead was all that was necessary to mark the day. Existence among the community assured that you conformed to the demands of time. In this fashion, existence is timeless. There is no beginning to work, no end to work, no retirement, no career. The life of a Russian peasant was eternal. But then, time was worth little because it was not scarce. The evidence for the small relative value of time is that it was only measured grossly—a day, a half-day, a moon. Something with little value is not finitely subdivided for measurement.

Time in a Russian peasant village was a manifestation of the movement of a network of people, and the measurement of time was community property that was communicated to all simultaneously by the ringing of church bells. An individual moved according to the meter and custom of those around him, and those customs were centuries old. Each individual surrendered to the community and to the community's maintenance of time and calendar. The future was an abstraction and would be indistinguishable from the present, once it arrived. The past was a measure of the sameness of the present.

The Russian peasant even recorded time according to an anachronistic calendar. Until the Bolshevik Revolution of 1917, Russia used the Julian Calendar. At the time of the Bolshevik Revolution, Russia's calendar was 11 days behind the Gregorian calendar, which had been fully adopted in Europe by 1753. In the nineteenth century, it was of little importance that Russia managed according to a different calendar. Nor did it matter that most of the civilized world (China and the East) used different calendars from the West. Time just wasn't that critical.

The entire world is now bound to one clock that measures in nanoseconds.

Compare this timelessness, this eternal existence, with today. Once you are finely and minutely tethered to a Palm Pilot, your thinking begins to change. You no longer think about the future, because you have "organized" it. You link the Palm Pilot to your computer, receive mail, and schedule changes. You have surrendered to the present and to your network. With this surrender goes the need for memory. Why remember anything that can be accessed instantaneously with unerring accuracy? If Darwinian selection works, future humans will have enlarged and rapid mouse fingers, and smaller frontal lobes devoted to memory. If you bake your Palm Pilot in a parked car in Atlanta during the summer, there is a chance you will have no idea what to do next—literally.

This surrender is both similar and different from the surrender of the Russian peasant. It is similar in that there are no longer time boundaries to work. It is different in that we are not bound to a place of work. But we are now bound by a global understanding of time. The geosynchronous satellites, the cesium atom clocks (five of which span the globe), and the precise requirements of data transfer and telecommunications all combine to bind the world to one clock, racing and counting away in billionths of a second.

> Unlike an automotive assembly line, a knowledge product has no limit to the amount of time that can be contributed. Also, unlike an automobile assembly, it is difficult to measure time consumed in knowledge production.

Knowledge workers exist in an edgy netherworld of work-in-progress. An automobile progressing through the final assembly line presents tangible evidence of completion. There is a precise schedule for production, and the progress can be viewed, touched, measured. The completion occurs as the product rolls from the line. A knowledge product—be it software, a financial package, a legal contract, a performance—does not have the same tangible quality of measure. There is no measurable beginning to the seed, or idea, of a knowledge product; there is no easy way to monitor the progress of production.

In this environment, we are encouraged to yoke ourselves to the effort at any hour, and in any place. We can now work during our commutes, while at home, while watching our children's swim meets, any place where we can balance a computer on our laps or maintain reception of a cell phone. We sometimes attempt to describe the progress of our work using project management techniques, which are very good at displaying the events of the past, but still poor in describing future effort. However, these reports always provide some comfort to management or to the buyer of service and impart an aura of science in the greasy trade of project management. And, in project management, what is a day? Is it the 8 hours of daylight spent in endless status update meetings? Or, should it include the next 8 to 12 hours into the darkness spent actually doing the work that provides the changes in status? This kind of relativistic day is reminiscent of the white nights of Russia during the summer solstice when there is no definitive night; rather there is a pale, milky twilight, ample for working. Thus we have new kinds of workdays: the eight-hour day, and the project day. Anyone who has been involved in the installation of a major software program will verify that the future use of time is extremely difficult to predict. Anyone who must estimate the future use of time begins to appreciate its relativity.

We work anytime and anyplace. The 12-to-16-hour days of the industrial sweatshop seem relaxed by comparison with the grueling hours associated with releasing a new product, negotiating a deal, or finishing a creative work to a deadline. The evidence is all around us. Performances of the Metropolitan Opera have been stopped while the performers pointedly await the cessation of a cell phone in the audience. The beach is littered with personal computers. It is possible to receive e-mail while in traffic.

Like the Russian peasant, we have surrendered to the present, but unlike the peasant, our present bears little resemblance to the past. Our future, also, will be different from the present. We organize the future, memorialize the past, and maximize the present. This contrast in itself is a manifestation of the value of time. Formerly, when past and future were indistinguishable, the passage of time was immaterial. But now, according to the calendar, we are able to leave Asia by airplane and arrive before we took off. This is an anomaly of the calendar, true, but we can now work both in *the present and the past!* In this environment, our construction of the calendar plays a special role in global knowledge work. Because of our need to synchronize a disparate world, calendars, formerly surrogates for the movement of society as a whole, will become surrogates for individual life. And calendars, formerly static bulletin boards and a convention for describing the future, will become living appliances.

Calendars and community: The active calendar is replacing the passive calendar.

Calendars are ancient civilized achievements. To construct a calendar, it is necessary to understand the movement of seasons, and by extension, the movement of celestial bodies. The calendar embodies the attempt to manage the future by describing and framing it. The calendar also helped to demystify the yearly death of the sun through the shortening of days and its renewal in December. The lengthening of the days after the winter solstice was thought to be a miracle in pagan cultures, and led to the creation of solstice festivals. Roman paganism termed this feasting time of twelve days, the Feast of the Saturnalia, which has become synonymous for celebration. Religions have maintained calendars throughout history. Even now, there has been little change in the calendar since Pope Gregory XIII formulated our modern 365¼ day calendar in 1583. Indeed, there has been little utility in changing it. So the calendar was formerly a public instrument, maintained by the church. During the industrial revolution, the calendar moved into the home and denoted the days of work, more so than the days of worship. With the advent of the Internet weather, the calendar is again moving into the public sphere, but in a different way. The Internet calendar will exist among your network of family and friends, maintaining your movements and time similar to the ringing of the Russian village church bells.

The classical calendar is static. It is a document with a matrix of days inside a matrix of months that make up the year. Its primary utility is to mark commitments and future events. It establishes a common understanding of when events can be scheduled, and provides a shorthand for scheduling. No one misunderstands a day, month, and year designation. This kind of static calendar was necessary to use the future well when place and time separated us. We are no longer separated by place or time. Using the Internet, we can communicate with nearly anyone, anywhere, at anytime. Events are immediate, data are voluminous, and our existence is leveraged by immediacy.

> **The active calendar can present the minutiae of living. This can make the "traceless time" become visible and well measured.**

The calendar—through electronic devices such as the Personal Digital Assistant (PDA)—is evolving into a living memorial of the immediate. Imagine the sweep of an airport searchlight. It flashes by overhead, illuminating a huge scope of land and atmosphere. The calendar will evolve to be a perpetual searchlight of the present. Your own electronic calendar will be perpetually "on." It will sweep the schedule of events around you in real time, across hundreds of dimensions. It will be housed on a data server, with linkages of your calendar with your friends, family, and business colleague network. There is unlimited potential for your calendar to exist among this network. There is likely to be a permanent calendar living in cyberspace for each of us. It will become a fluid appliance of the future, present, and past and will become common property of members of your own community. As with the church bell of Russian villages, the calendar will encompass an immediate communication mechanism, broadcasting the movement of time to all within your community. ICQ (I seek you), an Internet community device, was one of the first open communication channels. It was purchased by AOL and became the kernel of AOL's Instant Messenger, an open channel among friends and family. The logical extension of IM is the projection of future activities. With the addition of truly mobile commerce—the real-time Internet links via mobile devices—a calendar becomes a form of communication and commitment to a community.

However, because of such an appliance, we will live in an amplified present. Activities that otherwise occurred in the future will be brought forward to the present. The immediacy of the world will further accelerate actions and activities. The constant of the future is the immediacy of our data envelope, and the immediacy of the world.

> The abundance and ease of communication places new demands on individual time. It is now possible to send a communication to the entire world. It is also possible for the entire world to respond individually.

Keeping pace with calendaring is the technology of one-to-many. Broadcasting e-mails is a small example of one-to-many technology and, in general, this technology deploys time efficiently for the communicator, not necessarily for the receiver.

The technology of the one-to-many function, that of one person communicating with vast numbers of people, is rapidly advancing. The most obvious example is the video broadcast, such as a presidential broadcast to the nation. What is different in the Internet weather is that this technology is available to the masses. It is fairly easy to establish a webcasting video on an individual Web site. And this is nearly free. You can make a personal state of the union address to the Internet, and thereby the world, each year. You can do it each day, if you care to.

The many-to-one function is much more challenging. If we should receive an e-mail from every individual on the Internet, how would we process this information? This function is a way of stating, "How do we increase our ability to experience?" At a certain point, we will have optimized the use of our precious time. There will be marginal return for identifying and deploying otherwise idle time.

> The use of time to communicate individually has been greatly enhanced. But trust cannot be achieved by words alone. Trust usually requires presence, and presence consumes time.

There remain, and probably will remain for a long time, circumstances that require personal touch. Much of human communication is nonverbal, as anyone who has been married a long time can attest. A situation that tests all the abilities to communicate and to run in the wheel is the IPO road show. This is the presentation by the venture capitalists and chief executive officer of a new company to prospective institutional investors. Its purpose is to create demand for stock to be issued in an initial public offering. It is critical that the demand for the newly issued shares surge well above the price determined by the investment bankers on the first day of trading. To do this requires presenting compelling stories, in person, about the new firm to these investors. And this requires all the armament of vocabulary, charm, suasion, and charisma that a person can muster. Since these trips are usually frenetic, encompassing presentations to the maximum number of investors in usually an extremely short time, the road show is a special test of stamina, stress management, and presence. Much of the test, then, is not about the words spoken, rather, the test is in the alacrity of presentation.

Imagine the following trip involving investors in Asia, North America, and Europe:

- **Saturday, May 15, 1999**
  Fly from Chicago to Bangkok, arriving at 10 P.M. Sunday night, May 16.

- **Monday, May 17, 1999**
  Meet for breakfast Monday morning with a group of Thai investors, then fly at noon to Hong Kong, dine with Chinese investors. Sleep in Hong Kong the evening of Monday, May 17.

- **Tuesday, May 18, 1999**
  Tuesday morning, take a four-hour plane ride to Tokyo and address a group of Japanese investors for lunch. Then jump a plane for Chicago that takes off at 5:00 P.M. Tokyo time on Tuesday May 18 and arrives at 2:30 P.M. of the same day, effectively arriving before it took off. That allows you to present your investment pitch to a group of investors who have assembled at the Palmer House Tuesday

evening. Later Tuesday evening, you fly to London, arriving at 11:00 A.M. on Wednesday, May 19. Note that on the day that bears the name Tuesday, and bears the date May 18, you have spent time in three world cities—Hong Kong, Tokyo, and Chicago—flown at least 20 hours, and lapped 11 time zones.

- **Wednesday, May 19, 1999**
  Wednesday at noon Greenwich mean time, pitch to a luncheon of London City investors, catch the three o'clock to New York and face a Wall Street dinner crowd, then fly home to Chicago, arriving at 11:30 P.M. on Wednesday May 19.

Let me recap the sequence of cities: Chicago-Bangkok-Hong Kong-Tokyo-Chicago-London-New York-Chicago. During this frenetic trip, there were only two hotel stays in five days. That observation provokes a "Where's Waldo" kind of question: When and where were the hotel stays?

Your Chicago colleagues would have seen you on Friday afternoon, May 14, and again the following Thursday, May 20. You were gone from their sight *only three business days* and five calendar days, yet you have just flown 26,492 miles! This is equivalent to having flown completely around the world at the equator, and then immediately having tacked on a round trip between Chicago and Montreal.

There is a rapid increase in these global travelers—the world's guests, essentially—who weave the world economy together. For these weavers, one of the best gifts anyone can give is time. Time, in a world like this, is priceless.

Why didn't our intrepid traveler use point casting, or video display to perform the IPO road show of the earlier example? It turns out the technology is not good enough. Yet. In this case, time and trust are in conflict. To achieve trust in the minds of the potential investors requires being in front of them. Trust requires the investment of time.

Skeptical investors want to look at, see, question, and interact with the principals of the new firm. They want to see with whom they are investing. After all, there is no guarantee at all of receiving a return for this money. The road show environment, of being scrutinized while moving at the limit of your endurance, is a crucial test of conviction, character, and desire.

The free market will respond to demands for time with elegant technology products.

Assume technology that currently exists will be assembled to assist the harried business traveler. The challenge will be to create a mechanism that can capture the nonverbal nuances of communication. This technology will leverage the fixed amount of time each of us is granted.

Let's scroll forward in time and replay the tape of that trip. It is four years from now, in May 2005, and you are planning the same presentation requirements in the same six cities. You have previously sought permission to attend four of the presentations via your *Gemini Bot*.

Possibly a Gemini Bot would be sold using the phrase, "Next best thing to being there." Its function is to become a stand-in for individual wetware (geekspeak for humans). It is a holographic display that combines the best features of a chatterbot (a bot that can manage a social interface). The Gemini Bot is supported by a neural network—a computer that can learn. This neural network learns enough about the individual to mimic the person. It becomes a facsimile and interactive alter ego. Its purpose is to mimic your nonverbal charisma.

Your Gemini Bot was given to you in beta version, two years prior. Now, it is eerie how much like you it sounds and acts. So much so that you have decided to change certain of your habits, such as clearing your throat before speaking. Because of its credible performance in front of the newly merged (in 2004) Goldman Sachs-Morgan Stanley-HSBC, you feel it is ready to take on Wall Street and the City. This way, all meetings will occur on Monday, May 17. The sessions in Bangkok, New York, and London will be presented by your Gemini Bot, and you, the original wetware version, will handle breakfast in Hong Kong, lunch in Tokyo, and dinner in Chicago. The cost of production will be about the same, but there is the enormous saving of two business days. You will be able to make the presentation in Hong Kong on May 17 and still return to Chicago on the same calendar day. The purpose of such a technology would be to build trust and minimize time.

The basic load is two gigabytes of program and database, which is less than required for some video games. This basic load is part program and part a database about you that you have created by your begrudging existence in cyberspace. It has been accumulated by the cookies of all your Web interactions, by your purchases, by your travels, and by your friends and family networks, which have been recorded by your telephone carriers. However, the Gemini Bot can learn and improve its service to you by a constant feed of data from you. Each keystroke of your computer, each graphic handwritten note is fed to the neural network. All your purchases, reading material, movements, and trips, as well as all business correspondence to you and from you is fed into the neural network to better mimic and serve. Everything about you, *everything*, can be fed to the neural network to improve its service to you.

As the old saying goes, you can now meet yourself coming and going: a virtual chatterbot based on you. You/it could attend events while sleeping. You can coin money while you sleep. A Gemini Bot is the ultimate lawyer's dream: billing 24 by 7. In fact you can bill 24 hours for each of these wonders, so why stop at 24? Why not 48 by 7? Or 144 by 7? The ultimate Gemini Bot could make appearances in court to file routine motions. Imagine. . . .

The piece parts of technology to create a Gemini Bot already exist. Currently, it is a matter of price. Cobbling together a holographic display and linking it to the programming of a Deep Blue capability for interaction would consume tens of millions of dollars. But Moore's law will take care of price. This law, named after Gordon Moore, a founder of Intel, states that silicon chip processing power will double every 18 months.[2] With this exponential *increase* in processing power comes a dramatic and exponential *decrease* in the cost of computing. Already nascent technology exists to construct a Gemini Bot. Examine the Web site actuality-systems.com. The following is excerpted from this site:

Volumetric autostereoscopic displays create volume-filling imagery which can be seen without goggles. Industries using spatial information will experience a significant time savings by viewing 3-D information in true 3-D: for example, molecular visualization, mechanical CAD, air-traffic control, and medical visualization. Actuality Systems, Inc. is developing a high-resolution volumetric display and suite of software which will turbo-charge our customer's visualization experience.[3]

This technology relies on holographic display and produces a full, "volumetric" display of an object. With this technology, it is possible to walk around, under, over, and about a displayed object. How soon will this be displaying people?

To have a Gemini Bot hawking start-ups to venture capitalists seems a bit far-fetched. But once conceived, there undoubtedly will be some who think that would be a perfect use of such a capability. However, I can think of better uses. Imagine having access to medical care instantaneously via your home computer/ television/ personal digital assistant. A medical Gemini Bot would allow doctors and nurses to multiplex themselves without limit. Such a bot system would probably enhance human diagnostics. Bot systems don't ever forget, and their search engines can compare and present potential reasons that would cause the symptoms that are reported. This kind of comprehensive memory is valuable when encountering rare or exotic diseases outside a physician's normal experience. Diagnostics are already headed this way; a bot-like system is just one method of delivery.

Or imagine being able to project yourself to your family. Do you suppose your mother would enjoy seeing you more often? Or, would you like to see your children while you are traveling for business? Would you like to see your spouse while you are traveling the world like a chipmunk in the wheel of time?

Cooperation with the electronic atmosphere will enhance your prospects for employment. But maybe not the way you think it might. With such systems, it may no longer be necessary to "be" anywhere. Such systems will change the dynamics of working, learning, and governing. Time devoted to travel will be invested in other, more productive uses. Moving to a job may no longer be required, since a person can gain presence by video immersion. Business travel as a whole will dramatically decrease.

The increasing value of time, by itself, provokes profound changes in products and behaviors.

The Gemini Bot flight of fancy is a plausible and logical conclusion of technology to optimize the use of time. I have extrapolated from existing technology to demonstrate that technology devoted to one simple value—time—can effect profound changes in the way we interact in society. Only two technologies were involved: a Gemini Bot and an electronic calendar, and the associated data repository to link them.

These technologies can improve the way an individual uses the limited, finite allocation of time each person has been given. Can they actually give us more time?

Or, stated another way, can technology help us experience more during the time allocated to us? Of course, technology will improve the time overhead of living enabling us to experience more in the time we have. However, what about the time devoted to experience? By increasing our capacity to experience, can we know more, live more? We can now project our thinking and our presence to millions. Can we now experience interactions with millions? Will technology enhance our ability to experience and thereby extend our lives?

What is experience? How do we experience something? According to philosophers, experience is the *totality of the cognitions given by perception; all that is perceived, understood, and remembered.* Cognitions given by perception would include seeing, touching, hearing, smelling, tasting. What is perception? Certainly, perception changes over a lifetime. The hue and nuance of understanding changes as the prism of age colors cognitive perception. When we speak of understanding someone, we speak about an experience of multiple dimensions. We perceive someone's communication from the tone of voice, the inflection, the pauses, the silences, the pitch of the voice, the movement of the eyes, the movement of the body, and the movement of the hands. When we speak of understanding an idea, yet even more complex and evanescent factors are at work. However, technology is assaulting all these experiences, perceptions, and cognitions. Technology is racing forward to increase our very ability to experience.

Technology is also invading the perceptions. We are rapidly assembling the capability to provide alternative perceptions. Flavoring is a commonplace way to provide tastes. Fragrances are a commonplace way to provide aroma. Sound is precisely produced by digital disks. Visions are created in Hollywood that mimic both reality and fantasy. Mimicking human touch has yet to be accomplished, but there is growing understanding of touch. Amputees report continued feeling from their nonexistent limb. Surely this nerve sensation is a precursor to mimicking touch. The research being conducted in re-creating optical nerve signals to conquer some forms of blindness may lead to associated discoveries about how the brain processes signals associated with touching.

I think there will be simulators of increasing power to provide perception and understanding. We are pursuing technology to accelerate the elusive harmony between thoughts and perceptions. In this way, technology is also increasing the experience of life.

Time has become priceless because of the inordinate rewards for speed. Remember Metcalfe's law. The winner, the one who comes in first— first to market, first in time—is rewarded with fortune beyond measure. Examine the fortune of Amazon.com. The stock multiple of Amazon.com is one and a half times *revenue*. There is no meaningful price/earnings ratio since Amazon has yet to make money. Savvy Internet investors believe that Amazon.com has arrived first to command the network of Internet consumers. The bet placed here is that Amazon will achieve sufficient mass to command the first retail network of *billions* of people. The rewards of this network will be exponential. Even if the rewards were simply traditionally linear, the sheer scale of this endeavor assures magnificent reward.

But only if Amazon.com is, in fact, first.

A reward for speed to market is not, by itself, a new phenomenon. During the mid-nineteenth century the China tea trade led to the development of very fast sailing ships, including the class known as the "China Clippers." The first ship to arrive in London with the fresh harvest of tea commanded the highest price. This reward for speed engendered great engineering innovation in sailing ships, and eventually steamships. But this return for speed in the tea trade applied only to one shipload—the first one. If Metcalfe's law had been applicable to the tea trade, the investment capital available for innovation in sea transport would have been enormous. I imagine that steamships, turbines, and even jet skis would have been invented as much as a century earlier.

Like the tea ship captains, we seek faster and faster means to market. Travelers jet around the world so frenetically—26,492 miles in five days—*not because we can*, but *because we must*. So for each of us the central question of technology, and indeed, of our lives, becomes how to use time. We are increasingly aware, through the very technology meant to afford us more time, that we have an exquisitely finite gift of life time. Our gift of technology has brought us numerate precision. The summation of an average life's heartbeats, about 2.7 billion beats, is less than a third the number of vibrations of a cesium atom counting off one second. Just this small comparison of finite numbers causes us to pause to consider the ephemeral quality of our existence. The superlative nature of our technology, indeed of our society, highlights the relative scarcity of our heartbeats.

Scarcity creates value. No more time or less time is available to anyone. We now have more demand for the uses of time, and the demands pile up, competing for the ubiquitous present. What is scarce is idle time that can be used for nothing at all. Scarcity creates value, and contrast creates beauty. Time is priceless, and its beauty can be remarked by a pause. The sheer beauty and pleasure of life will be the pauses. Solitude, silence, and stillness will assume incredible value.

Summary

How have we become chipmunks in the wheel of time? We did not intend for this to happen, and it did not happen overnight. We have made this choice because the rewards of working at Internet pace can be so great. At the same time, this is becoming a binary choice: Work at Internet pace, or secede from the Internet world.

Knowledge workers of today exist in an edgy netherworld of work-in-progress. An automobile progressing through the final assembly line presents tangible evidence of completion. There is a precise schedule for production, and the progress can be viewed, touched, measured. The end occurs as the product rolls from the line. A knowledge product—software, a financial package, a legal contract, or a performance—does not have the same tangible quality of measure. There is no measurable beginning to the idea of a knowledge product, and there is no easy way to monitor the progress of production.

In this environment, we yoke ourselves to our work anytime and anyplace. We seek technology that reduces the time overhead of living—the time devoted to paying bills, to grocery shopping, to laundry, and to moving from home to work. As this technology becomes more robust, we begin to create technology that can extend our capability to experience. In this way, technology can, in some ways, give us more time.

Stated another way, technology will enable us to experience more during the time allocated to us. Technology will improve the time overhead of living. And by increasing our capacity to experience, technology will provide means to know more and to process more information.

No more time, or less time, is available to anyone. Our accumulated lifetime heartbeats are less than a third the number of vibrations of a cesium atom that we use to measure the passage of a second. We now have more demand for the uses of time, and the demands pile up, competing for the ubiquitous present. Idle time that can be used for nothing at all is becoming precious. Scarcity creates value, and contrast creates beauty. Time is priceless, and its beauty can be remarked by a pause. The sheer beauty and pleasure of life will be the pauses. Solitude, silence, and stillness will assume incredible value.

CHAPTER 5

Fast Facts and Factoid Fiction Crowd Out the Truth

The past decade has seen an explosion of information. As data become free, voluminous, and ubiquitous, what becomes scarce? When data can be free, in any volume, anywhere, what is crowded out? The answer is that truth is crowded out: Truth becomes scarce.

What is truth? In this book, I am not talking about the eternal verity: Truth. I am focusing on truthful processes that produce reliable, reproducible observations or that submit statements, based on data, to verification. Two time-tested processes produce the kind of truth I am referring to: journalism and the scientific process. They produce more truthful, reliable assemblies of data into information, but both of them consume precious time. Thus a conflict: The cost of time is increasing, and the volume of data to be worked is also increasing. These combine to escalate the scarcity and value of truthful information, and such information is the keystone of knowledge.

It is ironic that the cornucopia of data would compromise knowledge. It is a problem of volume combined with selection.

When asked to assemble information from data, which data do workers select and how do they execute the selection? Then, once they select data, they must tackle the problem presented by data volumes. Processing the data that are now routinely available is akin to digging a tunnel through a sand dune using a thimble.

Beware of the shortcuts that our accelerated business pace requires. The pace abbreviates the peer review of information, the submission for edit and critique, the repeated experiment and proving of concept. In particular, beware of *factoids*. A factoid is a statement wearing the clothing of fact. Very often, statements that are no more than reasoned assumptions or even swags have the aura of fact and are treated as such. The besotted projections for the size and growth rate of the business-to-consumer Internet market relied on a few actual data points that were clothed with regression and projection, and propagated with the speed of light. The din of these factoids crowded out the seasoned voices and data of business-to-consumer veterans (heretofore called retailers). This reliance on tainted data cost billions in investment, billions in personal careers, billions in enraged customers, and billions in devalued, stranded inventory.

The search for the truth, as memorialized by Diogenes and his lamp, has always been illusory. Diogenes set off to discover the big Truth—the quality of verity itself, the eternal, invariant correlation of belief and reality. To this, our technological prowess has added the correlation between belief and *virtual reality*. We can now mimic reality with video images and digital recording—an ability caricatured in the movie *The Matrix*. This mimicry can mislead us, or enrich us. These technological wonders can make us question what is actually true, virtually true, and not true at all. But the overwhelming proliferation of data and images is crowding out truth.

There is so much new data each year that new words are being invented to describe these incomprehensibly big quantities.

Dr. Hal Varian, Dean of the School of Information Sciences at the University of California at Berkeley, is leading a study entitled "How Much Information."[1] The purpose of this study is to accurately describe the amount of new information the world is producing each year. According to Dr. Varian and his colleagues, the world produced 1.5 billion gigabytes of data in the year 2000. A gigabyte equals one billion bytes, and a billion gigabytes is called an *exabyte*. Data production has become so outsized that we must continually create new prefixes for these quantities. This amount—1.5 exabytes—is about 250 megabytes of unique information for every man, woman, and child on earth. Formerly, the trillionbyte (terabyte) watermark was unthinkably big. If it is shown that information is, in fact, doubling every year, we can expect the world to produce 3.0 exabytes of data in 2001, 6.0 exabytes in 2002, and onward to *1,800 exabytes* in 2011, just 10 years from now.

Just how big is 1.5 exabytes of data? If each person on earth were to yearly print a book to store his share of 250 megabytes, each person would produce the equivalent of 100 books the same size as Tolstoy's *War and Peace*. The human race last year created the equivalent of 600 *billion* such volumes. To visualize how gargantuan this amount of data is, create a train of rail cars, each filled with these volumes (a rail boxcar can hold about 100,000 volumes). The resulting train required to hold all 600 billion volumes would consist of six million boxcars and stretch 79,000 miles, or well more than three times around the earth. The Sorcerer's Apprentice of data has been loosed: Next year each of us, on average, will create 200 such books; then 400 the year after; then 800; then 1,600 and so on.

So much new data are being created that raw data have become the devalued ruble of the information age.

Data are both discovered and created. Once data are in hand, they are "warehoused" and "mined," each term implying the inordinate toil involved in sifting, refining, and preparing the data for use. The data are sometimes created, sometimes discovered, yet every sector of society is guilty of data profligacy. In our individual lives, we are most often creating data. One of Dr. Varian's key findings is the importance of the amount of information produced, stored, and accessed by individuals. They account for about 80 percent of original print documents, and about 55 percent of electronic data stored on disk drives. Dr. Varian has termed this the *democratization of data*. The execution of science usually involves the discovery and use of data as yet unavailable to measurement or capture. New measurement techniques often produce mother lodes of hitherto inaccessible data. Witness the space program in all its technology. Witness the data on subatomic particles. Witness the modern hospital and its minute capture of the biochemistry of life. Witness the human genome project and its mapping of our genes and soon the unique proteins of life. Businesses create, discover, and consume data.

Data provide the ammunition of economic combat—the raw material of knowledge and fact-packages. Given the continuing acceleration of business, data must be converted to fact-packages with increasing speed. While there is increasing demand for the knowledge encapsulated in fact-packages, the rising tide of data makes the acquisition of fact-packages more time consuming and thereby more costly.

We are experiencing a peculiar data quicksand: We stand still, yet data rise around us. It would seem in the knowledge economy that an abundance of data would increase our wealth. However, sowing and growing data is analogous to a bumper crop of corn. As farmers grow more and more productive, the vast oversupply of corn drives down the price per bushel. So, the vast oversupply of data devalues it.

Ironically, this vast oversupply of data also compromises truth.

First-class journalism requires editing processes prior to words appearing in print. Necessary corroboration also is required, and fact-checking is performed to assure accuracy and truth in print. The errata columns that appear in every newspaper are testimony to the effort expended to assure the information presented in journalism is true.

The scientific method has two truthful mechanisms in place: replication and peer review. A statement of scientific effort must be replicable by a similarly skilled individual under like conditions to be considered to be true. This statement is also subjected to peer review prior to being accepted by the general scientific community.

Both of these processes consume time. The accelerating nature of everything exerts constant pressure to release or use information without assuring its soundness and validity. In addition, there is the rapidly growing volume of data to process. As a result, the average truthfulness or reliability of data has decreased, rather than increased. Although there have been rapid increases in the computing power to verify and process this rising volume, thus far computing power has lagged the increases in new data.

This growing volume presents a problem for computing technology that, on the one hand, creates data at near light speed; then, on the other, is required to recall, sift, and evaluate it. The processing of data into a fact-package is a tug of war between volume and processing power—between Moore's law and the exponential growth of information. According to Moore's law, which has been accurate since 1972, processing power doubles every 18 months, or a year and a half. Meanwhile, the amount of information doubles every 12 months. Information is outstripping the power to process it, and the relative gap between production and processing power is growing. From 1970 to 2000, there was 1,024 times greater information growth than processing power growth. As far as we see into the future, data will grow faster than our ability to work with it. And the distance is becoming greater every day, every week, every year. The differential between information volume and computer processing power doubles every three years.

These observations are counterintuitive for many people. The miracles that technology has wrought and the abundance of information would seem to enhance decision making. This is true to a point, although data can also be used as a cannonade to create a Mine-Eyes-Glaze-Over factor to convince or exclude. For any decision on matters of substance, a process of doubly verifying data, assumptions, and conclusions needs to be instituted. Such matters could be the annual plan process, the launch of new services, and in particular, the evaluation of markets.

In addition to the challenge to truth presented by an increasing volume of data, there are the traditional challenges of the quality of the data, the challenges of its durability, and the challenges of our human frailty when thinking and comprehending information.

Data quality is critical. The presentation, storage, and transmission of data is prone to introducing error. But there are also special circumstances where the facts represented by the data change. Certain fact-packages drift over time. An unlikely drifting fact is the mileage trucks use between two points and addresses in the United States.

How could mileage change?

The mileages used by truck drivers to determine pay and prices were not scientifically measured; they were agreed on by law. Formerly, a tariff agency, the Household Goods Carriers Bureau, issued a map stating the mileage between any two points in the United States.[2] It was published annually under a sole source arrangement with Rand McNally Corporation. The household goods trucking companies and the Interstate Commerce Commission agreed to use this mileage when paying drivers for mileage driven and to compute prices according to this mileage. This map use began in the 1930s, well before any computerization. During the 1960s, the United States began digitizing the land of the United States; zip codes are one form of this digitization. Each zip code has a unique longitude and latitude, and over the past four decades, the resolution of this X-Y coordinate system has become finer and finer. During this period, mileage began to be computed using Euclidean distance formulas, and adjusted using a circuity factor that produced a statistically accurate mileage over thousands of mileage readings. However, any individual mileage reading produced by this computational method could be quite inaccurate. For example, a small community that is accessible only by a bridge would have inaccurate mileage readings, since a circuity factor cannot account for unique, small geographic wrinkles. This mileage database has been gradually narrowing the difference between computed mileage and actual measured miles, as disgruntled truck drivers report the egregiously short miles. (They rarely report the long miles.)

Mapmakers have now adapted computerized graphics to streamline their production processes and thereby have subsumed the inaccuracies of the computed miles into their graphics database. A similar erratum in the mapping and location of addresses often occurs because of continuing new construction or the increasing resolution of location and measurement tools. This erratum is extremely important to utility companies who must dig trenches for utility cables.

Not only can data drift, it also can age. This acceleration of aging is the result of the decreasing half-life of software languages. John Boddie, quoted in *Software Development* (July 1999) recounts his experience on a project involving diverse sources and quality of data:

> In my current project, the data sources include Wang, Oracle, Microsoft SQL, Excel spreadsheets, Access databases, direct feeds from telephone switches in the network, direct feeds from Cisco and Newbridge routers, Lotus Notes, proprietary databases, and flat-file outputs from mainframe systems. . . . No requirements document starts with the assumption that the new system will be initialized with bad data, yet this is often the case in practice.[3]

The half-life of data management systems is now less than five years. Given the volume and complexity of software, data ages as it is migrated from system to system. It becomes riddled with incomplete fields, transposed entries, and other faults. Also software languages can have very short lives. Does anyone remember Borland? Ashton-Tate? Foxpro? Because of the network effect (described in Chapter 2), software languages must become monopolies or die. The odds of choosing the long-term winning software are well less than 50 percent; therefore, many times data is created and maintained in obsolete software. At the time of Boddie's article, Wang had been defunct for more than a decade.

One of the few examples of near-permanent data storage is the Rosetta Stone. This particular file—a slab of black basalt—has been able to maintain its data for nearly 2,200 years. It was equipped with perpetual software embedded within near-perpetual hardware—the basalt. Side by side on the stone was a message scripted in two languages (software) and three alphabets. The languages are Greek and Egyptian; the alphabets are Greek, hieroglyphic, and demotic, a form of cursive hieroglyphics. By careful comparison of the Greek text to the characters of the ancient Egyptian, Jean François Champollion, a French linguist, was able to begin deciphering the demotic script of the Egyptians, and thereby the language itself. The Egyptians chose the hardware and software for data storage wisely. The hardware (basaltic rock) is impervious to nearly any radiation, weather, sunlight, and the curious play of children. However, the most brilliant and lasting contribution was the choice of software. Of the three softwares—demotic Egyptian, hieroglyphic, and Greek—one, the Greek language, has survived the 2,200 years. Greek still lives and is used by millions of people today.

Present-day data storage is nowhere near as permanent as the Rosetta Stone. The medium for electronic storage itself is part of the challenge of maintaining data. The first medium, tape, becomes more and more fragile with age. Tape is vulnerable to magnetism, sunlight, and various injuries. Digital disk storage, while more robust, is also susceptible to magnetism, sunlight, and other injuries. Who hasn't experienced a treasured CD of the Beatles that has been played so often it skips? Who hasn't experienced the jerky skips of a flawed DVD? Then examine the software. The Social Security administration has trillions of data encoded in assembler. At a certain point, there is a risk that Social Security records of millions of Americans will be as inaccessible as the demotic script of the Egyptians. We currently are producing a constant Babel of software, and the shelf life of a software language is measured at most in decades, compared with the eons of spoken and written language. The demotic Egyptian lost to antiquity had a provable useful life of at least 4,000 years. Does anyone believe DB2, Oracle, or SQL will survive for even a hundred years?

Truth can be stranger than fiction and therefore rejected in favor of factoids.

Although we desire truth, we often cannot recognize it, or we reject it because the truth seems too implausible. Often our thinking is at war with our need for truthful information. In part, this has to do with our accumulated biases, and in part it has to do with fundamental ways we categorize information.

First, how do we accumulate biases and what impact do they have on truth? There has often been conflict between what is believed and what is true. For eons, it was believed that the world was flat, that the world was the center of the universe, that time was fixed, that all matter comprised five essences. This conflict between fact and belief seems to be rooted in our mental architecture. We are bred to believe. Beliefs provide shortcuts for survival. We learn biases that provide shortcuts for dealing with our environment. For example, wet, humid air is *lighter* than dry air. When we first think about this, it just does not seem correct. It seems much more reasonable that dry air would be lighter than wet air, since we can picture a wet towel versus a dry towel and cannot picture or sense the difference in the weight of dry versus wet air. So our mental resting state always reverts to assuming that wet air is heavier than dry air. This is an example of the unconscious cognitive reasoning that never sleeps. These biases have somehow developed over millions of years and have engendered our survival as a species. But the pace of change was formerly glacially slow.

When we use data, we often rely on mental techniques that categorize data and "factual" information according to our previous experience. This reliance on our experience results in factoids—observations wearing the clothing of fact. This occurs although precise data exist for answering nearly any kind of question.

This accumulation of experience and expertise often leads to "expert bias." In a famous experiment in 1977, Baruch Fischhoff, Paul Slovic, and Sarah Lichtenstein observed an interesting reverse correlation between certainty and accuracy.[4] A group of people were asked various questions and also asked to rate the certainty of accuracy of their answers. As the subjects became more certain of their answers, they became less accurate. As experts often spend careers engaged in the mastery of a discipline, an "expert bias" plays a role in their viewpoint on events, outcomes, and even factual material. This is explained both by the investment an expert has made in his viewpoint and by the economy of processing information according to these ingrained and tacit biases.

Expert bias can help explain some of the exquisite challenges outlined in *The Innovator's Dilemma* by Professor Clayton Christensen of Harvard.[5] Once an understanding and investment has been made in a technology, a solution, or a product, it becomes difficult to recover a naive, and fact-based viewpoint about alternatives.

These natural, inborn human tendencies are exacerbated by the profound volume of data from which to choose and command for decision making.

We have gradually adapted to the natural world. This adaptation has not required our processing power to change much in thousands of years. The innate abilities to see, hear, sense, and think are much the same as they were 400 years ago or even 4,000 years ago. The relationship between input data—our senses—and our ability to process this data was roughly balanced. Yet, commencing with the industrial age, the need to process more and more data has increased exponentially. From the time of Columbus until the end of the nineteenth century, data and knowledge doubled every *century*. With the industrial age, data accelerated, first doubling every 50 years, then every *decade*. Currently, data is said to *double every year*. But what is the value of all this data? Is it all true? And how can our eons-old equipment deal with this explosion?

Remember the stunning videos of the Patriot missiles during the Gulf War. Is it true that the Patriot missiles shot down the Scuds during the Gulf War? Despite our seeing the explosion, in "real time," of Patriots destroying Scuds, it was not true. The discovery of truth in this case took thousands of hours of scientific analysis and verification. Our equipment for determining the truth is too frail to process images of missiles moving at 100 miles per second at 30,000 feet against the black void of a desert night sky. All of our current technology could not provide the truth as we viewed the event. The truth was a small fact-package: the location, at a precise nanosecond, of two missiles in flight. The precise nanosecond was the time of the explosion of the Scud. The billions of bits that compose the videos of these events were boiled down to a few observations of four numbers: longitude, latitude, altitude, and time. The economy of the fact-package that resulted from thousands of hours of analysis belies the expense and effort to produce it.

At least two cautions are in order for any businessperson faced with making decisions based on any volume or quality of data. The first would be to initiate a procedure for validation and trusted peer review of data assembly, processing, and logic train. The second would be to watch carefully for the expert bias that we all exhibit in varying degrees. In many cases, this bias is a cruel lens and not a discerning filter.

These accumulated biases make our minds fertile ground for factoids.

Factoids can be kin to white lies such as "I believe you have lost weight," or they can be major flaws in reasoning or data. Often factoids are trivial abbreviations for belief. Factoids such as "It is illegal to drive barefoot" exist because data is doubling every year, and our equipment to process the data remains medieval. We are not equipped to reason through most factoids and peel away to the kernel of truth, if it exists.

The clothing the factoid wears is usually beguiling and plausible. Do you believe that it is illegal to drive barefoot? I have believed it for at least 20 years. This seems plausible; after all, legislators have devoted themselves to far more trivial law making. Yet, I have no factual foundation for this belief. Actually, it is not illegal to drive barefoot in *any* state. Never has been. (This, among other quirky fact-packages, can be found at urbanlegends.com.[6]) This site investigates urban legends and other sayings to determine their veracity.

Factoids often arise when playing lottery numbers. Assume you win a bet with a friend and the price of victory is a lottery ticket. Your friend asks whether you want a quick-pick, which is having the lottery computer generate a random sequence of 6 numbers. Or, he asks, do you want him to select the 6-number sequence 1-2-3-4-5-6?

A randomly generated quick pick of any old 6 numbers would seem to have greater odds of winning than a ticket with the highly unlikely sequence of 1-2-3-4-5-6. Which ticket has a higher probability of winning?

Neither. Both tickets have *equal* probability of winning. *Any* selection of 6 numbers from 49 numbers has roughly a 1-in-14 million chance of winning.

It is tough to believe that the sequence of 6 numbers in a row has an equal probability of being picked as a randomly selected group of 6 numbers on a quick-pick ticket. In this case, we are bound by mental illusions. A mental illusion, as defined by Massimo Piattelli-Palmarini in his book, *Inevitable Illusions,* is a track, or tunnel, that our minds use to process information and make decisions under uncertainty.[7] In this book, he masterfully outlines numerous examples of a "cognitive unconscious" at work that efficiently dispatches decisions for us, almost despite data, rather than using data.

Our mental illusions make it difficult to immediately embrace this fact regarding a sequence of 6 numbers. When we think of the sequence of 1-2-3-4-5-6, we think of the special relationship each number has to one another. Such a sequence is a sure winner in poker, and imparts emotion for some people. Each number is defined by its relationship with the other numbers. Instead of numbers, think of 49 pictures of completely unrelated objects. Imagine pictures of such diverse things as a garbage scow, a tulip, a cat, a dictionary, a car, a blast furnace, a bolt, a telephone pole. If a lottery were constructed to pick 6 unrelated pictures from a selection of 49 pictures, we would not hesitate to begin thinking about any sequence of 6 pictures being equal in chance to any other sequence. When we use numbers, however, our minds automatically impart values to these numbers. We choose even numbers, prime numbers, birthdays, ages, lucky numbers, odd numbers, and other numbers with meaning to us. We cannot overcome the years of conditioning that arithmetic has brought to us.

We are predisposed—our minds are wired—to accept certain kinds of factoids. As Piattelli-Palmarini illustrates, our thinking has developed to accept and imprint certain mental illusions. One such example is our viewpoint on geography. In the United States, most of us visualize San Francisco as simply being north of Los Angeles.

Actually the city closest to being straight north of Los Angeles is Fallon, Nevada, *some 150 miles east* of Reno, Nevada. Most of us would assume that São Paolo, Brazil, or Rio de Janeiro is due south of Boston. However, the South American city due south of Boston is Santiago, Chile, which is on the west coast of South America, and nearly 1,600 miles from Rio. If airline pilots flew on their presumed knowledge, rather than on compass readings, airline travel would be much more adventurous.

So far, we have spoken about the inherent problems that recur with data. Data is rarely pristine; it usually has some small percentage of corrupted data mingled within it or has sectors of data that have been damaged or altered by any of a thousand incidents that degrade data. Then, this less than pure data is often propagated and multiplied, further compounding errors. Finally, our own cognition has not been designed as a digital logic switch, but was set up with cognitive illusions that nurture factoids.

Data is crowding out truth. Further, we are inherently limited in our ability to comprehend, as evidenced by mental illusions and the propensity to cling to factoids. Data is so abundant that we now need to develop a method to preindex data in some way. This preindexing forms what is called *metadata*: data to describe or prescribe other data. Metadata behaves like a genetic map to a greater body of data, and often provides reliability, economy, and manageability.

Metadata, peer-to-peer computing, and emerging truth systems are the first emerging tools to help process truth consistently and economically in the Internet weather.

> **Data is bursting beyond all storage capabilities. It is becoming necessary to store and process *data about data*, rather than the source data itself.**

It is yet another challenge to store this data. The National Center for Atmospheric Research in Boulder, Colorado, has a daunting mission. The center—referred to by its initials, NCAR—monitors the vital signs of the earth. NCAR was formed by more than 60 universities around the world to be the premier center for atmospheric research. NCAR accumulates data from hundreds of sources including weather satellites, ships, airliners, and its proprietary aircraft. It measures the vital signs of the atmosphere from the bottom of the ocean to the surface of the sun. One of NCAR's continuing projects is a long-term climate simulation. This simulation displays a likely temperature pattern, by day, for the coming century, given the current data available. The simulation is depicted as cyclonic, moving blobs of color (red for hot equator, blue for the frigid poles) that move away from the equator for the coming century. Naturally, the greater the data and the more precise the data from which the simulation is built, the more accurate the long-term simulation will be. NCAR is one of a handful of institutions whose charter is to evaluate the impact of greenhouse gases with respect to global warming. It is important to all humankind that NCAR and similar institutions accurately portray this simulation. However, the volume of data challenges even NCAR, home to some of the most powerful computing assets in the world. Formerly NCAR could store the source data and a simulation, and be able to call up the stored data from the simulation. With increasing data, NCAR often has to choose whether to store the source data or the simulation, but not both. It turns out that the most economical method is not to store the simulations, but rather to rerun them each time scientific work requires data from the simulation. NCAR then stores the source data and the initial conditions, or assumptions that drive that simulation.

NCAR and other entities that deal with enormous data files are beginning to work with metadata, which can be described as Cliffs notes about data. The data file that stores the initial conditions for a long-term weather simulation is metadata. The initial conditions, when applied to the source data and the simulator, produce a unique data file, which is the long-term simulation associated with its metadata.

If NCAR can pack simulations of one hundred future years of weather into a relatively small gigabyte file, then this application of metadata has utility for distilling reliable kernels of information from immense data files and advancing our achievement of truth.

A metadata capability for video was made notorious at the 2001 Super Bowl in Tampa. The entrance gates to the stadium had high-speed video cameras and video identification software from Viisage.[8] Each of the more than 100,000 persons who entered the stadium was photographed digitally. The faces were then compared with a database of known terrorists and criminals. This technology uses what is called Principal Component Analysis, patented by the Media Lab at the Massachusetts Institute of Technology. According to Viisage's Web site, "The Company's software translates the characteristics of a face into a unique set of numbers, which is referred to as the *eigenface*." This eigenface group of numbers is composed of the ratio of distance between eyes, the ratio of distance between ears and nose, the ratio of distance between mouth and eyes. For the Superbowl, the Tampa police were interested in matches between any fan and a database of known criminals.

Viisage supplies an algorithm that treats the data in a way that greatly simplifies searching databases. Viisage creates metadata for image files, in this case images of faces. The storage in this case is not the amorphous video of millions of faces, but a table of unique numbers. Instead of storing several megabytes per face, the eigenface requires only a few bytes of numbers. The fact-package is a unique group of numbers associated with a unique face. I assume the assignment of an eigenface to each of us is not that far away and may be desirable, since such metadata can positively identify an individual in many situations. This particular use of metadata can provide truthful identification and help also protect privacy.

We can minutely measure, record, and store infinitesimally small observations, and are approaching unlimited capacity to warehouse this data. By harnessing every computer hooked to the Internet, we can achieve immense processing power to mine the data. As our power of observation has increased, so has the difficulty of deduction. We will hoard the trusted sources. As the volume of raw data increases, so too does its frailty. It ages faster, is susceptible to corruption, and is too dense for comprehension. The software tools meant to mine this data trove become enfeebled as various softwares around them age and expire. We have complicated our search for fact-packages with powerful and alluring factoids, verisimilitude, and cyberexperience.

> Methods are emerging that can greatly enhance the truth
> and reliability of information used for decision making. One
> involves harnessing idle processing power and the other is a
> virtual journalistic and peer review process.

The first improvement is the development of peer-to-peer computing. With peer-to-peer techniques, it is theoretically possible to employ all computers linked to the Internet to process data. This method gained fame from its use in the SETI program at the University of California at Berkeley.[9] SETI is an abbreviation for Search for ExtraTerrestrial Intelligence, and this program has been accumulating radio signals—via a radio telescope at Arecibo, Puerto Rico—from deep space for more than a decade. The intent of the search is to listen for radio signals from intelligent life. The search involves finding patterns within radio data that could not have been generated by known natural processes. Once any patterns have been identified, then those patterns must be subjected to further statistical tests to determine the probability that the patterns were created by an intelligent life form. As can be imagined, within a few years, the quantity of data, which was about a terabyte per month, overwhelmed the ability of even the largest supercomputers to process it. Data tapes were arriving at Berkeley from Arecibo and being warehoused until such time that a big enough computer was built to process this flood of data. In 1995, two brilliant Berkeley graduate students conceived the idea of using the *entire Internet* as a data processing engine.

A modern personal computer, at any one moment, uses a small fraction of its central processing unit. The large majority of this power is idle. These students conceived a method, now called distributed computing, to harness this idle power from machines hooked to the Internet. Anyone who wants to can sign up and donate processing time while logged onto the Internet. Tens of millions of computers have contributed processing power to SETI. This method, called SETI@home, assigns vectors of data to computers to work with during the cpu idle time. Since SETI@home has access to several million computers at any one time, it is effectively the most powerful supercomputer on earth, with processing power said to average 15 teraflops (a teraflop is one trillion floating point operations per second). By contrast, the largest available supercomputer is IBM's ASCI White, which is rated at 12 teraflops and costs about $100 million dollars (as of February 1, 2001). The investment in SETI@home has been about $500 thousand, roughly one half percent of ASCI White.

This power has allowed SETI to pass through its data file and to maintain processing of new data. At the same time, it has allowed SETI to reexamine certain data files that show promise of patterns. This gleaning operation is critical to finding any patterns and may eventually be responsible for the discovery of an extraterrestrial communication.

The idle processing power of the computers using the Internet is incomprehensibly large. If 100 million computers are linked to the Internet, then the idle processing power that can be tapped by distributed computing techniques is about 200 teraflops, roughly enough to process the entire SETI data file each second. We are challenged again by something we can describe but cannot comprehend: Even if the entire Internet were harnessed, the exponential growth rate of information dictates that information will outstrip our ability to process it. This is because the addition of all the computers using the Internet—whether 50 million, 200 million, or a billion—is a linear function, and the exponential growth of data will always win out over a linear function.

Additional computing power, by itself, is a necessary but insufficient resource to deal with the growth of information. It is necessary to install peer-review processes, and there are a few well-developed examples that already use the communications facility of the Internet. It is instructive to examine and attempt to participate in these sites.

Although the disciplined process of journalistic editing has not emerged, per se, on the Internet, a system of peer review has. Slashdot (slashdot.org) is an online news site that defines itself as, *"News for Nerds. Stuff that matters."*[10] To assure quality, and to reduce the aimless and unstructured chat of many Web sites, Slashdot has developed a peer-review process for rating contributors. Although nearly anyone can contribute, becoming an online reporter whose material appears on the Web site includes a disciplined peer review. The first step is for a contributor to add commentary to a known writer's original content. This criticism is then, itself, submitted to review by the readers of Slashdot. Over time, certain writers are accorded expert status, and their comments are weighted with greater importance than unknown contributors. By this process, a writer's contributions are evaluated and judged for accuracy and reliability. As a writer gains stature, his words appear more often, and his comments help determine the fate of others' words. This electronic anarchic analog for the journalistic editing process is becoming an accepted method to increase the value and truth content of Web information.

The Slashdot model can be well adapted within corporations, especially when searching for experts. Often in knowledge management, documents by themselves are nowhere near as useful as the authors. Many corporate knowledge management databases are so bloated with devalued information that they are not used. Rather, individuals develop a small group of expert contacts who can shortcut the search for quality (true) information. This is an example of Gresham's law in action.

We have always searched for the truth. Curiosity has motivated us to ask questions and seek data for answers. We have sought explanations of everything, and the process of discovery has revealed more data, more questions, and more need for fact-packages. We have been searching for a mechanical method to determine the truth since the ancient mathematicians of Greece.

As the language of science, mathematics has been motivated by the search for truth. For thousands of years, mathematics believed its machinery to be true. Euclid's axioms and proof method for geometry were rooted in the conviction that the axioms were true, and the logic machinery produced results that were unassailably true. Mathematics assumed that it was near to the Truth at the end of the nineteenth century. Its quest was for a system of logic rules that could describe the truth or falsity of a statement constructed within the rules. And this search seemed near to the prize: a system of logical, complete, and consistent rules. Between 1880 and 1890, the Italian mathematician Giuseppe

Peano derived a handful of axioms that described the logic machinery of ordinary arithmetic. In 1903, Bertrand Russell and Alfred North Whitehead created a method to determine the truth-value of sentences that they called the *sentential calculus*.[11] Surely the Truth was just within reach. Then in 1934, German mathematician Kurt Godel proved that truth, as defined in a logic system, can *never* be known.[12] He showed that any system of logic robust enough to support the machinery of everyday arithmetic *must be logically inconsistent*. The belief in the absolute nature of truth was once again shown to be in conflict with reality.

These proofs mean humankind will never be able to determine truth with an algorithm. The truth, whether it is considered to be the reliable words of a good newspaper or the integrity of a scientist, will always require the participation of human wisdom. The truth will always take time, and humans will be sorely tempted to abbreviate the process of review and editing as tsunami after tsunami of data rises around us.

Summary

Data is doubling every year, yet the power of semiconductors doubles only every year and a half. This difference magnifies the problem of data processing since every three years the volume of data outstrips processing power of computers exponentially. At the end of three years, processing power has increased only by 4 times, while the volume of data has increased by 8 times. After nine years, the volume of data has increased 512 times, while processing power has only increased 64 times.

This surfeit of data causes truth—the careful, cautious, and principled assembly of data into knowledge—to be crowded out. While there is more and more high-quality data, this data, perversely, becomes more difficult to sculpt into information. Add to this the challenges of virtual reality, and what is true, virtually true, and not true at all becomes a unique issue for our times and for the foreseeable future.

This situation creates Gresham's law of data: Bad data drives out good. The wealth-intoxicated frenzy of dot-com business-to-consumer and business-to-business Internet market projections and assertions drove all common sense to ground. It was a hyper-inflated frenzy of skewed data.

We embrace factoids as comfortable abbreviations. Although we desire truth, we often cannot recognize it, or we reject it because the truth seems implausible. Often our thinking is at war with our need for truthful information because of our accumulated biases, and the fundamental ways we categorize information.

A key challenge is that electronic data wear the clothing of electronic authenticity. A factoid is an observation wearing the clothing of fact. Given the sheer volume of electronic information and images, we will begin to treasure "true" sources and hoard them.

Making good decisions requires sound, reliable, consistent information. It requires information free from bias of any kind.

CHAPTER 6

Taxis, Technology, and Trust

Trust is an experience good. We cannot assert trust or claim it, and we cannot purchase it. Trust is earned and perceived. Trust is accumulated through time and reliable behavior. The electronic distance of cyberspace, the anonymity of transactions, and the gradual demise of truth are making trust scarcer. Unlike the other verities, trust cannot be bought. It is possible to purchase time, privacy, and truth through various products and processes. Trust, however, is dependent on truth and reliable behavior over time, and is then related to these verities. There are many markets where privacy also is critical to achieving trust, in particular health care and financial services.

A key challenge for Internet commerce is the achievement of trust. The freewheeling, open, anarchic, fast pace of the Internet is inimical to trust. Only a few Web site and dot-com companies from the dot-com boom have achieved trust—among the most notable being Amazon.com, eBay, Travelocity, and Schwab.com. All of these firms have achieved trust by consistent performance. Yet each has also relied on slightly different service features to gain consumer trust. Amazon, dealing in small dollar purchases, has focused on providing superior service and selection. eBay has been among the first to provide reputation rating of its sellers and buyers.[1] This rating system has become a valued indicator of the reliability of the seller or buyer. Travelocity prominently features its affiliation as a Sabre company, and Sabre is the first and largest travel reservation system. Schwab provides three channels of access: the Web, phone, and in-person through their office network. And each has focused on near flawless Web execution.

Achieving trust is one of the most difficult challenges for businesses using electronic channels. Several of the biggest concepts that propelled e-commerce investment in the past five years did not focus on trust. Many of these businesses focused on time and novelty and did not invest in building consumer trust.

One of the first big ideas was the "last mile to the home" as it pertains to Internet retailing. When the dot-com boom escalated in 1998 and 1999, some highly optimistic projections placed e-tailing volumes at reaching as much as 30 percent of retail sales, which is about four times catalog retail volumes. This kind of increase in volume would be a boon to UPS, FedEx, and the U.S. Postal Service. But it could be a bonanza for an entity that could control the last mile delivery, that of warehouse or truck dock to an individual home. The common strategy that emerged to own "the last mile" to the home was through online grocery business. This has stalled due mostly to failed trust.

Another big idea was the projected explosion of online electronic bill presentment and payment. Because Internet users now number as many as 75 million in the United States, it was assumed that this savvy community would quickly subscribe to individual paperless payment systems. It was assumed that this group of wired consumers would accept electronic invoices and executed payment for all household bills. This service also has stalled primarily due to lack of trust.

Yet another concept was the projected conquest of commerce by e-marketplaces. The jury is still out on the success of these massive collaborative ventures. These ventures, such as Covisint in the automotive industry, Exostar in aerospace, Transora in consumer goods, Elemica in chemicals, are consortia of competitive companies formed to leverage frictionless commerce on the Web. To succeed, the forming companies must trust each other, and any users must trust the consortia. Simply moving competitors to become co-opitors requires trust, let alone ceding to one another decision authority over such issues as procurement, specification, and design.

The e-marketplaces are harbingers of increasing alliance formation in all industries. The sheer pace, innovation, global expansion, and complexity of business are causing alliances and joint ventures to form, and trust is fundamental to the success of any alliance. While alliances have been formed for centuries, they were formerly rare—a last-resort measure. The requirement to ally to complete a product or service offering is now commonplace—alliances have become the least worst measure. Mutual trust among partners is essential to achieving a successful alliance. Yet, according to various sources, including a *Business Week* special report on partnerships (October 25, 1999), more than half of all alliances fail outright, and less than a fifth of alliances are unqualified successes.[2]

The last mile to the home: Whom do you trust to enter your home?

The dot-com boom led off with online retailing, which was renamed *business-to-consumer,* and then referred to as B2C. Most of these e-tailing concepts focused on the value of time to the harried citizen of the Internet weather, since it is acknowledged that most of us have less and less unassigned time. It was assumed that the extraordinary time value of online service would overpower compromises that must be made elsewhere in the service.

One of these compromises was trust.

The first successful online retailers focused on mailable items such as books, music CDs, clothing, jewelry, and other small items. The most important characteristic of such items is that they can be delivered by the U.S. Postal Service, or alternatively by such carriers as UPS and FedEx. All of these services are trusted delivery agents; therefore an e-tailer of mailable items was not required to create a trusted-agent delivery system. Also, all three of these services leave packages without entering a home and have established long service records. Those e-tailers that chose mailables were faced with traditional retail challenges such as handling back orders, shipping the correct merchandise, and having the correct inventory. Catalog retailing is a business of "eaches." Failing to receive an item ordered from a catalog retailer causes more disappointment than a stock-out in a retailer's store. Many mailable e-tailers underestimated the difficulty of maintaining inventory and shipping perfect orders. For these particular e-tailers, building trust is the challenge of fulfilling exactly what a customer ordered, time and again. Amazon has excelled at this and has gained consumer trust as a result.

There are also successful online retailing ventures in goods or services that can be delivered electronically, such as airline tickets, event tickets of any kind, and financial services. Trust has been less of issue in airline and event ticket purchases, but has been a critical hurdle for online financial services. The growth of these services still face considerable barriers of trust.

The online purchase of groceries seemed appealing because groceries are a weekly purchase, and thereby a service could be established with assured frequencies and a weekly visit to its consumer base. Almost any other household purchase is occasional and unpredictable. Given this weekly frequency, the use of weekly grocery delivery was assumed to provide ownership of "the last mile to the home." The weekly grocery delivery would provide the platform for assuming all other e-tailing deliveries.

In retrospect, these business plans were fantastic. Most online grocers acknowledge that grocery home delivery is a tough, low-margin business with a perpetual and elevated service requirement. The investor was asked to hold his breath, however, because the grocery deliveries would allow ownership of the last mile to the home. Based on this ownership, the next business model built from this unique piece of real estate would be high-margin, easy, with little discerning service requirement. No online grocer was able to describe this nirvana business although attempts were made to include dry cleaning, video rental, and other implausible products. Another way of saying this is, "The current business we *must* do is really lousy, but it positions us to command a wonderful business that we can't quite describe."

Essential to any possible success of the grocery business is a repeat customer, and the online grocer faces a double trust challenge. The first trust challenge is the selection of perishable food for someone else. The second trust challenge is allowing a stranger to repeatedly enter the home.

Usually when perishables are purchased, the decision to purchase is made on the spot. A consumer looks over the various vegetables, fruit, or meat, and makes a purchase based on the presentation of the food at the time. This is not possible when purchasing online. Many consumers use online grocers only for such noisome purchases as bottled water, beer, canned goods, and other relatively heavy merchandise. The consumer actually shops for the high-margin perishable in the store. While this may seem to contradict the business model—that of harried consumers never entering the grocery store—it does fit a model of a consumer's optimizing trust, and never having to carry heavy items to and from the car. Also if there are no perishable items in the purchase, it may not be necessary to be home to accept the delivery.

The second compromise on trust is the driver. For all intents and purposes, *the driver is the service.* For the vast majority of customers, the driver is the only person they will ever meet from the online grocer. The first time a driver shows up wearing a baseball cap with an obscenity emblazoned on it, that consumer is lost forever. Consumers do not leave online grocer services for technical reasons. They leave because the produce is mottled, the order was incomplete, or the driver was unacceptable.

Among the most important lessons from this surge of e-tailing ventures is that technology will not be the differentiating factor for long-term success. More traditional attributes such as selection, perfect orders, and trust will provide the competitive advantages.

We are seeing the maturation of e-tailing. The first challenge was technical, that of establishing robust Web sites linked to enough server power, with enough bandwidth, to handle hundreds of thousands of online activities simultaneously. In the first phase of e-tailing, many new ventures faced "success crises" wherein overwhelming demand paralyzed the order management technology. The next phase—and the next series of success crises—tested the limits of physical capabilities associated with these new businesses.

Many of them could not fulfill orders because of insufficient warehouse space, process, or inventory. Among these notable failures were eToys.com and Furniture.com. Now, the maturation of e-tailing requires achieving, growing, and sustaining trust. The same multistage process is also true of business-to-business e-commerce, which lags e-tailing by a few quarters.

In making deliveries to the consumer at home, UPS, FedEx, and the U.S. Postal Service all are trusted intermediaries. However, their role hasn't been put to the test that a weekly grocery delivery demands. They haven't been tested with the delivery and setup of furniture or appliances in the home. Basically, these three make quick stops at homes. In many cases, other home delivery services require the performance of services in the home, such as placing groceries in inventory. The performance of this service, each week, into the foreseeable future, requires that the driver earn a much higher level of trust than a postal carrier. The key challenge for the future is acquiring consumer trust and guarding it as the company treasure, for it is.

Can a trusted service be mimicked by technology? Are trust and technology in conflict?

Technology rarely enhances trust. Just think about your recent experience with the telephone. How often have you called to an airline, a hotel company, an electric utility, a gas company, a department store—you name it—and actually been greeted by a person? Most often, we hear a recorded menu of selections that require a phenomenal memory, the attention of someone hypnotized, and the time to actually listen. Amuse (or infuriate) yourself by calling customer service at your telephone company to see what technology has wrought in the name of customer service.

Technology often means distant and impersonal. Even inside a taxi, which is as close as two strangers will usually allow themselves, especially in New York City, recorded messages start to play as soon as you shut the door. Formerly, NYC hacks were as voluble as any on earth. Now, sterile recorded messages remind the passenger to buckle the seat belt and thus replace the reason for initial contact. Taxis provide intimacy, and thereby provide an interesting example of establishing trust, or not, devoid of any technology. And, for trusted services, the Black Cabs of London by far outrank any other in the world.

The Black Cabs are one of the world's most venerable services. Anyone who has been to London certainly remembers the squat, unique cabs and their unusual cleanliness and quality. Is it possible to mimic the features of a Black Cab and still retain the unusual level of trust afforded to the cabs by the riding public? Would the Black Cabs be enhanced by the recorded voice of the Queen? Of Tony Blair or Paul McCartney greeting you as you close the door? The idea is ludicrous.

As you travel around the world, the taxi ride often becomes the most memorable part of the trip. There are pleasant memories, and there are remarkable memories. It is remarkable when your taxi driver completely leaves the six stalled traffic lanes on a superhighway near São Paulo and jumps to the berm, which is not level and sometimes not paved, and rockets past traffic at 60+ miles an hour. It is remarkable that Moscow cabs drive at night with their lights off. It is remarkable when your taxi in Miami quits twice between downtown and the airport because the driver is adding a quart of gasoline at a time. Taxi drivers in Miami must pay for their own gas, so it is an art to return the taxi running on just vapors. A quart of gasoline will power a car about three or four miles in hot, humid, jammed Miami traffic.

The world traveler will remember these cab rides, but will always identify the London Black Cab as being among the cleanest, safest, and most trustworthy of all taxis anywhere in the world. While there are other clean, safe taxis (notably Tokyo), the London Black Cabs are different in one fashion from any other taxis: The entrance requirements to become a Black Cab are extremely strict, archaic, and technology-free. One of the requirements is a prodigious memory. The Black Cabs are one of the few, if not the only, jobs in the world today that rely on a major feat of memory. Thus the institution of Black Cab is based on an anachronism that can be easily replaced by technology. But doing so could not replace the trust these drivers have earned.

To become a Black Cab operator in London requires that an individual pass several tests. An applicant must submit to an intensive background investigation by the London Metro Police, demonstrate an impeccable driving record, pass a medical exam, and attain *The Knowledge*. Of all of these tests, attaining The Knowledge is by far the most difficult.[3] The Knowledge is an archaic feat of memory: the complete memorization of London streets, including the alleys, the one-ways, the peculiar streets that change their name, and the changing construction of new streets and rerouting of streets. Even the best minds require two years of concentrated effort to achieve The Knowledge. It generally takes three years for a good mind to accomplish this feat, and it often takes four years. Once you claim to have attained The Knowledge—through a kind of apprenticeship—you submit to a road test with the worst curmudgeon Black Cabby that can be found. If you survive the ordeal of trial by curmudgeon, you buy a Black Cab and become both the owner and the driver of the cab. This process necessarily limits the supply of Black Cabs since someone must be able to devote up to four years committing The Knowledge to memory. Becoming a Black Cabby is like joining a guild. The result is an institution of impeccable credentials and public trust.

Current satellite and navigation technology can easily replace The Knowledge. It would be easier and less time-consuming to equip cabs with street-graphic displays and navigation capability to direct a cab around London. With such systems, the minute-by-minute directions can be delivered with voice. One voice could be programmed for the driver; one voice for the passenger. The passenger voice could be programmed for the language of the passenger, along with taped messages to buy Microsoft Office or to shop at Harrods. This technology would radically increase the supply of Black Cab drivers, who would not have to dedicate several years to apprenticeship. Even the drivers who could not memorize the streets would be eligible to drive a Black Cab. As with the native language passenger voice, the driver voice could be programmed for any of the more than 200 major world languages. More drivers would mean lower wages, and, thereby, a combination of lower fares and higher profits for the taxi company.

So replacing The Knowledge is not that difficult; the technology already exists and is deployed in millions of vehicles elsewhere. However, of the entire package of attributes that make the Black Cab a charming institution, The Knowledge is the least public. Most of us do not question that a taxi driver actually knows how to get to and from place to place within a city. Acquiring The Knowledge is similar to acquiring a professional degree. At three years, law school is similar to the time and effort required for The Knowledge. Because of this extraordinary requirement to become a cabby in London, very high caliber talent is driving the cabs. The result is courtesy, cleanliness, efficiency, and trust.

Of all the attributes, the hardest to duplicate is trust. That we care can be established by polling world travelers. Ask world travelers about the best taxis in the world. London will always rate.

In service industries that are driven by technology, trust is more difficult to acquire.

Financial services provide an interesting example where technology is in place, but trust is not.

The technological environment of financial services is the best of any industry. Due to the risks associated with financial transactions, financial services firms have been early adapters of security technology. The financial industry's encryption and Internet security is far more advanced than that of any other industry. A recent (January 25, 2001) report by the U.S. Security and Exchange Commission entitled *Examinations of Broker-Dealers Offering Online Trading*[4] found that all online trading firms offered some form of encryption, and nearly all offered very strong encryption. The security surrounding wire transfer of funds is nearly uncrackable, and there have been few, if any, technological heists of funds. This is despite Hollywood's depiction of Sean Connery's and Catherine Zeta-Jones' technological heist of several billion dollars in the movie *Entrapment*. Nearly all financial thefts involve breached security process, not breached technology.

Given the technology in place, electronic bill payment and presentment (EBPP) would seem to be a perfect product for the

Internet-enabled consumer, of whom there are more than 75 million. These are among the savviest and most affluent consumers and thereby constitute a desirable target market. The EBPP products allow bill consolidation and payment while using just the computer. There are no envelopes, no retrieval of bills from a mailbox in the rain, no placing envelopes in a mailbox, no writing checks. This allows someone to execute the time-overhead chore of bill paying while flying, waiting for a plane, or riding a commuter train. The services offer varying degrees of proof of payment. In fact, Epinions.com reviews of EBPP services are generally positive. It would seem that such services are poised to take off.

However, only about 100,000 consumers in the United States are using online bill presentment.[5] This is an immeasurably small percentage—well less than 1 percent—of the 75 million Internet users. If the industry has information technology security, and product reviews from early adapters are positive, then why has electronic bill payment and presentment been so slow to gain market share?

Security concerns account for some of the slow market penetration. According to Jupiter Research's James Van Dyke, 58 percent of online consumers did not make purchases on specific Web sites because of security concerns. Van Dyke states, *"Attention focused on online security incidents has led consumers to believe that fraud is approximately 12 times more prevalent online than it is offline."*[6] Separately, Jupiter Research has reported that 54 percent of consumers don't trust a third party with sensitive billing information. Forrester Research also has reported that 73 percent of consumers continue to deposit checks, in person, with a human teller.[7]

Obviously, the barrier is trust. Despite sound evidence that online financial transactions are as safe, possibly safer than those conducted in person, the majority of Internet-enabled consumers will not place their trust in such systems. This is due to what's at risk versus the convenience gained. Most electronic theft has been of credit cards, and in the United States and many countries, an individual's financial exposure is limited. But many of these thefts have been traced to Russia, the Philippines, Thailand, and other distant nations. A technological incursion into your money is silent and stealthy, and likely to go undetected for a few days. By that time, your funds could be on deposit in a Moscow bank, or anywhere in the world, untraceable. The fear associated with this kind of event overpowers the convenience of using online financial products.

Can trust be vouchered?

A group of third parties interested in the outcome of EBPP market penetration are the world's postal services. In most countries, the postal services have trust but little technology. In the developed world, the postal services are life-threatened by technology, in particular e-mail and EBPP. The large majority of postal profit is derived from first-class mail. The majority of first-class mail is bill presentment and payment. Thus postal services have a significant stake in the outcome of electronic bill payment.

Recognizing this threat, both the United States Postal Service and Canada Post have entered the electronic bill payment market. USPS has allied with Checkfree, an Internet-based payment service.[8] Canada Post has formed a joint venture company called ePost, which can accept bills and pay bills electronically.[9] As one of Canada's most trusted entities, Canada Post is vouching, through its accumulated consumer trust, for this service. The logo for ePost contains the implied voucher from Canada Post—a winged chevron that is the same as the one used in the Canada Post identity. ePost is openly affiliated with Canada Post and is also associated with the Bank of Montreal, one of Canada's four largest banks, and Telus, a major Canadian telecommunications company.

While not specifically advertising itself as an electronic bill payment facility, ePost positions itself as an electronic mailbox with features such as electronic bill payment. The EBP capabilities are just one feature of a mailbox system, including the ability to accept real mail, send real mail, and to filter advertising mail according to preferences. Throughout any transaction on the system, the link between the individual personal computer and the ePost server is protected by strong encryption. ePost has been designed so that no activities occur on the personal computer; all transactions occur within the fortress firewalled boundaries of ePost servers.

This particular joint venture highlights some of the unusual outcomes caused by technology. Canada Post, a trusted entity, is contributing trust to ePost. At the same time, the Bank of Montreal and Telus are becoming electronic post offices. Canada Post has recognized the threat of EBPP to its core letter mail franchise and is openly cannibalizing it with a sound virtual product. Behind the scenes of this product, other allied companies are providing such technologies as hosting, security, and encryption. But for this venture, Canada Post is capturing value and equity from its storehouse of consumer trust.

Can trust be vouchered? Can it be bought and sold? ePost and other alliances and joint ventures demonstrate attempts to execute just that—the sale or trading of trust for equity. Whatever the outcome of this electronic mailbox and EBPP facility assembled by a real postal service, a bank, a telephone company, and several information technology firms, forming alliances in response to markets is becoming paramount to success.

Alliances have transitioned from being measures of last resort to becoming preferred forms of entering new markets. Technology warps the shape of markets. It creates wholly new markets and destroys old markets. All industries are facing similar challenges. Responding to these rapid changes requires speed over cost, and ergo, alliances are the preferred method of execution. Or, better stated, alliances are the least-worst method of entering new markets.

It is a significant possibility that technology will reduce, or even replace, the traditional postal service. In this example, it is easy to see the impact of technology: E-mail takes seconds versus days for letter mail. E-mail is nearly free while letter mail costs upward of 34 cents per letter. The postal services cost time, which is a cardinal sin in the Internet weather. However, they still have trust. Their responses are demonstrating their attempt to harvest trust and privacy, having ceded time to the Internet or even to former dreaded competitors. For example, in November 2000, USPS and FedEx announced a major alliance that, in effect, ceded to FedEx much of the postal service's expedited parcel business. FedEx will place its familiar purple drop boxes in tens of thousands of post offices around the country.[10]

To see Canada Post forming alliances with a bank is not astounding. To see the United States Postal Service forming an alliance with FedEx is astounding. To see Ford forming a joint venture with General Motors stretches credulity.

Alliances are forming to gain economy of skill.

The Industrial Age was powered by economy of scale. The Information Age is powered by economy of skill. Formerly, increased margins, pricing power, and market share were gained by economy of scale; and vertical integration was the fastest and cheapest method of meeting production need.

One of the most notable outcomes of the information economy has been the disaggregation of industrial companies; the automotive original equipment manufacturers (OEMs) provide one of the best examples. Formerly, the OEMs were vertically integrated. Each of them manufactured nearly every part needed to assemble a car. But almost from inception, Ford was the most vertically integrated. The famous Rouge complex conceived and built by Henry Ford included the ability to make steel, glass, and virtually every part necessary for a car. Iron ore entered the steel mill on the River Rouge, and finished automobiles exited the Dearborn assembly plant. All activities were performed within the Rouge complex, and no partners were required. When the only car offered was a Model T, such a complex presented Ford with considerable economies of scale.

As with many industries, fashion, innovation, and technology have seeped into the automotive business. It is now far more important to produce fashionable cars and to balance supply with demand. There are now many styles of cars, making long production runs difficult to accomplish. The profitable path now is to create a car that the public demands and to respond by building only cars that are ordered. In this environment, a massive assembly complex can become a millstone rather than a competitive asset. These assets are like the Queen of Spades in a game of hearts.

The disaggregation of Ford began with the sale of the steel plant on the Rouge complex to form Rouge Steel as an independent entity. It culminated in early 2000 with the spinout to shareholders of Ford's parts operations called Visteon. This follows similar actions by General Motors in forming Delphi Corporation.

A visit to Ford's Web site includes a special index for "partnerships and alliances" that lists dozens out of several hundred alliances. Included are Microsoft, Qualcomm, America's National Parks, Top Driver, UPS, Internet Capital Group, Yahoo!, iVillage Auto Center, and Covisint—a joint venture of General Motors, Ford, DaimlerChrysler, Nissan, PSA Peugeot Citroën, and Renault.

These alliances bring economies of skill to Ford that are difficult or impossible to acquire otherwise. Microsoft has sold a minority equity stake in CarPoint.com to Ford. This allows Ford direct communication with automotive customers. Without this kind of channel, it must rely on its dealers for customer insight since Ford is enjoined from selling directly to consumers in most states. CarPoint is not a Ford company; it is allied with Ford, and thereby is more trusted as an independent adviser for an automotive consumer than is Ford itself. iVillage is a Web site devoted to women, and women buy nearly 60 percent of all new automobiles.[11] By allying with iVillage, Ford hopes to become more trusted by women and increase sales to them. The alliance with Qualcomm provides in-vehicle navigation and wireless communication for cars, in response to the capabilities brought to General Motors by its subsidiary Hughes and their joint On-Star capability.

It is Covisint, however, that provides the best example for the future. And one of the key challenges for the success of Covisint, and hundreds of other vertical e-marketplaces, is the trust of the partners. At each stage of alliance formation, building and maintaining trust is the most critical quality necessary for success. Its takes mutual trust and candor to address these alliance issues:

- Who will direct the alliance?
- How will contributions to the alliance be valued?
- What is the value to the market of this alliance?
- Who will own the customer relationship?
- How will profits or losses be shared?

Imagine the discussions among the owners of Covisint regarding the governance of the alliance. The owners are the world's largest industrial firms who have been competing with each other across the entire world for a century. Despite the need to collaborate, these competitors cannot easily come to the table and trust each other. Yet Covisint and the other e-marketplaces cannot succeed without the mutual trust of the partner-owners.

Alliances are rapidly increasing and thereby increasing the demand for trust in industry. The electronic distance of transactions and the sheer pace of business are challenging the supply of trust. Taken together, these forces mean that trust is radically increasing in value.

Summary

Of all the verities, the most difficult to achieve is trust. Truth, time, and privacy can be purchased and managed by individual effort. Trust, on the other hand, cannot be purchased, asserted, borrowed, or improved by individual effort. Trust is perceived and is a measure of numerous interactions over time.

The nature of technological industries is inimical to achieving trust. They are young, entrepreneurial, fast-paced, and based on electronic interactions. All these factors make achieving trust more difficult. In this sense, the supply of trust is dwindling. Despite the envelope of electronic communication, trust still requires face-to-face interaction.

Many Internet-enabled ventures have underestimated the difficulty of achieving consumer trust. It is the "touch" part of customer relationships, and no amount of software, technology, data mining, or algorithms can replace a person's empathy. In particular, online grocers have been faced with a double trust challenge—selecting perishables for someone else, and of consistently and courteously entering someone's home. Online bill presentment and payment— despite a powerful increase in convenience and lower costs—has stalled because a majority of consumers do not trust electronic intermediary services even though the financial services industry has an admirable record for online security.

To achieve trust is to be authentic, responsive and, above all, honest. As part of a sterling service record, one of the best ways to win trust is during resolution of problems. In many cases, a long, long service record is not noticed, remarked, or remembered. However, the judicious, empathetic, and expeditious solution to a problem will be remarked and remembered. Service is measured at the margins, at those few events that stand out in a track record of good service. Beware of electronic distance from customers. Electronic distance may cause current customers to divorce you rather than embrace you and may cause prospective customers just to click on by.

New technology, new business relationships, or new forms of service all place pressure on trusted relationships. To reduce this pressure, it is instructive to learn from the world's most trusted institutions, which often have built trust through careful selection and motivation of their people.

Many of the world's most venerable services and products are technology-free. In fact consumer trust in the Black Cab institution of London would more likely be reduced by technology than enhanced by it. Trust cannot be mimicked with technology, and technology often diminishes trust.

Novelty, innovation, and pace of the Internet weather require firms to make alliances to succeed. There is now too much information technology landscape for one firm to master, often leaving alliances as the only option to compete in a market. Even IBM has ceded information technology space to competition and acquired much more through alliances with hundreds of firms. An alliance milestone was marked when General Motors, Ford, and Daimler-Chrysler announced the formation of their joint venture, Covisint. The formation, execution, and success of these thousands of alliances require trust. Given the proliferation of alliances among competitors and collaborators, there is an entirely new set of demands for trust in business. In this respect, the demand for trust has increased across the board.

Trust is facing dwindling supply and increased demand, and thereby has increased in value.

To achieve trust, even in our technological industries, there are no shortcuts. Trust requires time and consistent, honest information; it requires authenticity and intimacy. These things have not changed—their execution has. It is tempting to abbreviate these disciplined and perpetual behaviors. When faced with novel technology, resist the temptation to increase the distance between your firm and your customers. Distance decreases trust and must be overcome for a business to be successful.

CHAPTER 7

Individual Sovereignty

In a few hundred years . . . it is likely that the most important event historians will see is not technology, not the Internet, not e-commerce. It is the unprecedented change in the human condition. For the first time—literally—substantial numbers of people have choices. For the first time, they will have to manage themselves. And society is totally unprepared for it. . . . Throughout human history, it was the super-achievers—and only the super-achievers (such as Mozart and Da Vinci)—who knew when to say "No." They always knew what to reach for. They knew where to place themselves. Now all of us will have to learn that.

—Peter Drucker[1]

The atmosphere of technology that characterizes the Internet weather places incessant, profound force on the way we work and the way firms organize to accomplish work. Since data and communication are becoming free, individuals now have the freedom to perform work at home, according to their own schedules. The economics of technology accelerate the pace of work, requiring firms to execute faster. To be faster, firms must access the best intellect, the best creativity faster. To be nimble, firms must pare away the time overhead of routine functions that simply sustain the firm.

Firms are opening up data access for individuals and requiring workers to become more independent and decisive, since this is the only way to gain speed of work. This provides more sovereignty to workers. At the same time, this trend has accelerated the reduction of full-time employees. These employees are being replaced by people working on individual contracts and on a project-specific basis. The conclusion of these trends is worker sovereignty, whether desired or not.

Sovereignty is an ironic gift: It provides more freedom and more enrichment, but requires more individual responsibility. It requires an individual to command his career as if it were a product portfolio.

We do not have to wait a few hundred years for *"unprecedented change in the human condition."* Substantial change has already occurred. We have already developed a class of sovereign workers—elite programmers, consultants, writers, lawyers, educators, artists, musicians, trainers, meeting planners, and salespeople. They are mobile, branded mercenaries. These individual sovereigns rule over their work life, workplace, and work time. They have earned freedom, security, and insecurity. This class of people has grown from a mere handful in 1900 to several million in 2000. Their percentage of the workforce swelled from immeasurably small (effectively zero) to more than 8.3 million, or almost 7 percent of workers in the century from 1900 to 2000 (Bureau of Labor Statistics: "Contingent and Alternative Employment Arrangements"[2]). Peter Drucker notes changes *that will have* occurred in several hundred years; the changes *that have already* occurred are remarkable.

At a certain point, the sourcing of people becomes the sourcing of intellect, processes, knowledge products, or knowledge outcomes. Firms must learn to source these activities rather than employees. Throughout all these relationships, whether short- or long-term, business will accelerate. To maintain or conquer this pace, firms and their vendor-sovereigns must share data openly and truthfully, and must develop trust. Candor and trust are the only ways to execute quickly.

Some 8.3 million or more people already execute their work using alternative arrangements instead of full-time employment. These individuals are already aware of the need for building an individual product or capability portfolio. In this context, individuals must be concerned about their product, their brand. Above all, this brand will be manifested through a trusted reputation. It is also necessary to build unique knowledge and to keep current in that knowledge.

Sovereign workers, once successful, are difficult to attract as employees. These successful sovereigns are often the most talented.

Tom Vick is an example of such a sovereign worker. He has been an information technology professional for 20 years, of which 14 years have been as an independent contractor. These 20 years include three stints as an employee, but he has been independently contracting for the past 9 years. Vick's history is typical of many independent information technology professionals.

In high school, he began writing code for games on the Commodore computer, one of the first home computers available in the early 1980s. It was primarily a game computer, and Vick became expert in the Commodore operating system by the time he was 16. While in high school, he worked part time from the home developing games and other features for the Commodore. He attended college for one year, but the allure of making money was too great. He left college to start a software services firm with his father and then moved to become a partner in another small software services firm. Between the stints with these firms he independently contracted.

At age 36, he is well established as an individual talent. The rates for services in the markets where he chooses to compete range from $75 per hour up to $225 per hour. His work has averaged 50 billable hours per week, just a bit more than the average American employee. If he could produce 2,000 billable hours a year—which is in line with an attorney's billable hours per year—he would enjoy gross income of $450,000. While not always able to charge $225 per hour, Vick has been able to command prices for his services at the high end of contracting rates for 9 years and, as a result, has become financially independent. Now, he is already contemplating retirement, his next career, or possibly starting another firm.

Vick can contemplate retirement, or at least restructuring his work life, because he has established a brand. His branded product—his skills and reputation—is well known among several buyers of such talent, and among other sovereign workers. Vick is established within a network and does not have to rely on one company for workload and compensation.

Vick's contracts come through personal referrals and traditional third-party contracting firms. Although jobs are available on the Internet, he has established himself well enough that he does not need to use the Internet to obtain jobs; his personal network is robust enough that he is never without work. But he monitors RHI.com, Dice.com, and Computerjobs.com to check the market.

Because of the balance that sovereignty provides, Vick would not consider becoming an employee. This balance includes being able to work as much or as little as desired, working at home, and setting his price according to market demand. Because he has positioned himself on the high end of the informational technology services spectrum, he rarely has trouble obtaining work contracts and has great latitude in the conditions of the contract. The primary benefit, though, is higher income working independently instead of as an employee.

The way Tom Vick is managing his work life would be totally foreign to Tom Rath, the main character of Sloan Wilson's classic novel, *The Man in the Gray Flannel Suit,* published in 1955. The excerpt from the book jacket describes Tom Rath's work life:

> . . . the man in the gray flannel suit is a fairly universal figure in mid-twentieth century America. The gray flannel suit is the uniform of the man with the briefcase who leaves home each morning to make his living as an executive in a nearby city. Tom Rath's wife appreciates the security this job provides.[3]

Although this novel captured the essence of being a company man in New York City in the mid-1950s, this role and the classic relationship of employee did not begin to really change until the advent of the personal computer in the mid-1980s.

The concept of lifetime employment with a firm has gone the way of Cadillac fins and hula hoops.

When a person became an employee of a Fortune 500 firm in the 1970s, it was assumed that person was signing on for life. Inherently, the firm and employee assumed a parent-child relationship, with the firm supplying health care, wage, pension, and community. The firm was omniscient, and the entry workers looked to it for definition and role. We conformed to moiling over a small set of code, to following the rote of the assembly line, to training in the practiced art of the firm, to earning our steps on a well-defined ladder. The Hay System codified wage in terms of numbers, tradition, and tenure. The system of working and getting ahead was one of normative actions. The firm became central to our lives, and its needs were paramount. We moved to places where the firm needed our presence. We used our time in synchrony with the beat of the firm itself. Overall, this was a system of a parent raising a child.

The erosion of the classic employer-employee relationship began in the information technology departments of major firms. These departments are the mine canaries of the sovereign worker trend. They are on the frontier of technology and perform on the frontier of worker sovereignty with a fluid amalgam of talent—permanent employees, contractors, and project-oriented consultants. Any firm, regardless of size, must conform its IT employment to the ambient weather of the IT market. Every major firm arrives at an optimized mix of the three kinds of talent, but no firm I know of depends solely on employees, or on contractors, or on consultants. An information technology department becomes the nerve tissue of a firm, and, as such, is a silhouette of the firm itself.

The consulting firms that live from IT consulting—and that is the majority of revenue in big league consulting—are ceding sovereignty to their workers because of the work ecosystem they perform in. The consulting workplace provides a small market study of the greater cybermarket. To begin with, a consultant has no permanent workplace. The client site is the workplace, and it changes with the project. Many times, the site provided is an unused room so small and cramped that working off site, at home, is preferable to listening to the breathing of every consultant on the project. The consulting office is becoming a place where little client work is performed. Instead, it is devoted to the life of the consulting firm itself. The office is the source of the firm's community, culture, and collegiality.

Many of the largest consulting firms no longer declare a headquarters location.[4] Because the work occurs at client sites all over the world and a notable quality-of-life issue for many consultants is the availability of nonstop flights to and from the home city, the erosion of headquarters as a specific location can be predicted. The next time you are in O'Hare Airport and have time between flights, examine the meeting room announcements at the O'Hare Hilton, a hotel within the airport itself. Dozens of meetings are always being held by consulting firms, many of whom have offices in Chicago, but find it simpler and faster to meet on the airport property. Some firms have even eliminated offices and chosen "hoteling": They simply call in and make a reservation for an enclosed or open space, depending on availability and the priority of their need. No files remain in an office location, no telephone extensions; there is just an elaborate system of telephone forwarding and file forwarding. The office is no longer the place of work, but a place to meet other members of the firm and to participate in "community." In this environment, an employee is more a guest of the office than a resident. This kind of work is not place-constrained; it is peripatetic, global, and time-constrained.

In this environment, it is difficult to build trust between a corporation and its workers. Distance is inimical to trust. The freedom to work at a distance, tethered electronically, does not allow for the personal interactions that build a firm's culture and create trust. The solution chosen varies from firm to firm, but often these companies have instituted a concept of communities formed around skills, geographies, industry market activities, or various other affinities among people. The communities are budgeted to meet together in person, and share burdens of training, mentoring, and building a culture. These activities are essential to binding a firm together with trust, but were taken for granted when all work was performed together, at one location. In that environment, communities form naturally.

A pervasive envelope of communications and data is elevating employees and bringing information democracy to work.

In one generation, there will be a dramatic increase in the population of sovereign workers, released to their own wits, freedoms, capabilities, and initiative. These changes are profound and rapid. The visible change is where work is performed. Sovereign workers do not need to be in any particular place. They do not need to be in cities, although many choose cities for reasons other than work. The less visible changes are no less profound. Because the sovereign workers like Tom Vick will move into and out of employee status and be difficult to entice as employees, the organizing principles of a firm must change to attract and retain talent. Sovereignty appeals to the most talented, and firms must recraft their approach and relationship with those individuals. In the long run, these changes in organizing principles are the most powerful ones that will occur.

The factors that create sovereignty as a viable option are numerous, but free information is one of the most powerful enabling forces behind worker sovereignty. A major attribute of being boss has been access to information. It was formerly more cost-effective to segment information and provide it sparingly, in rigid format, according to the schedule of the data provider. Now cost is not the issue. It is faster to broadly provide information, in particular in knowledge product development, delivery, and maintenance. These products and their problems are each a puzzle, and the more data (clues) provided, the faster the delivery or solution occurs. Thus information is broadly shared across the organization changing the boss-worker relationship to more a relationship of peers. People who perform at the outer circle of the firm, interacting with real customers, must be empowered by information and authority to act. Ergo an increase in sovereignty. Other workers then perform less as bosses directing activity, but as spokes on the circle, assuring good communications and supplies for execution at the front line.

Technology enables this transformation, but the technology itself is not the transformation. The change is the change in role and the centrifugal movement of power, authority, and information throughout a firm.

Information that was costly in time or money is now widely available with a click of your mouse. It includes raw material for work, leads for finding work, and help in finding workers. A free market is emerging in knowledge work—witness Dice.com and Computerjobs.com. Numerous sites also match skilled professionals with client needs, examples of which are Lawyers.com and The Creative Group®, which matches advertising and media freelancers with assignments. Each of these markets matches knowledge professionals with assignments, both long term and for projects.

Another force enabling sovereignty is the rapidly decreasing cost of communication, which is tending to zero. In 1991, telephone service cost as much as $0.50 per minute and 1-800 service was considered extremely cost-effective at $0.30 per minute. Compare that with recent offers by Verizon, Cingular, and Sprint. These firms offer packages of 2,500 minutes for $29.00 per month, which is a little more than a penny a minute! This is a 98 percent reduction in price in just a little over a decade. Data services are reducing price by orders of magnitude greater yet.

With virtually free telephone service has come free video projection. Just 5 years ago, no one would have proposed attending a videoconference from home using the Internet. And, 10 years ago, the Internet was still the domain of geeks. To get information, to work, to produce, to account, an employee had to go to a workplace. Now, with streaming video, you don't have go anywhere to attend a meeting. You can face the camera in your PC and view your meeting on the screen. As video over the Internet becomes more robust, the need to meet in reality will be replaced with the capability to meet virtually. The convergence of computing power and telecommunications means, for more and more of us, not having to "go to work." In a few decades, we may not even use the term and may not associate work with place. It is more likely that we will work according to time and our expressions will be more like "that is his work time," or "I don't want that work because it is set according to European Central Time."

> **A pervasive envelope of communications and data, combined with the acceleration of network effect markets, is dissolving firms.**

Meanwhile, companies are coming apart; the same free information and free communication that liberate the workforce have become solvents of firms. The increasing velocity of business produces incessant centrifugal forces. The sheer acceleration of business means shorter and shorter half-lives of technology products. The skill associated with integrating these technologies into a firm keeps becoming more specialized and more exogenous. Most firms cannot invest to stay current in these technologies. For a person, then, mastery comes with movement. For firms, staying current in arcane technology is too expensive. It is best to source the specialist skills as needed rather than to invest in the escalating needs of technology competence. These forces combine to cast technology specialists into the cybermarket.

The very concept of place is changing. Place is now a sector on a hard drive of a server. It is a Web address that is local everywhere, global everywhere, and nowhere. The place of work is a notebook computer that can weigh less than three pounds. The workplace is in the car, while walking to the plane, while checking in for the plane, while listening to the boarding announcements. Place of work is being exchanged for "community," and these new communities are affinity groups forming IM (Instant Messenger) buddy lists. They participate in chat rooms, supply each other with jobs, and in turn work for each other. We are in the unusual position of being able to precisely state an address for work that never changes, without being able to state, or even know, where that address actually is. Some firms are "placeless" now, with several consulting firms leading the way.

Although this method of organizing work economizes time for an individual and for a firm, it increases facelessness and distance among associates. This is a considerable challenge to trust creation.

What exactly is work? What will work look like? How can we tell that work is being performed? Do we even need to observe that it is being performed? These questions are rarely asked in the day-to-day battle of finishing a project, making an automobile, or digging a mine. Nevertheless, the work environment is a manifestation of the contributions, desires, and capabilities of millions of individuals employed by thousands of firms. We do not notice infinitesimal shifts in behaviors in any short period of time. But over a longer term—and a long term is now five years—there are dramatic shifts in what we think of as being work and how work is performed.

First off, work and movement are no longer synonymous. Silence, meditation, and daydreaming are essential to knowledge work. Some of the stormiest clairvoyance occurs while a person may otherwise appear to be comatose. However, meeting behaviors and office behaviors indicate our inherent belief that movement is associated with work. We inherently move when under inspection in the workplace. In 1979, I was collaborating with one of the Big Four tire companies then based in Akron, Ohio. Their purchasing department was arranged like an enormous junior high school study hall, with pods of desks butting against each other, workers facing each other. The desks and people were spread across a floor space larger than any indoor stadium. No matter what these people were supposed to be doing, they were evidencing movement. As a result, this vast sea of desks and people was very noisy and surely inimical to thinking. The modern consulting offices I have been in have similar open pod arrangements. Even today, there is more motion among the pod-izens than there would be if they were hidden by higher walls.

In the early 1980s, I had occasion to walk around inside several of General Motor's assembly plants. This was the beginning of the Japanese invasion of the American market, and articles about the demise of General Motors were everywhere. A veteran manufacturing consultant had given me a quick tool for evaluating the productivity of a workforce while touring a plant. This tool was to count the number of people in motion versus the number of people motionless. All the GM assembly plants I visited demonstrated more than 80 percent of their people in motion. Based on this observation, I concluded that the problems of General Motors did not revolve around individual worker productivity. General Motors certainly had problems during the 1980s but they weren't reflected in the relative motion of workers in their plants.

We will be cured forever of the notion that movement is work. For a sovereign worker, work is the use of time for money. Since motion consumes time, and time is the fundamental divisor of knowledge work, there will be less motion among knowledge workers. This implies fewer meetings, since the motion involved with meeting—in particular airline travel—is becoming prohibitively costly. The worst cost is not the airfares, which are increasing, but the cost of the time.

Travel is often an abuse of time, and sometimes abuse of the individual traveling. If an individual lives in a secondary airline market with few nonstop flights, then any city is about five hours of travel away including stem time. As an example, Indianapolis is five hours from Detroit if routed through the hub cities of Cleveland, Cincinnati, or Chicago. (It is possible to drive this distance in less than four hours.) Thus 10 hours a week—25 percent of a 40-hour week—is invested in the stop-start activity of parking, checking in, boarding, waiting, flying, renting a car or taxi. The herky-jerky of airline travel makes it nearly impossible to accomplish meaningful work while flying, and moreover, there is no privacy on an airplane. An independent contractor should raise rates by 33 percent to cover the cost of the time overhead of travel. That rarely is possible, so the cost is borne or reduced other ways.

This kind of time is a cost for anyone, not just someone who is charging for time. But face time builds trust. It is difficult to brainstorm over a telephone. The conditions for serendipity rarely occur on the telephone. The challenge is building trust without face time.

Will work be silent? solitary? Whatever the style, we will not need to know what work looks like. Sovereign workers will not be "supervised." There is not, and cannot be, a watchful eye over the work. There are methods to monitor work, but this will be a market for intellectual piecework. The outcome of knowledge work is not a behavior within the confines of walls surrounded by banks of telephones or workstations. The outcome, the result, is the knowledge product being delivered.

Sovereignty changes the relationship of employers and employees from that of parent-child, with attendant provision of needs, to that of sovereigns negotiating economic treaties and alliances between the firm and the sovereign worker. Certainly the relationship between a multinational corporation and an individual who is contracting his or her talent is not an equal relationship. But the market determines the price for skills because the market is fluid. Unique skills in high demand will command premium prices and contractual conditions. Each individual can have access to the price of the skills in the market, and to the kinds and volume of opportunities in that market. There is no company so large that it can dictate the terms of the market for knowledge work. The market favors no one.

Firms will not be parents and will not provide fixed places for work, so we will be looking to each other, much more so than ever before. Knowledge work is rarely produced, purchased, or sold as a continuous process—there is lumpiness to such work. It is usually a series or group of projects be they a software install, a modification, an invention, a manual, an advertisement, or other intellectual product. Projects are conceived that require an individual just for part-time work, up to projects that require hundreds of individuals. In this environment, it is critical to have trusted partners who will share your work and who will share their work with you.

This network—call it the friends and family network—is the only true recurring source of security. It is not possible for any firm to guarantee long-term employment, and almost no firm does. So individual security is becoming part skills, part network, and part playing the odds. The larger and more active your network, the greater the chances of income. This network can be global and virtual, but an individual's success within this network will depend on sharing. A knowledge worker will have to give away knowledge to gain valence within this network.

Guild like communities will provide the work procurement and security formerly provided by firms. These communities will be loosely linked with information and tightly linked with trust.

Although sovereign workers are often solitary soldiers, their welfare depends on each worker's valence within a community. This valence will be developed through trust, the investment of time, and consistent performance over time. Trust is essential to becoming a member of a work producing and sharing community as well as for gaining stature within that group. Communities, or associations, will form to meet the needs of independent workers. The first need will be information about the market itself, and Web sites such as Dice.com, Computerjobs.com, RHI.com, The Creative Group®, and Lawyers.com, are but a few examples of hundreds of specialized skill Web sites-cum markets. As soon as these Web-based markets achieve a certain size and competitive position, they will be motivated to increase their service offerings to both the supply (the sovereign workers) and the demand (the firms buying contracts). For workers, this will likely mean health insurance, training, and mentoring. For firms, this will likely mean quality assurance and skill certification mechanisms. The mechanisms that emerge will be analogous to tried and true forms of skilled trade organization, albeit with a key difference: the fluid electronic web that enables the association and makes possible scale and scope beyond the reach of any previous method of organizing skilled professionals. The skill building and quality assurance desired by firms will also have a portion of reputation, a form of "trust rating."

According to Arthur G. Moore, a partner with Knowledge Partners Inc.:

> For every knowledge worker process and relationship that currently exists, a virtual analog can be envisioned, in many cases one that is much more fluid and reliable than current common practice. . . . Absent our more familiar modes of establishing trust, others will develop to enable knowledge and skill brokers to certify their wares. Envision, for example, a resume where each assertion is validated by a disinterested third party, as being certified by the (anonymous but valid) organization for which the service was performed. Other standards, and certification processes can be counted on to spring up, along with the web of informal, virtual connections that mimics our current interchanges.

A virtual association of sovereign workers can take several forms, but the most likely are the benevolent dictator, the guild, and the partnership models. These virtual organization structures are analogous to their namesakes in the real world.

The community of Linux developers is a global, open community, whose objective is the propagation and continuing development of the Linux operating system. By contributing to Linux and having contributions accepted by the Linux community, an individual gains stature among the community, and thereby a measure of trust and certification of skill. This community, although open, loosely associated, global, and free flowing is presided over by Linus Torvalds, the creator of Linux. Torvalds has assumed the position of benevolent dictator. He has been allowed this position due to his stature among the Linux community and his principled behavior. Although alternative benevolent dictatorships may arise to compete with Torvalds, there have been none so far within the Linux community. This association of sovereign workers is bound by a shared interest—the development of Linux—and advances by the fiat of Torvalds.

The Linux development model is facilitated by the extremely complex and technical nature of the work itself. Hacking an operating system is more black and white than, say, describing a superior market strategy for a brand-new consumer good. Market and strategy skills are no less intellectual than hacking, and variations of trusted communities will emerge that better serve this kind of skill.

These communities may be ones where deep trust in one another is as important as demonstrated skills. These private networks may well be entirely open regarding personal information with entry only by vouchsafement from several of the current members. This kind of private market would act like a current partnership or a guild.

Although the benevolent dictator model anticipates peer review and commentary, a guild model and the partnership model use peer review to advance in stature within the association. A partnership model would entail sharing the risks, expenses, and rewards of operating the association; whereas a guild would operate much as a condominium coop. The guild would generally be involved in ad hoc governance; whereas a partnership would require predetermined governance and process for managing the association.

We will need to be concerned about our "brand." When we are representing ourselves in a cybermarket, what exactly is being represented? The brand we build is associated with an expectation in the market, and the buyer will anticipate that the branded product will behave in a certain way. As with authors and pen names, sovereign workers may often have disparate capabilities, directed to overlapping markets that require the establishment of more than one brand. An address associated with C++ capability will be different from an address associated with an ability to referee hockey games. Any independent worker will need to focus on what capability is being sold, to whom, and what that representation is. The publishing industry has historically blended the concept of brand with pen name. Evan Hunter is a well-known writer of critically acclaimed fiction. Using the name Ed McBain, he is also a bestselling author of police detective novels. Tom Clancy, the famous spy novel writer, has created one of the strongest brands in publishing. He is using this brand for several product lines, including lines of books that he endorses but does not write. Various Internet pioneers have well-established brands, including Philip Zimmerman for Public Key Cryptography and John Perry Barlowe, who is associated with the Electronic Frontier Freedom Foundation. John Perry Barlowe has also a distinguished brand as a rock song lyricist for The Grateful Dead.

Dissolution of firms and the emergence of brand as the critical property are occurring in nearly every industry, even the automotive industry. Bob Lutz, the Chief Executive of Exide, and a former Vice Chairman of Chrysler, has launched Cunningham Motor Company. This company will produce a luxury sports car with an estimated price of $250,000. However, the company will have no factories, no engineering department, and no selling staff. All these functions will be contracted out. It is assumed that an automotive parts supplier will perform the actual assembly of this car and the retail network will be franchised among existing sales channels. Lutz intends that Cunningham Motor Company only have 20 full-time employees—it will become the first virtual automotive original equipment manufacturer.[5]

Although Cunningham is the most dramatic example of the trend to leaner, more virtual and more flexible firms in the automotive industry, the Big Three are all moving in that direction. They each are ceding more and more responsibility for part design, subassembly, and manufacturing to their suppliers. Suppliers, in turn, are devolving their firms and relying on contracted engineering, manufacturing, information technology, and marketing.

Worker sovereignty is easiest to describe and understand when speaking about the high-tech and information technology industries where it is an accepted practice and an individual typically moves easily between stints as an employee and stints as an independent contractor. However, this trend toward devolution of job and disassembly of firms is occurring in all industries. Its pace is accelerating in the automotive industry. If it can happen there, it can happen anywhere. Indeed, one of the bastions of independent contracting has been the trucking industry. Owner-operator truckers have always been a significant percentage of truck drivers and have often been referred to as "kings of the road." The Internet has enabled these owner-operators to find loads more quickly and with less expense than ever before. Free information provided over the Internet is changing the rigid command systems of managing owner-operators. Formerly, all information necessary to work and find the next load was controlled by a dispatcher. Now much of that information can be viewed and used while connected to the Internet at a truckstop. Meanwhile, satellite communications with trucks provide a method to maintain continuous contact with the shipping market. Pervasive communications have provided truckers an ability to self-direct their work. At the same time, truckers have lost their privacy on the road, as previously described. In this way—freedom of action and loss of privacy—truckers provide an interesting example of technology's mixed blessings.

This trend to worker sovereignty will continue because creative intellect, combined with speed, is the killer application for the future. Even the largest firms cannot claim to have *the* smartest people; it is simply mathematically improbable. Even IBM, with some 350,000 people, employs well less than 0.003 of the U.S. workforce, thus their mathematical chances of employing *the* smartest people is arithmetically tiny. To source intellect, firms must compete in the open talent market. In turn, if an individual possesses a rare and in-demand skill, that individual will continually assess capturing the premium available in the open market for freelancing work versus the more assured income stream from employment. But the impetus for sovereignty will be driven by the needs of the talented. To become an employee, is not in the best interest of many of these people.

Nearly everyone will experience periods of freelancing, independent contracting, or other forms of individual sovereignty. The Internet did not create the needs of the labor market, nor did it create the needs of firms. It has, however, certainly accelerated the already existing trend to sovereignty.

These trends are accelerating because information is easily available, and it is the raw material of knowledge work. But what binds associations of sovereigns together is trust built on truthful transactions and sharing. Within communities of sovereign workers, more value will accrue to those workers who sustain and increase the verities. Those who can economize time for a firm or other individuals will prosper. Those who are trustworthy and build reputations as such will prosper. Pervasive communications will accentuate the value of trust because reputation can be broadcast to millions. The event that loses trust can also be broadcast.

Summary

Information and communication are becoming free, surrounding us with an atmosphere of data. Free data coupled with free communication enable many knowledge tasks, formerly performed at a place of work, to be performed anywhere. Tasks formerly performed on a schedule in concert with all other workers, now may occur according to a schedule convenient for the worker. Knowledge work can be performed anywhere, at anytime.

The economics of knowledge and information technology result in the acceleration of everything. This acceleration is necessary because there is no longer reward for second place. In this environment, firms must be fast and must be first. To be fast, they become smaller and more focused. Firms rely on alliances, partnerships, and outsourcing to remain lean and nimble. It means becoming flatter, with fewer layers of decision making. It means moving the ability to make a decision to the front line and making the individual worker more sovereign.

These forces—free communication and data, and the economics of networks—make individual workers become more sovereign. This sovereignty is a natural, logical, and inevitable conclusion of the Internet weather.

The ability to perform work at home, anytime, according to personal convenience, releases work from any single place and from a defined, repeated schedule. Technology is facilitating this release. It increases the freedom of an individual, but also increases responsibility and risk. The release provides more sovereignty to a worker, almost regardless of desire for such sovereignty. So an individual must assess his product—the career—in terms of the value he brings to a firm. At the same time, he must understand how this association further develops his product—his reputation, his brand, his truthful information.

The worker must ask these questions: Am I a trusted source of knowledge? Am I a unique source of something? Do I enhance time for others? Do I enhance privacy? Am I a trusted confidant of a customer? Does a firm increase one or more of these values for me?

Sovereignty is an ironic gift: It provides more freedom, more enrichment, but it demands more personal responsibility. It requires individuals to manage their careers as if they were a product portfolio: They must enhance the product, increase margin, and market their unique portfolio of knowledge, trusted customers, trusted colleagues, and time-saving skills.

So what makes a firm want a sustaining relationship with a worker? The number one reason would be the trust of a customer. Next would be unique, reliable knowledge—the truth—that can be transmitted faster and more efficiently than any other method of acquiring it.

So what makes a worker want a sustaining relationship with a firm? It cannot any longer be security and should not only be money. There is no security at a firm, and money is a poor substitute for learning. People will be working for themselves. They will be works in progress and will need to increase their truth and their impact on time, and they will need to build trust.

CHAPTER 8

Inbots and Outbots

Agents of Privacide

With pervasive communication go intrusion and the loss of privacy. Privacy is emerging as the key issue for consumers dealing with Web-based services. It is now time to raise awareness and action on privacy within firms.

The technology of intrusion—even benign intrusion—has raced well ahead of public policy, law, corporate strategy, and customary business practice. Not too long ago, it was possible to protect a vast landscape of corporate information due to centralized, stand-alone data processing. As recently as 1990, most firms had not implemented a corporate LAN (local area network), and few firms were actively linked to the Internet until well after 1993. Corporate Internet use was rare as late as 1996. Now, just a handful of years later, the only operative assumption is that *any and all electronic information is accessible by the public.*

This is an extreme assumption, but the remarkable capabilities of lonely hackers warrant extreme measures. Of these measures, it is critical to assess what kind of information must always be private. Technology and processes exist to protect these jewels, but the protective technology and measures are expensive and time consuming. Therefore, any firm must determine what those jewels are and develop a privacy strategy that protects important corporate data, yet does so cost-effectively.

A privacy strategy and action plan will then employ three broad activities: creation of a hardened information vault for the jewels; benign neglect of the data-scree that accumulates everyday; and "preemptive publicity" of certain strategic information, novelties, events, and developments.

A short review of the e-tailing environment can highlight the rapidity and profundity of technology impacts in commerce. Picture Sam Walton, an icon of retailing, practicing in the e-tailing environment. Walton was a former intelligence officer in the U.S. Army, and always appreciated the use of intelligence. Indeed, he personally conducted what would otherwise be termed field intelligence throughout his long retailing career.

Sam Walton was renowned for visiting both his stores and those of his competitors. During his reign, Sam Walton spent much of the year traveling around the United States visiting his stores, motivating Wal-Mart employees, and staying in touch with the shoppers. During visits to competitors, he wore a baseball cap to disguise his appearance. With a baseball cap, Sam Walton—the most dreaded competitor in retail—looked like any senior citizen and walked around competitors' stores unnoticed.[1]

A Sam Walton visit to a store poses interesting questions. At what point is Sam Walton trespassing? stealing intellectual property? misappropriating data? invading the business's privacy? Given the size of Wal-Mart, at what point do the actions of competitive shoppers from Wal-Mart constitute monopolistic, anticompetitive practice?

In fact, a store could not legally bar entry to Sam Walton. Nor could any store treat Sam differently from any other shopper. The store could not refuse to sell goods to him. It could not conceal price displays while Sam was in the store and revert to standard practice before and after the visit. Retailers are open to the public. Because of the public display commonly practiced for store operations, a retail business provides a wealth of information to anyone. Anyone with time and resources can accumulate it.

These questions become much more interesting when the business is an e-tail store such as Amazon.com or eBay, and the visitor is not a person such as Sam Walton, but a software robot—a bot. The store is then a virtual location, with virtual visitors. Over the past 18 months, eBay has blazed a legal trail involving the behavior of bots. It has initiated litigation against ReverseAuction.com, Bidder's Edge, and Auction Watch.[2] It has successfully obtained an injunction against bots from Bidder's Edge from entering eBay's Web sites in one of the first court actions regarding trespassing in the digital domain. eBay blocked attempted Web site access by Bidder's Edge and Auction Watch, which were using forms of bots called *shopping bots* and *crawlers* that search the Internet for price comparisons on specified goods. eBay charged that Bidder's Edge had trespassed on eBay's computers and misappropriated proprietary data. As reported by John Wilke in *The Wall Street Journal*, eBay issued a statement, "eBay must have the ability to disallow certain types of monitoring and copying of our site in the interest of protecting the integrity of the eBay system and your information."[3] In this case, "your information" refers to information that eBay users enter, such as address and name.

Meanwhile, in a separate action, ReverseAuction.com paid eBay $1.2 million to settle a complaint that ReverseAuction engaged in misleading business practices through the actions of ReverseAuction bots. These bots were scraping the addresses of eBay subscribers and then spamming them with ReverseAuction material. Compare this with the practices of Sam Walton visiting Target. Appropriating the subscriber addresses would be analogous to Sam's obtaining the name and address of every shopper from the store files and establishing a Wal-Mart mailing list based on this list.

The incursion of bots into a Web site brings brand-new challenges to the legal and commercial fabric of business. In general, the law governing fair trade dictates that all customers who present similar economic situations to a buyer must be treated similarly. Certain classes of customers can receive preferential treatment, but this treatment must be economically justified by such factors as purchase volume, commitment to terms of contract and other economic factors. In general, a potential customer cannot be excluded from access to a place of business. If you choose to open a retail store, you must serve all shoppers, not just the ones you like. If a business operates a catalog, it cannot select which customers can place orders. A business must provide information to all shoppers and must provide equal access. It cannot hide prices from Sam

Walton unless it hides them from everyone. Fair trade law, antitrust law, fraud laws have not been repealed because we can scour the entire world for information. These laws both prescribe and proscribe certain behavior. The laws have not changed, but common practice in the virtual store world is different from common practice in the bricks-and-mortar world.

No legislator, no business strategist foresaw the ability to assemble vast data that now exists using Internet agents.

The overwhelming power of Internet search agents is presenting serious challenges to the law as currently formulated. One of the most important and most common duties of a bot is to gather extensive information from Web sites. A bot queries, catalogs, and often stores this information. The Uniform Commercial Code did not anticipate the ubiquity and data-capture power of an army of bots. When constructing a Web site to sell to the public, you have in fact opened a store. If you sell construction supplies, trucks, or flowers, you must sell to your competitors on the same terms and conditions you sell to anyone. Whereas the Sam Walton method of physically visiting stores was slow and expensive, an army of bots can search the entire Internet within a few minutes, for effectively zero marginal cost. The information that Sam Walton could accumulate in 10 years can now be accumulated in 10 nanoseconds by a handful of bots.

No legislator anticipated that the accumulated actions of bots could strip an individual of privacy. Their primary functions are to retrieve data and to do a few simple actions with that data. Usually a bot will retrieve data and forward it to a program that classifies and stores it. If the indexing of the data files is a Social Security number, mapped to a telephone number, mapped to a driver's license number, mapped to a specific address, then each datum acquired by a bot is a piece of a jigsaw puzzle. The assembly of hundreds of these pieces creates a picture of an individual, and the individual's privacy is forever breached.

The viral atmosphere of bots—some friend, some foe—mean that businesses, too, have lost their privacy. Nearly anything a business executes using the Internet is now subject to surveillance. The only safe assumption is that anything a firm zips over the Internet has the potential to appear on *60 Minutes,* or as part of a trial record. Some of the most damaging evidence in the Microsoft antitrust case was the file of thousands of e-mails between Microsoft employees.[4] It should also be assumed that your competitors could trace every byte that has moved into and out of your firm.

The virulent bots of the Internet, if a firm is not properly protected, can strip a firm bare of its secrets in minutes. The price of privacy, as well as its scarcity, demands that a firm decide what must be private. Once that it is decided—and the scope of privacy must be limited because of its price—then all other information must be assumed to be public.

Bots are the spies and soldiers of the Internet. Webopedia.com defines a bot: "short for *robot,* a computer program that runs automatically." Botspot.com answers the question this way: "In short: A *bot* is a software tool for digging through data." It continues, "The term bot has become interchangeable with the term *agent,* to indicate that the software can be sent out on a mission, usually to find information and report back."

How many kinds of bots there are? Does anyone really know? There are chatterbots, shopping bots, surveillance bots, e-mail bots, search bots, game bots, stock bots, news bots, and so on. There are probably as many kinds of bots as there are uses for information technology. Bots existed before the Internet, but the vast dimensions of Internet have led to an explosion of their use.

Bots always remind me of the "Sorcerer's Apprentice" sequence in Disney's film, *Fantasia.* Mickey Mouse portrays the Sorcerer's apprentice. While the Sorcerer is away, Mickey must carry water buckets from a well to fill the cistern in the basement. He sees the open book of spells and conjures a spell for a broom to carry the water buckets for him, and then falls asleep. He is awakened by the sound and feel of water lapping around him. During his nap, the broom had continued to execute its magic command and overfilled the cistern, causing water to course down on the basement floor. Mickey does not know the command to stop the broom. In desperation, he chops the broom into hundreds of splinters, each of which pops into a robotic magic broom, carrying yet more water to the cistern.

Bots are the apprentice's magic brooms, executing their sole task doggedly, without malice, without judgment, without remorse, without joy. We, the Sorcerer's apprentices, have loosed millions of bots into the Internet atmosphere without really knowing where they will travel, what sites will be breached, what sites embrace them, what sites will reject them. Bots travel with the inexorable precision of a digital clock and the remorseless efficiency of bacteria.

The Internet is a viral, organic, anarchic web of bots, databases, bits, and bytes. Now, imagine the myriad software applets—the bots—unleashed to roam the infinite vastness of the Internet. We have conjured the commands and breathed life into their missions. The Internet, with its bots, affects all people and all business, regardless of size. Two years ago, I attended a meeting in Atlanta with a tiny start-up firm involved in chemicals trading. There were only six employees. The president of this small company asked me, "What is your firm's bot strategy?"

This was the first time I had ever heard of the necessity of having a bot strategy. I was momentarily nonplussed because I was not expecting such a sophisticated question from a six-person firm that bought and sold chemicals for utilities, steel mills, railroads, and heavy industry. This small company was debating internally which bots to allow access to their catalog and which to exclude. They were both buying from and selling to many of the largest integrated chemical firms. Were the information requests and quotes they provided being used to undercut their prices? Given these large firms knew both their purchase price and their selling price on many chemicals, at what point could these same corporations know their margins? At what point would an outsider be able to derive their profit and loss statement?

This small chemical company was concerned about its privacy. It was one of the first in that market to have developed an online catalog for buying and selling chemicals, and had established a clever taxonomy for chemicals. The indexing software allowed anyone, unsophisticated in the purchase of chemicals, to detect the right chemical to purchase. One of the key features of this taxonomy was the ability to ferret out spelling errors and duplicate names for nearly 15,000 common chemicals used in heavy industries. For example, they had links so that muriatic acid was known to be hydrochloric acid and vice versa. Further links prompted the user as to the application of the acid, molarity, shipping and handling characteristics, and the like. At the same time, a user would not be able to mistake muriatic or hydrochloric acid for anhydrous hydrochloride. Such a mistake could be devastating since anhydrous hydrochloride will explode simply if left sitting too long. They were investigating licensing the taxonomy to such e-commerce portals as e-chemicals.com, Chemconnect, or ICG Commerz. But at the same time, they were buying from the major chemical firms, selling to them, and buying and selling from competitive chemical distributors.

Given the breaches of privacy that have already occurred, firms must immediately assess what to protect and what to allow to be public.

A bot strategy is about the presence of a firm on the Internet. Firms need to develop a strategy for dealing with the inbots pinging a firm's Internet presence, and with the outbots deployed by the firm to execute specific missions. A bot strategy is about a firm's privacy. To develop a bot strategy, it is necessary to address two questions: What is the benefit of privacy, and what is the benefit of publicity?

Each firm is a unique assembly of knowledge, practice, and culture. This knowledge encompasses trade secrets, patents, copyrights, trademarks, brands and the unique processes that weave the firm together and breathe life into it. Wal-Mart's competitive advantage did not derive from access to competitive information; it derived from its unique assembly of information, knowledge, practice, and culture. Much more of Wal-Mart's competitive advantage has derived from listening to the market and to the wants of individual consumers, and providing those goods than has come from knowledge of prices or practices at Kmart or Sears. When

Sam made those trips, he observed the shoppers as much as the stores and used the information to tailor Wal-Mart's offerings to fit more precisely what consumers would buy. Because of the symmetry of information in the retail business, even Wal-Mart's practices became widely known. Yet, despite having this competitive information, Wal-Mart's competitors were unable to stem its growth.

Another example of well-exposed corporate secrets exists in the automotive industry, which is possibly the most studied in the world. Ford has few secrets from General Motors, which has few secrets from DaimlerChrysler. The Toyota process for manufacturing cars is widely known, yet nearly impossible to duplicate. This process has become familiar by communication with suppliers to Toyota, discussions with former employees, the journalism of the automotive press, and the efforts of business schools. Nevertheless, the other big automotive firms have been unable to reproduce, let alone exceed, Toyota's manufacturing performance.

> **As Wal-Mart and Toyota demonstrate, information's use in conjunction with other firm assets and practice create the competitive advantage. Often even trade-secret information is fallow outside its firm.**

We are experiencing privacide. Individual privacy is all but gone, and business privacy is in its death throes. As corporate privacy evaporates, it is critical to address the importance of privacy for a business. The best assumption is that *any* information within your firm is public, and then begin applying tests to determine what information should remain private. Information should be protected if it has value by itself, separate and apart from any relationship with your firm. In this class are some patents, some copyrights, unique but unpatentable practice, and what I will call corporate memes. Memes are credited to Richard Dawkins in his 1976 book, *The Selfish Gene*.[5] As he defined them, memes are units of cultural information that can spread through a culture rather as genes spread through a gene pool. In the corporate body, memes are units of information that define the corporation. It is critical to identify these packets of information and practice, for they are the jewels worth protection.

When we think of privacy in business, we often think of secrecy. And, one of the most famous trade secrets in the business world is the formula for Coca-Cola. What is this the benefit of this secrecy?

The formula for Coca-Cola is *priceless*. Although this implies extraordinary value, it simply means that *no price can be determined for this formula because there is no market for it*. Who would buy it? The former KGB? PepsiCo? Ironically, the value of this secret is protected by Coke's worldwide fame and publicity! The theft of the Coke formula would be as public as the theft of the Mona Lisa. Should anyone claim to have the actual formula, it would be reason to assume a theft of the formula had occurred. If you experimented until you thought you got it right, how would you know it was the same unless you had the secret formula? In this case, having a trade secret—the formula for Coca-Cola—is fallow outside Coke itself.

In the book *For God, Country & Coca-Cola,* Mark Pendergrast revealed a formula for Coca-Cola taken from the formula book of Dr. John Pemberton, the inventor of Coca-Cola.[6] As Mr. Pendergrast recounts in *The Wall Street Journal,* Coke's reaction was, "They practically yawned in response, issuing a bland release saying that this was just one in a long series of Coke formula wannabes, and that, like the others, it was inaccurate."

Coke's famous formula is a trade secret. However, it does not meet my criteria for the extraordinary effort of protecting its privacy, because the formula has no value outside its association with the Coca-Cola Company. Counterexamples exist, however, wherein trade secrecy is essential for a firm's existence.

Trade secrets can also apply to methods, processes, and other differentiating knowledge. Non-Stop Logistics is a software firm that has documented powerful supply chain savings for its clients. It has chosen to retain trade secrecy for its algorithms and scientific insights. This software package has enabled several firms to achieve large savings in inventory while improving many other service attributes of logistics. Dr. Hau Lee, of Stanford University, one of the founding intellects of Non-Stop, claims that the composition of science, algorithms, and supply chain insight is Non-Stop's "secret sauce."[7] It is publicly known how this software works—it addresses the "bull-whip" effect, for which Dr. Lee is renowned. The math and management science behind the bull-whip effect are widely known. What competitors do not know are the correct ingredients for a program to cure this effect while increasing customer service. Dr. Lee's fear is that the eureka insight provided by a patent application would immediately allow similar inventions and thereby dilute the market space currently occupied by Non-Stop. With trade secrecy, the secret sauce of the software will never be revealed and not then easily imitated.

Trade secrecy, by itself, may or may not qualify as a corporate jewel. A key test regarding the value of a trade secret is whether it can be used competitively against the firm. If it can, such as the secret sauce of Dr. Lee's science, then privacy measures, technology, and process are warranted. It is not easy to determine this, and in many firms, just asking the value of trade secrecy will be viewed as heretical. However, as the price of privacy increases, this kind of question is necessary. Although Coke maintains a secrecy system for its formula, its defense is simply a "bland release" denying the breach of secrecy. Such denials are not costly.

> **Privacy and corporate secrecy are often equated with the protection of intellectual property such as patents and copyrights. Ironically, the protection of innovation often involves active *publicity*.**

Another kind of information worthy of protection is an invention. Some patents, such as that for xerography, for aspartame (called Nutrasweet), and for numerous drugs are worth billions of dollars by themselves, without association with their creators. Nearly any large chemical or consumer package good firm would have been able to capitalize on the large market potential of Nutrasweet. These blockbuster inventions that provide a solution for a huge market require a cloak of secrecy during their conception and development. Indeed, the patent law itself requires secrecy.

Patents must be conceived in secrecy yet deployed publicly. An invention cannot have been publicly disclosed prior to the patent filing. A trade secret sometimes has patentable novelty about it, yet remains secret forever. The decision to patent or retain secrecy depends on the strength, breadth, and novelty of the invention itself. Many inventions are like the answer to a puzzle. Once disclosed, the innovation spurs other creative people to conceive a little bit different way to achieve the same innovation. Many times, a patent does not provide the exclusive market intended by the inventor. Rather, clever imitators innovate around the patent and gain a share of the market. Thus, privacy and publicity become critically important.

The benefit of privacy and secrecy for patents is embedded within the patent law itself. For an innovation to be patentable, the innovation must not have been publicly disclosed prior to the patent filing. It therefore must remain secret up until that time, and then it must be published. Thus a patent presents both sides of the privacy problem: the benefit of privacy and the benefit of publicity. In both cases, privacy and publicity are prescribed by law.

An invention cannot be patented in the United States if:

- The invention was described in a printed publication before the applicant conceived the invention.
- The invention was patented or described in a printed publication in the United States or foreign country, or in public use or on sale in this country more than one year prior to the date of application for patent in the United States.

The body of publicly disclosed technology or practice is called "prior art," and the existence of prior art prevents patents from being issued. Prior art is the practice of artful disclosure. Up until the time of your patent application, the highest level of secrecy must be maintained. At the time of application, widespread publication of the patent itself and associated technology that is prior art is in order.

Say you have an invention for a gasoline additive that increases fuel mileage by 15 miles per gallon. This invention will be worth a great deal of money. At five cents a gallon, it will be worth more than $7 billion per year. None of the major oil firms will easily submit to your invention; they will try to innovate their own and patent around your technology. At this point, you must move from secrecy to publicity. Once you have determined what your patent application will describe, then it is timely to think about surrounding the technology of your patent with disclosures of prior art. By so doing, you have made patents impossible on any of this technology, and you have scorched the earth around your invention.

Thus, in the realm of secrecy, innovation, and treasured business practice, *publicity is a powerful weapon*. This is especially true for high-technology firms. Each patent should be measured according to its franchise value, and each novel business practice supporting that invention should be evaluated. Those novel practices that provide competitive advantage but are not deemed patentable should be widely publicized as prior art. Ironically, *publicity provides protection*. Defensive layers of prior art should buffer each patent.

If no patent is granted or applied for, each firm must still evaluate defensive publicity or trade secrecy for a unique business practice or art.

Privacy and secrecy have often been equated with intellectual property. But even the best technology and the leading intellectual property will be unproductive without means, leadership, and the vision to implement them. Xerox's Palo Alto Research Center is renowned for having invented much of the technology that subsequently was used by others to create personal computers, Adobe Print utilities, screen graphics, and many other innovations. Being able to create innovations is only part of success and the protection or promotion of those innovations is only part of a privacy strategy.

What are the true competitive advantages of a firm? Information is only part of competitive advantage.

Possibly the most important kind of information is what I have called *corporate memes*. Memes are the information, practice, and process gene pools of our firms. The great firms have great memes. Among great firms, I would place Berkshire Hathaway and UPS.

Both of these firms have distinctive process, practice, and use of information. Warren Buffett, the Chairman of Berkshire Hathaway, cloaks the information within Berkshire Hathaway with candor. United Parcel Service is the most massively engineered firm on earth, and its processes, discipline, and standards create an obsession with performance. Both of these firms share extensive information widely with the public. Berkshire Hathaway's annual report even shares wisdom and opinion in form of Buffett's annual letter to shareholders. The information that Berkshire Hathaway focuses on cash flow, earnings, and the concept of a business franchise is publicly available to anyone. Yet, this information has been deployed uniquely better than any other firm over a 35-year period: Since Berkshire's first annual report, the compound annual growth rate of book value has been 23.6 percent, compared with 11.8 percent for the S&P 500. UPS publicizes its prices and its service matrix. Its operating methods are fairly well known. Nevertheless, UPS produces 12 percent pretax margin, roughly double that of FedEx, its nearest competitor. The practices—the memes—of both firms protect their privacy.

> **Given the virulent nature of the Internet, how does a firm protect its privacy?**

Three tactics can protect privacy: Active Privacy, Benign Neglect, and Active Publicity. Active Privacy includes the information and practice jewels of a corporation. These must be surrounded with tough encryption, tight secrecy procedures, and warning systems against incursions. The security technologies and processes that can accomplish tight secrecy are expensive and add processing and time overhead. It is impractical to adopt these practices for all information. Certainly, personnel data fall in this category because of representing a fiduciary responsibility to employees. Individual customer data fall in this category for similar reasons, and also because such care will be recognized and will build trust.

In the category of Benign Neglect can be placed much of the information overload of a firm, including e-mail, both external and internal. A caveat on e-mail, though. All corporations should employ technologies that obliterate e-mail automatically after a specified time, whether that is three months, a year, whatever. These technologies defy forensic technology and do destroy e-mail. As the Microsoft antitrust trial demonstrates, there can be deep veins of incriminating e-mail within a firm, even though that e-mail was actually innocently produced. In a large firm, there is probably enough content in e-mail, when sifted by a diligent attorney, to prove a firm culpable of many inadvertent or unknown transgressions. Likewise, the same e-mail files can likely prove the opposite for whatever an attorney can mine. Also, some trade secrets fall in the Benign Neglect category. I am not sure if Coke's formula is in this category, but protection of it can be assured with a bland denial.

A privacy strategy must include a tactic of Active Publicity. This category includes the important innovations that need to be made public as a defense against patent by a competitor. As a hypothetical example, suppose that IBM were able to patent "The Supply Chain." All consultancies and hundreds of software firms would then owe royalty on existing supply chain practices to IBM.

Certain data can be subject to Benign Neglect or Actively Publicized. Industry indexes, such as the J. J. Kinney/Perform Municipal Indices, published by Standard & Poor and Investor Tools, Inc. use data to entice the use of other services within a firm. Often raw data are not useful alone or are publicly available through other means.

The following table shows examples of the three categories:

Active Privacy	Benign Neglect	Active Publicity
Trade secrets	Trade secrets	Innovative prior art
Patentable innovation	Raw data	Data used for promotion
Product development	Industrial customer lists	Successes
Pricing intelligence	E-mail (with expiration)	Product launch
Truth		Financial figures (public firm)
Financial figures (private firm)		Truth
Personnel data		
Retail customer data		

What vaults can hold secrets? No server hooked to the Internet can behave as a vault. There are simply too many incursions by competitive bots. The Coke formula is likely inside a real vault somewhere, with access granted to precious few. Perhaps the employees who mix the formula are separated and each is kept ignorant of the ingredients and processes used to create Coke. There are numerous ways to compartment, divide, and hide such information.

Yet each firm is, in effect, a vault. The memes, the unique processes, the unique assembly of each firm become a form of vault. IBM's customer list has little value to EDS, one of IBM's largest competitors, in part because EDS should already know most of IBM's customers. This information is not actionable by itself. Knowing why those companies are IBM customers would have far more value. The compensation of every person at EDS has almost no value for Computer Sciences Corporation, one of EDS's largest competitors. Without a record of job responsibilities, scope, and experience, compensation information is practically meaningless. The compensation at a consulting firm has little meaning to an automotive firm because the terms and conditions of employment at an automotive firm versus a consulting firm are so different. Competitive information satisfies curiosity but rarely provides actionable insight.

Unless you are ACNielsen and are selling information, it is rarely valuable in and of itself. Most of the information within a firm cannot be acted on by anyone else with the same result.

There is a class of information that is like uncut diamonds. Much of this information comes from dealing with real customers. The accurate determination of the direction of a market and what customers really value is far more important than patents, trade secrets, and formulas. I have a standard for the use of the term *value*: Value is determined by the exchange of money. Until a customer will pay for something, no value has been established. This definition lays waste to broad swaths of "value-added services" claimed during the selling process. Information about what a customer is willing to actually pay for is the most precious business information on earth. This information should be surrounded with impenetrable encryption, a moat of oath and confidentiality documents, and threat of economic death.

For example, what are consumers willing to pay for delivery on demand to their homes or places of work? Are consumers willing to pay $5.00 across the board for the convenience of receiving an order the same day it is placed? Are consumers willing to pay $10 for home delivery of groceries, but not $11? Webvan.com, Kozmo.com, and Urbanfetch spent several hundred million dollars in search of these consumer insights. If any one of these firms could have determined the prices consumers will pay for specialized on-demand delivery, possibly they could have avoided their magnificent financial flame-outs.

Competitive information, on the other hand, is mostly secondary information. Competitors are doing the same thing you are: They are listening to the market, formulating responses, and moving in the direction the market tells them. This movement is usually the first intelligence that you can access, and it is already a considerable time behind the market demand. Also, the secret sauce—your unique combination of personnel, corporate charisma, and character—and your market presence create capabilities that cannot easily be duplicated.

The death of privacy is due to the convergence of many forces: the virulent bots roaming the Internet, the sheer explosion of data, nomadic workforces, and the spreading collaboration of firms. Privacy has become scarce and dear, and no firm can afford secrecy for all its information. For firms in the future, privacy is about balancing needs against costs. This balancing begins with the assessment of what information is valuable by itself—those creative insights and innovations that can change markets—and what unique insights the firm has acquired about its customers and its markets. These two kinds of information reward their protection. All other information must be assumed to be free among the public.

Summary

In the Internet weather, the only safe assumption for a firm is that any and all electronic information is accessible by the public. While this is draconian, such an approach launches a pursuit of privacy and frames its value.

Privacy technologies and privacy procedures can be instituted, but to protect the secrecy of any and all electronic information is cost prohibitive. Technology has taken away privacy in a wholesale manner, and technology can give it back piecemeal. Privacy products and privacy procedures add cost and time to information flow. The technology of privacy, based on strong encryption, is excellent. Breaches of privacy are usually associated with breaches or laxity of process, rather than of technology. Given the expense of instituting privacy technology and process, such processes must be instituted carefully and selectively. A strategy for privacy revolves around three activities:

1. A vaultlike secrecy surrounding certain precious information, art, and practice.

2. Benign neglect of certain classes of information.

3. Active publicity and promotion of certain classes of information. This can also termed *preemptive publicity.*

Vaultlike secrecy and security of records must be enforced in any transactions with individuals, whether these transactions be for sales purposes or for personnel purposes. Privacy and security are the key barriers for financial services firms to overcome prior to their propagation of Web-based services. Certain classes of innovation and intellectual property are worthy of privacy protection and the pursuit of patent. Trade secrets can range from recipes, to procedures, to steps of craft, to highly advanced mathematical formulas. Ironically, both patentable innovation and trade secrets are often best protected by preemptive publicity. Innovative intellectual property surrounding patents should be publicized as prior art to protect the patentable innovation, or protect the trade secret. This is a strategy of scorching the earth around innovation so that a competitor cannot patent away a process already in use.

How much truth—reliability, veracity, verification, replication—have data been subjected to? How much time has been invested in processing data? These questions are necessary in thinking about whether to preemptively publish data, subject it to benign neglect, or shroud with secrecy.

Privacy is emerging as the key consumer and individual issue when dealing with Internet transactions. Firms must have an effective privacy strategy in place that is pragmatic, workable, and enforceable. Currently, many firms have a "let's sue" policy, which is a blanket injunction on anything and is as unenforceable as trying to own the air we breathe.

CHAPTER 9

Trustees of Time

We are allowed choices about the use of our time. We can choose to run in the wheel of time or to exit the Internet economy. Our businesses, however, do not have these same choices. The pace of business is accelerating now and will forever more. Businesses must, and do, react to the business climate as cicadas react to the summer temperature. As the summer temperature rises, cicadas sing faster. They have no choice and it is not a conscious act; their biochemistry itself dictates the increase in song. So, too, our businesses have no choice, but are accelerated by their existence within a global business climate. Their business chemistry accelerates behavior in this Internet weather. There is no shelter for business from this global change.

Acceleration has created enormous stresses within existing old-line industries such as automotive manufacturing, energy, and utilities, to name but a few. In part, this stress occurs because these organizations have thought of time as an immaterial management measure. As innovation moves faster, each of these industries faces dire threats to its continued prosperity.

The future belongs to those firms that adopt a model I call *principled agility,* one of whose primary roles is the role of a *trustee of time.*

The high-tech electronic industries have created the leading examples of this model. The model is emerging by Darwinian

selection because it is the fastest way to work. No one would intuitively choose a form of anarchy to create fashionable, innovative
products faster than competitors. However, the Internet weather
demands speed beyond any other organizational attribute. Firms
that do not practice a principled agility cannot sustain the pace of
business. It is as simple as that.

The culprit in this drama is the structure of time as practiced
in a traditional corporate business organization.

> **Hierarchical organizations are products of the Industrial
> Age. They developed when information was costly.**

Most corporations are organized according to a vertical, traditional structure that can be depicted by an organization chart.
Nearly always, this chart is a pyramid, with 5 to 10 layers of authority between the chief executive and the lowest (most productive) worker. The organization chart is also an information flow
map. The Boss is at the top, and various managers report to her.
Each manager, in turn, has a layer of persons that report to him.
The organization has tight, well-regarded, and well-known methods of communication. A subordinate never sends a communication directly to his boss's boss. This is political suicide, as well as
counterproductive in a hierarchical, vertical organization. This
skipping of a layer of communication often slows down a process,
since the rules of careful and deliberate organizations dictate that
a boss would share any communication with his direct reports,
which came from a layer down the organization. These rules minimize misunderstandings and lay out clear channels for communication and decision making. The hierarchical style of management
organization evolved—in the same Darwinian fashion—over the
last few decades of the nineteenth century and the first few
decades of the twentieth century.

This method was the most efficient management model for the
huge industrial enterprises that grew from the rail, oil, steel, and resource industries. With this organization, delegation and role are
critical. Information is processed upward, and decisions are passed

downward. This form of information management and decision making allowed clarity when deciding on actions that impacted a broad range of the organization. Alfred Sloan Jr., one the most brilliant managers of the twentieth century, perfected this kind of corporate autocracy when he became president of General Motors in 1923. Under his firm and disciplined direction, General Motors unseated Ford Motor to become the largest automotive corporation in terms of vehicles built and revenue, and still maintains that lead some 80 years later.

Hierarchical management has strict rules of communication and organization. In the classic organization chart of boxes, each box depicts an individual. The Boss occupies a sole box at the top of this pyramid. Generally, information is compartmented. A department and its management complement will have access and control over a category of information. This compartmenting of information requires special communication between the specialist holder of the information and the next level of management.

Because of this compartmentalization, the Boss must spend time with her individual managers to receive information and judgments from each department. Let's say that the Boss chooses to receive information and make decisions for the subordinates, one day a week with each of her four managers. Assume further that these meetings average four hours of discussion. Assume that Boss and Manager A schedule their "one-on-one" every Monday and, further, that Boss and Manager B have a standing one-on-one on Tuesdays. This is a classic, linear use of management time. Manager A and the Boss would have consumed eight hours of their time—four hours each—simply nurturing their communication. Manager A would be "reporting" to the Boss, and the Boss, presumably would be making decisions, becoming better informed, and asking for more information. Let's say that one piece of additional information required from Manager A was only available through collaboration with Manager B. However, since B is occupied on Tuesdays, A will have to wait until Wednesday to collaborate, then wait again until the following week during his Monday session with Boss to share the new information for a decision. Meanwhile, three business days will have elapsed, and there probably will be no decision since it is likely that A will have to cycle back to the Boss.

While Boss is waiting for A to "get with B," time goes by. It is mostly a linear, sequential process. Information moves up a level in the organization and is processed. Possibly it moves higher for more processing and permission; possibly a decision is taken. A decision moves back down the hierarchy in a mirror image to the way information moved up. At each step, there are three potential outcomes:

1. The information is complete, a decision is made and sent.

2. The information is processed and moved up one more step.

3. The information stops completely with that last process.

This kind of organization is meant to reduce risk. It surely is deliberate, but this style creates dwell time while waiting for communication. Information is processed and passed forward. It is usually processed once and even several times prior to a decision falling back down the same steps that the information climbed. Each sequential action takes time and because the time between actions cannot be predicted—the interruptions caused by travel, conflicting schedules, and the like—there is tremendous variability in this chain of actions.

Information in a hierarchy moves up and down the organization pyramid like a Slinky. First it recoils itself and moves up one layer. After recovering—the processing time—it slinks up one more layer. Should it reach the very top of the pyramid, it will enjoy a long, easy end-over-end down to the base. In nearly all corporations, the base of the pyramid, the line, is where everything happens. Product is created, customers are served, invoices are sent, and bills are collected. Product ideas, new customer needs, and new market ideas are generally first recognized at the lowest level of the organization. If an organization has seven layers of management, simple feedback for a novel customer idea could take 14 business days, or nearly three weeks. In fact, this would be a fast track if the idea actually required all seven layers of management processing, since it would accommodate no dwell time between layers.

Graphically, this will look like an assembly line of ideas. An idea will be generated somewhere down in the field and course its way along the assembly line of management. The idea will be buffed up, colored, shined, ground off, bolted together, and filigreed with clauses and disclaimers. During this process, minutes turn into hours; hours turn into days, then weeks. The idea itself gains weight and bulk, and is shorn of identifiable risk. The Slinky-pyramid assembly line of the organization will, at some time, roll the decision off the process, or move the idea to the cripple lot.

I have purposely exaggerated the example to highlight that the traditional hierarchical organization cannot act quickly. It is simply, structurally, too difficult to sustain fast action. It is like asking elephants to dance ballet. It is not that the people in such an organization work any slower; in many cases, they work as long hours as any high-tech executive. It is not due to any difference in raw talent, nor in work discipline, nor in desire. It is simply that such a structure cannot sustain sufficient speed. There are crisis teams and certain fast track teams, and so forth, but these usually achieve speed by being allowed to compromise the rules of the organization.

At the turn of the twentieth century, when hierarchy was implemented, this form of organization was the fastest. Hierarchy parsed information into precise packets and moved them up and down the chain of command very efficiently. At that time, and until very recently, communication was expensive and relatively slow. Telegraph charged by the word, resulting in a colorful staccato language used only in telegrams. This method is not sufficient for relaying the complex bundles of information necessary in a huge corporation. Written word traveled inexpensively but slowly by mail, and the telephone was beginning its penetration of the nation. But the telephone also was expensive. Long-distance rates were formerly as much as 40 to 50 cents per minute. So channeling communication with precise rules, and compartmenting the information were the most efficient use of communication that existed.

When information becomes free, hierarchical organizations are less appropriate.

Now enter the Internet, and the World Wide Web. Information on the Web is provided raw, in real time, free, and voluminously.

Information on the Web is provided anarchically. The Internet revolution provided a means to broadcast vast amounts of information to an entire organization. To act on such pervasive communication, organizations began to change. Picture, instead of a pyramid, an organization like a spiderweb, like the Internet itself.

In such a web organization, each node represents a person, and all persons are connected to all other persons. Management, in this case, is a node in the network. In this way, *everyone* in the organization sees the same information at the time the information is available. Such a management structure acts more like a web, or an immense scrum, tugging, pulling, and pushing with hundreds of actions creating a Ouija-like movement of the organization to a collective decision. Movement becomes a form of decision, and the organization is characterized by momentum, flow, sharing, and, most critically, speed.

Such a method of organizing would not have a traditional organization chart. Instead, it would be depicted best as a network flow diagram, or as an immense, interconnected grid. Boss is centered in the web, and Managers A, B, C, and D, are now interconnected nodes within the organization. Boss and managers do not spend time sequentially. They spend time together in real time. Information flows through the web like a summer breeze through a screen. Each person receives an equal view; each person must act to keep current. *Each person must act simply to stand still* in such an organization.

This kind of information transparency and organization structure is designed solely for movement. The organization swarms around decisions with experiments, corrects, and moves. An idea does not move like a Slinky, it moves like an electric current. The idea wafts its way into the information flow that is available to all. Then, with information broadly shared, without edit, an idea can be acted on within minutes or hours of its birth. This fluid use of information creates tremendous response capability to changes in the market caused by fashion or innovation. A customer's idea can be acted on within hours, as management scrums its way around the idea.

This kind of organization performs according to principled agility. Movement and speed, celerity and nimbleness are paramount values. High-tech firms such as Cisco, Adaptec, Taiwan

Semi-Conductor Foundry, and others demonstrate this kind of celerity. They have been successful in part because of their speed. They have allowed the market to push them into swarming nodes of management action. It has been widely stated that, among high-tech firms, it is no longer the big eat the small; it is now that the fast eat the slow. Speed is more important than size. Further, time is more important than money or cost. Speed has become the secret sauce: Speed raises revenues and reduces costs.

Principled agility has arrived in the high-tech and information industries because these industries have been on the frontier of innovation and fashion. These are industries where you must run simply to stay in place. Moore's law and Metcalfe's law were both formulated by important scholar-business founders (Moore of Intel; Metcalfe of Novel) from these industries. According to Moore's law, innovation in semiconductors will produce a doubling of transistors on a chip every 18 months. This has led to a dramatic decrease in cost of processing power, at the same time as delivering an immense increase in performance. In the case of semiconductors, fashion follows function. The absolute dollar value of chips has not changed in 16 years, yet the performance has increased by a factor of six thousand times. This innovation has spread into the personal computer, creating a need for new models each year. Indeed, I have spent my way through the various designs of Intel chips through my purchase of home PCs to supply computing power that matched the games my sons were buying. Moore's law means fashion driven by innovation.

Metcalfe's law outlines the reward for creating a network effect for a company's product. Since the creation and maintenance of a network effect usually translates to monopoly rewards, companies use innovation to achieve a network effect. Only one company can enjoy a network effect in a particular market, thus all companies race to achieve a network effect. This race is motivated both by fear and desire—the fear of losing a market to a powerful network effect owned by a competitor, and the desire for the rich rewards of being first.

Innovation is driving novel products in all industries. With innovation, product life cycles are shorter and obsolescence more frequent. As consumers, we experience innovation as fashion, and thus fashion, fickle fashion, is becoming the driving force in all markets. Product innovation is accelerating, delivering more features and functions in products at declining prices. Fashion and innovation, then, become close cousins. This relationship ratchets up the pressure to become first to market, to design a novel and winning product, and to stay ahead of the fashion desires of the market.

At the same time, innovation is seeding old products with new virtues, adding to the cacophony of consumer choice. We have seen examples of refrigerators, toilets, and microwave ovens each become information appliances. We have seen the same movement in automobiles, and certainly the dizzying improvement in cell phones and personal computers speaks to rapid and accelerating innovation.

Even warehouses are being changed by technology and industrial fashion. Warehouses formerly were square, low buildings. This design optimized real estate more than the labor of storage. As a result, when moving goods, travel paths for forklifts and warehousemen can be longer in a traditional building. Today's faster flow of goods demands more rectangular buildings that are meant for goods to flow through them. A rectangular design facilitates travel time between dock doors and accelerates the movement of goods. They are meant to function more like a truck dock where goods do not stay in storage. They facilitate the re-sortation of goods that move from one truck to another within an hour or so. This kind of flow-through operation, and the attendant modern electronic sortation systems require longer and narrower buildings than the former design of warehouses. The former stalwart building, a low cube, is becoming obsolete.

If fashion can impact the construction of warehouses, certainly very little is immune to the fickle fates of fashion. In particular, automobiles are now increasingly subject to the whimsy of fashion. The automotive industry is among the most rigidly hierarchical in all manufacturing, and the second largest in terms of revenue, globally. However, the automotive industry is competitive, capital-intensive, and subject to the whims of fashion. A competitive, capital-intensive, fashion business: Could there be a worse combination? Very few industries exhibit all three of these characteristics to the same degree. Thus the automotive industry is experiencing magnified stress from the acceleration of business. Each automotive company's approach to accelerate its business is the key determinant of that company's future. Those that don't "get it," that don't understand fashion, that don't understand speed, will have received a terminal dose of radiation. As with such a dose, the death spiral is at first imperceptible, lingering, but inevitable.

Innovation and fashion demand fast production, and greatly reduced cycle times.

In 1999, there were 2,400 vehicle models available from 15 major automotive manufacturers. General Motors alone markets cars under seven nameplates, leading to 300 models just from General Motors. There is no longer such a thing as a model year. Formerly, September marked the beginning of a new model year, and all nameplates rolled out new cars during the fall. Now, new lines roll out each month of the year, blurring the lines of model year and fashion. Detroit is beginning to compete on speed to market.

With the increasing emphasis on fashion and innovation in new vehicles, the key challenge for the automotive industry is to produce fresh cars. Innovation begets fashion, and fashion requires fresh. If you want a computer, you call Dell or Gateway; they assemble it the following day and deliver within a few days. Both Dell and Gateway announce new lines several times a year, sometimes leading fashion, sometimes meeting fashion. You get a fresh computer from these companies. If you call an automotive dealer to order a car, it will take an average of 60 days to produce it, then another 7 to 12 to deliver. Your car can be 72 days stale. Yet, an automobile only spends a few hours on the assembly line once the bolting has begun. Why can't the auto companies deliver your car in less than 72 days? What happens to all that time?

The simplest way to answer is that no one is actually responsible for all that time. Numerous departments each own a piece of that time, and these departments are not connected. The automotive industry organization pyramid is exceptionally rigid, with precise rules of communication and decision throughout the chain of command. Each department within a major automotive manufacturer is the owner and steward for its information, be it manufacturing, sales, marketing, design, engineering, finance, dealer relationship, service parts, purchasing, and numerous other corporate departments. There also can be tremendous variability in the movement of information between these various departments. As a result, the order-to-delivery process has tremendous variability. So, of the 72 to 90 days required to order and to take delivery of a car, 10 different departments may take information and use it. Our Slinky—in this case an order for a car—must journey up and sideways through a corporate maze of information management and decision making before bouncing its way out the assembly line door and onward to the new owner.

The information flow in the automotive industry is configured to reduce the risk inherent in complex, big-ticket manufacturing. The amount of time spent for the entire order-to-delivery process has been an immaterial management measure. In fact, the most passionately watched metric in any assembly operation is direct labor hours per car, which turns out to be a miniscule metric when compared with the total order-to-delivery time. Direct labor hours per car is a measurement of the amount of union worker-hours consumed during the assembly process, once a car is on the line. Currently, according to the Harbour Report, it takes about 17 to 20 UAW hours to assemble a car. If the fully loaded cost of an assembly line worker is $50 per hour, the direct labor cost of a car then ranges between $850 and $1,000. In 1998, the average price for a car was over $20,000 for the first time. Thus the most closely watched metric for the automotive industry comprises about 4.5 percent of the average selling price of a car. If you look at ads for new cars in the Sunday paper, it is nearly certain you will see numerous offers of rebates, cash incentives, zero percent financing, and other price discounts that sum to much more than $1,000 per vehicle.

The auto industry has become expert at precisely and quickly building cars that no one wants. The culprit, again, is the structure of the way time is used within the industry. To survive, the automotive industry must take itself apart and adopt principled agility. The hierarchical structure of the industry cannot support the sustaining speed to survive and prosper as innovation begets fashion.

The automotive industry uses time just as Henry Ford did, some one hundred years ago. Ford produced just one model, the Model T, in just one color. The robust Model T was priced right, and was fully featured for its time and its market. Since there was no variation in model, it made sense to produce each as an exact clone, stamped from the assembly line like peas. Fashion did not affect cars. Thus, a car would move linearly down the line, parts sequenced one after another, each car exactly like the one in front of it or behind it. In this case, the black seat cushions could be ordered in massive quantities and placed in day-use quantities near the assembly line.

Now, at the Ford Taurus assembly line in Chicago, a white Taurus with beige interior could be followed by a red Taurus with a gray interior and sunroof option, which is followed by a green one with green interior. The line producing such a high-volume car as the Taurus may run at the rate of a car a minute. Every 60 seconds, then, the beige interior parts must be precisely followed by gray, then green . . . and so on, for a thousand cars each day, every day, all year.

The assembly of a car is one of the most complex manufacturing operations in the world. For each car, about three thousand parts must arrive at the side of the assembly line at precisely the right time, in the right quantity, and easily accessible to the car at the point of production. This operation involves incredible synchrony and, thereby, time management. For Ford Motor Company, whose annual production is about 7 million vehicles, this means that over 20 billion parts were precisely delivered, within the 2- to 4-minute time window, for a part's application to a car at lineside. This equates to about 10,000 parts arriving per minute at Ford's assembly plants worldwide.

> **Trustees of time are emerging to optimize time-consuming processes such as supply chain management.**

The synchrony of a modern automotive assembly, although a display of manufacturing virtuosity, is obsolete. This method was designed for the volume production of cars an automotive company *projects will sell*. It was not designed to produce *cars that have been sold*. The automotive industry was not structured to produce a fashion product. Should the automotive manufacturers focus on speed and produce cars that consumers want? Should they focus on margin per car rather than labor hours per car? Imagine the reduction in discounting if the customers could order the exact car they wanted for delivery within a week.

Numerous programs are developing within the automotive industry to accelerate the order-to-delivery cycle.

On August 5, 1999, Toyota announced a five-day car.[1] This car, a version of the Solera, can be ordered and produced within five days. Transit to dealer still can consume up to 10 days, but a 5-day order-to-production cycle is within hailing range of the make-to-order personal computer business. Within several weeks, Renault, General Motors, and Ford Motor Company announced dramatic programs to reduce order-to-delivery times.[2] Renault announced a program for make-to-order vehicles, delivered in the European Community within 16 days.[3] General Motors announced a massive program led by one of its most senior executives, Harold Kutner, the Group Vice President of Worldwide Purchasing.[4] This program is chartered to reduce General Motor's order-to-delivery time from more than 70 days, on average, to less than 15.

Ford Motor Company, too, has taken significant actions. On February 2, 2000, Ford announced that UPS, the world's largest parcel company was assuming the responsibility for outbound delivery of all Ford's North American automobile production.[5] UPS? UPS is now delivering automobiles? Where will they put them inside their drab brown delivery trucks?

Actually, UPS was contracted to manage the time consumed from the end of production to final delivery of an automobile. Once a car is ordered, UPS will monitor its place in the assembly queue and the line setup, then assume responsibility for all movement of the new vehicle once final assembly is complete. UPS has assumed a special role—it has become a trustee of time. UPS has been given stewardship over the critical process of new vehicle delivery. This final presentation to the consumer is one of visibility and trust. To execute this process, UPS must act as a trustee of time; in fact, they must act in many senses as a fiduciary. According to Webster's New International Dictionary, a fiduciary relationship exists when "one person justifiably reposes confidence, faith, and reliance in another whose aid, advice, or protection is sought in some matter: the relation existing when good conscience requires one to act at all times for the sole benefit and interests of another, with loyalty to those interests."

UPS was selected because it has the capability to monitor, describe, measure, and minimize this process time. Using their tracking, tracing, and decision technology, UPS will be sculpting a new use of this time, and both Ford and UPS have publicly announced that UPS will reduce the amount of time used by up to 40 percent.

On behalf of Ford, UPS has accepted being responsible for the amount of time commencing with the end of vehicle assembly through the purchase and delivery process. It is now UPS's duty to use that time as if it were its own and, in doing so, *to act for the sole benefit and interests of Ford.* Ford has ceded to UPS a process and, within it, the microevents that consume time. The time Ford has ceded to UPS is currently about 16 or 17 days, on average, and it is UPS's mission to reduce this time by 40 percent.

Ford has chosen a Gordian knot approach to a process that can consume 15 of the 70 some days from order to delivery. This Gordian sword is to recognize the capabilities of someone else— UPS and its management of time and movement—and cede to that organization a role of incredible responsibility.

Thus the automotive industry—the competitive, capital-intensive, fashion industry—is fighting for survival. This industry, the father of twentieth-century manufacturing and, the engine of victory in the world wars, is besieged by technology's pace of change and will struggle to enter the twenty-first century.

For guidance, it must look to the increasingly nimble, fleet, paranoid, and global high-tech and information industries, which, for the most part, have existed for less than a full generation. Microsoft, among the oldest, is barely 25 years old. Sun Microsystems was founded in 1982, Dell Computer in 1984, Compaq in 1982, and Cisco, for a while in the year 2000, the world's most valuable company.

These companies were born running. They were forged in fierce competition among the brightest people in the world, bent on ruling the world. Because of the magical alchemy of the network effect—the winner takes all—these high-tech leaders must race to rule. And the model that propels nearly all of them is that of principled agility. The high-tech world is one of rapid innovation, short product shelf life, and chipmunks on the wheel.

These companies must produce their product within a day of order or face extinction. How can these companies do in one day what an auto company takes 60 days to accomplish? These organizations, and the high-tech electronics industry as a whole, use time differently.

Gateway or Dell's main production asset is not an assembly line, but a position as a node between customers and suppliers. These computer manufacturers have become fashion merchants of technology. The fashion changes rapidly. If you are a college student, you may value power over portability to support such features as MP3 and computer games. If you are a graphics artist, you need a different kind of power. If you are a globe-trotting consultant, you will want the maximum power possible in a computer that weighs less than three pounds. To succeed in the fashion world of personal computers, it is necessary to be next to the customer—a node in the customer information network. This is a knowledge management position of design, information, engineering, communication, and character. Trust and open communications are implied. Information is less processed than presented.

Cisco Systems is one of the barometers of the high-tech industry. Cisco does not actually own factories. It relies on key suppliers to manufacture for it. These suppliers are linked directly, via the Internet, to the raw, real-time information stream of customer orders and supply status. These suppliers have increasingly linked their process flows and information flows to those of Cisco to gain speed.

Optimizing time requires openness, truthfulness, and trust.

Cisco is but a barometer because the high-tech electronics industry is a web of interwoven alliances. Your customer is your vendor is your partner is your competitor. The key to prosperity is speed. Speed is the single most important attribute for success. Because of Moore's law, processing power increases each year, and this increase correlates to a decrease in cost. Some semiconductor components reduce in cost 6 percent per quarter. So in this case speed and Moore's law combine to create a virtuous cycle: The faster you go, the more you can use fresh components that bring more capability and cost even less! In this case, you want to produce instantaneously, without inventory, since your inventory will quickly be obsolete. The high-tech industry is in a state of constant NOW. What is ordered now, is supplied now, and is sold now.

In this industry, a command-and-control organization cannot work. Such a hierarchy cannot sustain the speed necessary for survival. Instead, management's scrumming and Ouija-like movements are characteristic. These organizations are drawn together as a web, or grid of information, each person processing raw information and acting.

In high-tech industries, there has been a Darwinian selection. Slow organizations have been left behind as roadkill. The remaining prosperous organizations focus on speed. With speed come collaboration, sharing, trust, and transparency. There is no other way to be fast. The industry cannot wait for a chain of command. The remaining organizations in Silicon Valley have adopted principled agility.

The key principles that impel principled agility are openness, truthfulness, and trust. Together, these engender the collaborative scrum of movement among customer-owner-supplier.

Openness is a business community value. Dell and Cisco are best described as information nodes among a community of suppliers and customers. These firms receive information from a customer, which they share openly and instantaneously among the community of suppliers and employees who must produce the computer or the switch. The supply community and the production process are then keyed, not to a *forecast of what products a centralized function thinks will be sold,* but to *products that have been sold.* Because these firms share information from the point of entry, each supplier can respond to the customer faster. Openness has been selected as a value because of the broad uncertainty of technological fashion. With openness, firms have the advantage of the collective creativity and intellect of their suppliers, and gain the perspective of someone in a different position in the process.

Truthfulness has been selected because it is fast. Protracted negotiations wherein you game your supplier with deception, feint, and parry simply take too long. Stating needs simply, truthfully, and quickly saves untold time in procurement.

Trust is paramount because of the enormous responsibility each participant assumes in principled agility. A supplier who works both for Lucent and Cisco is in the unique position of knowing Cisco's order book. A Cisco supplier will also be informed of Cisco's production plans, its engineering, and likely its research. Suppliers who are manufacturing key components must know this kind of strategic information to keep pace with the overall market Cisco is trying to serve.

But just having information is not enough. Being able to act on the information—without the ladder of information up the chain and decisions cascading back down—saves days. Thus collaboration becomes naturally selected by Darwinian business survival as a key principle of speed. Speed then rewards with more fashionable goods sold without discount, which creates the need for more speed, which reinforces openness and collaboration.

In such a business landscape, the relationship between companies is increasingly fiduciary: Each must be capable of acting on the other's behalf. These business partners will be required to care for a process that is actually owned by the other, and care for it as if it were their own. At the highest level, companies will be trustees of time in another company's process.

I find it exquisite that the pace of technology is placing increasing value on the principles of trust, time, openness, and truth. I find it exquisite that new fashion, innovation, and creativity must rely on old values to succeed.

Summary

It is not possible for a hierarchical organization to be fast. The way information must travel throughout the organization precludes speed. To accelerate and exceed competition, hierarchical firms must become more anarchic and more weblike in structure, and must make more decisions closer to the customer interaction.

The automotive industry is interesting to monitor with respect to acceleration. This industry is one of the oldest, most complex, and most affected by technology, fashion, and global competition. Already a new role has emerged in the industry—that of trustee of time—and it will propagate to other industries. This role as a fiduciary for process time within another firm is exemplified by the UPS-Ford Motor partnership for outbound vehicle delivery.

While high-tech provides the leading examples of organizing for speed, the automotive industry is a better barometer for acceleration of the broader manufacturing economy. Roles such as trustee of time and organization styles such as principled agility will be proven once the automotive industry has broadly adopted them.

CHAPTER 10

The Color of Data

The horizon of knowledge is always receding beyond our grasp, despite the dramatic, accelerating, and incessant improvement of our reach.

As outlined in Chapter 5, information is being produced in unspeakable quantities. I say unspeakable because the amount of new information is so large that it requires the invention of *new names* for these quantities. This has caused the creation of *metadata*, which is *data about data*. While metadata is crucial to processing vast troves of data, it does not create human understanding. Even using metadata, vast troves of data remain beyond comprehension.

There is no choice but to employ the ironic servant, technology, to assist with producing meaningful information from these immense data mountains. The method is to deploy technologies that front the data with a human face. Emerging technology does and will utilize sight, sound, and touch to impart truthful information. The first of these kinds of technology utilizes visual display, imparting attributes such as color and movement to convey factual attributes of data.

Many technology developments are designed to increase the truth, engender trust, and husband time. Metadata is but one. Other technologies rely on displaying factual information in forms such as color and motion that more quickly provide information to our senses. These developments are the most important use of

165

technology to improve the supply of the verities as they increase in value.

We need these technologies because we are processing information using mental and sensory equipment honed to survive on the African plain. If you have any doubt that our basic mental equipment is frail, think about the following small illusions of the mind: Ask yourself, colleagues, and friends this question, "Are there more seven-letter words ending with *ing* than there are with *i* as the fifth letter?" This will begin a process of thinking about the seven-letter "ing" words such as darling, damping, dunking, etc. It is very hard to begin the process of thinking of seven-letter words in which *i* is the fifth letter, of which *selfish* is but one. So, automatically nearly all people will respond that there are more seven-letter words ending with *ing* than there are seven-letter words whose fifth letter is *i*.

However, reasoned examination shows that the opposite is true. Every seven-letter word ending with *ing* has an *i* as its fifth letter. Our minds find it easier to imagine words ending with *ing* than to imagine whole words just given the fifth letter. Therefore, our prejudicial answer is wrong, but entirely plausible.

Now, ask yourself, your colleagues, and your friends a question given the following information:

Steve is very shy and withdrawn, invariably helpful, but with little interest in people or in the world of reality. A meek and tidy soul, he has a need for order and structure, and a passion for detail.

From *Inevitable Illusions*, by Piatelli-Palmerini[1]

The question is, "Is Steve a librarian or a farmer?" Again, nearly everyone will answer that Steve is a librarian, although nothing in this information can direct that choice. There are shy, meek farmers. In fact, there are about one hundred times more farmers in the United States than there are librarians, so the more probable occupation of the two is farmer.

Beguiling, illusory questions such as these assault every business, everyday. These kinds of questions are close cousins to factoids, in that they travel as illusions and prey on our biases. The answers require pausing and filling in blanks with sound, factual information. These data should be available, given the unspeakable quantities around us, but are not, due to the investment of time required to mine data.

We are now being assaulted with terabytes of data each day, every day, all around us. At the same time, our brain capacity has not evolved much beyond that of our species of 10,000 years ago. Our perceptions as well as our mental processing evolved to help us quickly discern friend, foe, or food. Yet, our basic equipment—the five senses—has not changed, nor has the basic wiring of our brain.

Few people, however, are assaulted with as much data as Alan Greenspan and the other governors of the Federal Reserve Bank. Greenspan provides a complex model of human cognition. His mind can process a great deal of information. He can reason this information into a shape and take actions based on his reasoning. Although few of us could replicate his performance in the area of economics, most of us are now being challenged with a surfeit of data in the same way he is.

What has changed is that, like Alan Greenspan, we are facing daily decisions based on overwhelming information. We are facing these decisions without having time to consume the proliferating information. Those who can consume data effectively enjoy inordinate competitive advantage. In Chapter 5, I described a perverse kind of Gresham's law of data: Bad data drives out good. This law predicts we will change our behavior by withdrawing to a few trusted, hoarded sources of information; however, these sources will provide extremely high-quality information. We will not "surf" as much, which is similar to trying to boil the ocean. Ironically, we will derive actions based on less information rather than more. Information processing will be forced first to preprocess metadata, in order to consider the work effort of processing the volume of underlying data that metadata represents. We simply cannot process the information available to us; it must be preprocessed or prepared for our use.

One of the most powerful tools for presenting truthful information is color. Moving displays of color greatly enhance comprehension.

To describe this phenomenon, I devised what I call the *color of data*. Color can be an economical method of displaying extremely dense data and capturing meaning with just a glance. In many situations, such as stellar images produced by the Hubble Space Telescope, information begins as colors, is captured digitally, and is transformed for use into color again.

There are some tried-and-true shortcuts to enhancing cognition. There is a maritime saying, "Red sky at night, sailor's delight; red sky in the morning, sailor take warning." Here, color of the sky encompasses a great deal of information. In particular, at dawn or sunset, when the sun's rays are refracted through greater volumes of air, the difference in water vapor within the air will change the perceived color of the sun. More water in the air results in more absorption of blue and violet energy, producing a redder light. Through centuries of sailing, this color has become a reasonable predictor of the day's weather. A red sunrise is likely to produce a stormy day, since the morning air contains enough moisture to filter other than infrared red light.

The Weather Channel has made dramatic use of color to portray information. During hurricane season in the Caribbean, television viewers are now accustomed to the swirling colored pictures of a hurricane as it builds strength and moves toward the Americas. The dark reds indicate vast areas of violence. The cool blues indicate the areas of declining violence and taming of the winds. Such pictures capture trillions of bits of data in a way that quickly imparts what we need to know about the storm. The colors show the variation of power, and demonstrate the swirling violence of the storm.

The density of information incorporated in weather maps provides a good example of the ability of color to capture and convey facts quickly. The raw data that feed a weather map are multidimensional: temperature, pressure, humidity, longitude, latitude, and height of the air mass, wind speed, and wind direction. Formerly, weather maps were produced in black and white, using lines and symbols that depicted information. Such a map is called an isentropic chart, and was first used in the 1930s in Britain and the United States. Isentropic charts are built from iso-bar maps. They are a series of grid lines, each with numbers and small flags indicating pressure, wind speed, and direction. On such a chart, the closer the contour lines, the faster the winds. Only a very seasoned eye could scan such a map and quickly categorize the strength of a storm. The progression from this rigid black and white, two-dimensional graph to the swirling colored simulations of the Weather Channel has taken many decades. However, the resulting moving images quickly make available an immense amount of information that can be understood by the untrained eye. The display is in harmony with our equipment to process it.

The National Center for Atmospheric Research (NCAR) in Boulder, Colorado, has built a large-scale simulator of the earth's climate system. This simulator is used for long-term projections of average temperatures of the earth. I observed this simulator projecting the effect of an El Niño, which is depicted as a whalelike blob of red (warm) water swimming about the equator from Peru across the Pacific. Following within the next few years is a cool La Niña, which starts a cool blue whalelike blob of weather off the coast of Africa and moves across the Atlantic to the Caribbean. This was one of the many simulations that NCAR performs to project the impact of current trends on future weather patterns.

The effect of differing levels of greenhouse gases on future weather is one such simulation. To illustrate the effects of increases in greenhouse gas content of the world's atmosphere, swirls of weather are depicted in color, day by day for a century in the future. Each day that is projected to be above average temperature in the future is a shade of red. The cooler the day, on average, the more green/blue the day is shaded in a particular region of the world. It is, then, possible to see the color of the data. The projections demonstrate the gradient of the weather—always hot at the equator, then cooling as heat dissipates through climate and wind to the poles. The global weather system is depicted as a massive temperature gradient with heat moving to the poles from the equator. If the poles warm, there is actually some chance that the weather will become more benign, since there would be less gradient between the equator and the poles.

In this case, there is no chance of an illusion of the mind. The simulation demonstrates movement and color of data only. Color by itself depicts the relationship of predicted temperature to average temperature, and the changing color translates into the movement of weather systems from the equator to the poles. This kind of display is ideally suited for our vision and cognition. The heredity of our senses has selected for the ability to see color and movement with high precision.

Meteorology has been leading advances in the simulation of large systems and the display of data. Weather measurement has exponentially increased in volume, as weather data arrive from satellites, airliners, airports, ships, ports, navies, weather stations, and specific measuring devices. Both the number of measuring points and the frequency and precision of measurement have increased. The various universities, governments, and private institutions that produce weather forecasts have been at the forefront of supercomputing power applied to large-scale simulation. These institutions monitor the vital signs of the earth and project the health of earth based on the quality of its atmosphere and water. The execution of this mission absolutely requires unvarnished truth and the best science available.

Similarly, this kind of technology is assisting large-scale businesses in monitoring the vital signs of their business, their market, and their competition. Simulation and display is already occurring in electric power distribution, airlines networks, telephone networks, and railroad systems. BNSF Railway operates a huge nerve center and command center in Fort Worth, Texas, where its entire rail network can be viewed and vital signs displayed.

Visualization of data is no longer a luxury. In many industries, visualization technology has become a ticket to entry. This is especially true of the financial industry.

The financial industry leads businesses in the use of visualization of data.

A cousin to the global weather system is the global financial system. These systems are cousins because simulation mathematics can be employed to evaluate the impact of discrete events on the overall system. The interlinked electronic systems that compose the world's financial system are a financial ecosystem. This system mimics storms, calms, trade winds, fair weather, and chaos.

Each day, about a trillion dollars of bonds, currency, and stocks changes hands. This market is growing, instantaneous, and fluid. Money flows at the speed of light through the world's trading system, spanning all geography and time. Anomalies in these markets have the power to enrich those that can seize on them quickly. The currency and bond markets, in particular, are in constant search of anomalies such as a bond having a momentarily different price in Hong Kong from its price in New York. Or, a French government bond may be priced somewhat high, for 10 milliseconds, compared with bonds of Alcatel, the French Telephone company. Although the differential could be infinitesimally small, when applied to billions of dollars, this difference could amount to a considerable lightning fast profit.

Or, 30-year U.S. Treasury bonds could temporarily become convex compared with 10-year U.S. Treasury bonds. Or, the concavity curve flattens. In each case, it is difficult, if not impossible, for a human to "see" these changes with the speed necessary to act on them. A writhing ribbon whipping about helically above another writhing ribbon would be much easier to sense than a rapidly changing column of numbers. The relative position and curvature of these ribbons could portray an immense amount of data; changes in the color of the ribbons would further demonstrate facts and relationships among the data. If a trader could don a virtual reality helmet and watch the concavity or convexity of a group of bonds relate to each other as such ribbons, he could understand the changes in relation much faster.

The relationship among bonds could be configured as a landscape, which I will call a *bondscape*. The bond trader would see a living landscape in his viewer. She would see mountains that changed colors as certain features changed, such as convexity, yield, or price compared with another similar class of bonds. Price of the bond could well be indicated by the height of the mountain. Rivers running down the bond mountain could depict risk. In essence, the trader would not be looking at a landscape, but rather a bondscape. This method, using the color of the data, would enable the trader to comprehend massive amounts of correlated data and the changes in the data.

This is already occurring in the financial trading powerhouses of the world. The gain of millisecond pennies on trillions of dollars becomes enormous trading profits. Consider, if you will, that a penny on a trillion dollars is 10 billion dollars.

In financial markets, the term *hot money* is often used. This is a shorthand term for the activity of a certain kind of investor in the market. This investor moves money around quickly, actively trading stocks, bonds, real estate, and a broad array of financial instruments. His money is "hot" in that it rarely sits around very long. The activity of this type of trader, and the hot movement of his money provide the evaluation at the margin, which then provides the spot value of the markets.

What would be the temperature of money, then? Picture the striated wall of the Grand Canyon. This striation of color depicts age, composition, and relative length of time of an epoch in history. An important piece of information for an investor is the depth of trading in a particular security. What is of interest is float, which is the amount of securities available in the market, and the percentage of securities actually trading. Hot money provides the spot value and is often based on a miniscule sliver of total amount of securities that can be traded. A security could be depicted as striated wall, with each layer becoming colder and bluer in color, and more stable, as the picture moves to the bottom. The hot money, in red, again, would be furiously storming and crashing about on the top of the security and the relative depth of color would indicate the amount of the total security trading in a day. The deepest blue at the bottom could depict the authorized, but unissued stock, whose release would depress the price. The temperature of the money would be a critical piece of information to use to assist trading decisions.

Weather simulation and financial instrument trading are, at core, mathematical. The description of the weather is an accumulation of statistics about temperature, humidity, air pressure, wind speed, and chemical composition of the air. This plethora of statistics, however, quickly becomes too immense for human comprehension. It is difficult for a human to detect patterns among columns and rows of numbers. Like the weather, currency trading is impacted by global events. In the case of the weather, the trade winds developing over Africa have a decided effect on the American Southeast some days later. In the case of currency markets, the default of a major state-supported bank in Thailand has both an immediate and lingering effect on the entire global currency trading system. Such a default will have an immediate impact on Thai baht, then tangential and corollary impacts on the yen, the yuan, the dollar, and most other major currencies. This kind of global systemic effect cannot be "seen" by looking at raw numbers. However, the world currency trading system, at its root, is nothing more than numbers racing across trading screens. Although the chore is massive, there are tools to correlate the changes among these numbers. In the past, these relationships have been shown by graphs. Bondscapes and currency scapes are taking over.

These particular uses have developed because the root of the weather system and the financial system is numbers. The math and technology for correlating systems of numbers is well developed. Rapid increases in the power of graphic display, processing power, and data transmission are making living, breathing data possible—as long as its roots are numerical.

Technology is also being created to mine truth and trust from nonnumerical data. This represents the vast majority of information, and is currently fallow.

It is common for an individual to be tasked with determining, say, the market for hair conditioner in South America. Such a request is often urgent, and often the research has been performed before, within the corporation, but the information is inaccessible for a variety of reasons. Or, a request is made to research the characteristics of competitive hair conditioners and their producers in South America.

A burgeoning body of investment is being devoted to the type of knowledge called *tacit knowledge*. We know how to ride bicycles, but this knowledge is not really describable. We can speak to the action, and describe the action, but cannot describe how it actually works. In fact, the placement of the front tire in front of the turning axis of the handlebars is the physical architecture that makes bicycle riding possible. As we move our legs, we are unconsciously executing microturns that force the bike to remain upright because of the balance of centripetal forces that we introduce by pedaling. To actually simulate this action with a computer model is incredibly complex. However, we can develop a way to know this math and physics within the hand, eye, body, and pedal coordination that is manifested by riding the bike. This is tacit knowledge that most 5-year-olds master, but cannot describe. It is knowledge that is very difficult to capture.

Within most organizations, tacit knowledge is far larger than explicit knowledge. Part of the challenge of revealing this knowledge is its volume. But the biggest challenge is trust. People share information with people they know. An outcome of too much information is that personal networks supplant databases.

Many corporations, such as GE, Boeing, Ryder Systems, and Valeo, have instituted knowledge management systems. Typically, employees are incented to contribute to these databases, regardless of the quality, insight, originality, or importance of the data being contributed. A contribution to knowledge management databases is a punch on the compensation ticket. These factors combine to degrade the average quality of the information in such databases. Because of this degradation and the volume, employees usually short-circuit the system and begin to query their own network of friends. Word-of-mouth vouching for expertise will lead to people with reputations—by word of mouth—for expertise and reliability in a subject. While this probably increases the trustworthiness and reliability of the information, it costs a huge amount of time. Phone messages and e-mail expand exponentially as the data call rings throughout the firm.

Technologies are even developing to display trust and graphically impart trust values to these databases. In academia, a widely held manifestation of quality work is citations of that work in other research. This can lead to ranking the expertise and authority of the cited scholar and such statistics are reviewed at time of nomination for tenure, for awards, and other recognition. All transfer of knowledge acts in a similar way, except that the ranking is not formally captured anywhere—it is tacit. Building reputation within a firm is usually word of mouth. The most important technology developments in this area are methods to capture measures of authority of an expert, credibility, and acknowledged reference by others. The display of trusted networks look like skewed spiderwebs, with fat, variegated strands leading to and from experts. The deeper the color and the fatter the line, the more authority and vouched trust possessed by that person. A person gains weighting in this system by frequency and quality of interaction. Quality is measured by the ranking of a person's common correspondents. This ranking system provides a surprisingly accurate way to portray reputation and greatly enhances the average truth and trust of a database. Addressing these verities assures increased use of the database with an attendant reduction in time spent searching for expertise.

The rapid growth of tacit knowledge is a fraternal twin to the exponential growth of electronic information. It is also one of the most fertile areas of investment for software and artificial intelligence investment. Among the leaders in the creation of tools to organize tacit knowledge are the software firms Volantia.com, BrightPlanet.com, Autonomy, Tacit Knowledge Systems, Askmecorp, and Aurigin Systems. Each of these firms has developed a unique approach to finding meaning in the data-scree at the base of any surrounding data mountains.

Any organization develops tacit knowledge of its own even though it is difficult to capture and codify. An example is the body of knowledge required to successfully install a new software system, or to build, fill, and implement a new distribution center. In the case of the distribution center, the kind of knowledge required to implement new facilities and system spans several disciplines within the firm. Customer service functions often develop domain experts in certain technical problem solving that remains immune to knowledge capture in any systematic way. Knowledge becomes buried in volume. Proliferating e-mail is unretrievable in any systematic way. The knowledge embedded in graphic presentations in such software as PowerPoint and FreeLance cannot be captured by most software packages. Although the information in these disparate places and stored in disparate media may address the same subjects, there is no easy way to correlate them, index them, and harvest the accumulated knowledge. This immense reservoir of knowledge is quiet; it is tacit.

Emerging technologies display information in novel ways to capture factual relationships among nonnumeric data.

Examine the capability of newsmaps.com. This software depicts unrelated text files, documents, and graphics files by turning them into bas-relief visual displays. In effect, this software can provide a view of landscapes of the day's events. This capability is owned by Aurigin Systems, which has produced software to evaluate the relationships among vast quantities of unstructured documents.[2] Among these documents can be e-mails, Web pages, word documents, news articles, and spreadsheets. The software then produces Java language topographical maps that display the relationship among documents. The software clusters affiliated documents into hills, mountains. The distance between hills or mountains displays the similarity or differences among the information. There are competitors in this market, the most commonly cited ones being Autonomy and Semio. These companies view themselves as knowledge management companies.

They are attempting to become to knowledge management what online analytical processing (OLAP) has become to customer service and financial services data. An OLAP program provides some intelligence during the processing of a customer interaction. In the case of a call center, OLAP programs will determine and present to the call center employee a history of the caller's purchases or interactions with the call center. It is common for these programs to project commonly ordered goods, and suggest affiliated items that would be attractive to the caller, based on history. In the case of the Internet, OLAP programs evaluate the economic value of a user to a Web site and help customize the site to that user. These companies are attempting to provide knowledge analytical processing to harvest the otherwise silent knowledge within an organization.

Online processing of knowledge, or *knowledgescapes,* may result in the presentation of perpendicular information, or parallel information as the knowledgescape is being laid out. Information that had been parallel in content would now be aligned generally in favor of, or supportive of, the information in question. Information that was perpendicular would be in conflict with it.

An interesting use of the capabilities of Aurigin Systems and its knowledgescapes would have been in the document management of the Microsoft antitrust trial. This trial has produced a little over *100 million pages* of documents. Microsoft's attorneys could use the Themescape capability of Aurigin to group this massive stack of documents according to categories of interest. Such a category might be all documents that show decreasing software prices when Microsoft entered a market. This is a critical factual finding, because if it is true, then Microsoft did *not* use monopoly power to increase the price of its products. The viewpoint would create a mountain of documents among the pages of evidence that indicated Microsoft's entry to a market reduced prices for Microsoft's products and competitive products. Also displayed would be a distant mountain of documents that showed the opposite. Filling the valley between the opposing views would be bumps of documents unrelated to pricing matters. The Justice Department could use similar software for the same purposes. The Justice Department, using the same tools, would be looking at the mountains and hills of documents indicating that prices increased when Microsoft entered a market. The very same docuscape can serve both parties; since the mountain each was interested in would be placed far apart on the display.

Now, let's also assume that Bill Gates has been advised that he must soften his public image to blunt the wrath of the Justice Department. Such software could help the assembly and evaluation of the news stories used to determine Gates' public image and would probably be approached in two ways: retrospectively and prospectively. The first sort of the evidentiary documents would be for those that portrayed Bill Gates as a generous software titan, truly vigilant for innovation and intellectual freedom in the software industry. The docuscape would aggregate such documents in a pile, and move another pile further away . . . those showing his aggressive side. Then, prospectively, Aurigin or similar software could provide a moving and living time series analysis of how the public feels about Bill Gates. The docuscape could be sorted by the tone of articles: admiration, scorn, ridicule, envy, and neutral.

With the sort would come the relief map of the intensity of these articles; over time, color could be added to highlight changes in tone, height would indicate volume of articles, and so forth. This approach could be used to accumulate an index that might possibly be called the "Index of Public Affection" for Bill Gates.

Display technologies are emerging that can demonstrate the use of time.

Only the rare individual can inherently know how much time activities are consuming. A minute in some circumstances can seem to be an eternity. Try pausing midway in a speech in front of hundreds of people for a full minute. During this pause, do not do anything; just stare out at the audience. I have done this several times, and the audience always begins showing real discomfort at 30 seconds, which by itself seems like an eternity. At the end of the silence, when asked how long that was, most people guess it was 5 to 10 minutes. (The speaker will feel as if it were an hour, rather than 60 seconds.) Or, recall computer screen changes that take 5 seconds. That 5 seconds seems to take forever.

Our perception of time is relative. This relativity makes the management of time doubly difficult. Tasks that "should" take only an hour consume a day. Big tasks scheduled for 10 hours whiz by in 3 hours. Because of the inordinate increasing value of time, it is a true competitive advantage to be able to display the use of time as it is occurring.

Activities within an organization can be grossly divided into those activities that must be executed sequentially and those that can be executed simultaneously. It is essential that simultaneous activities move along. Likewise, the sequence of activities dependent on each other must be clearly identified and all necessary materials, skills, and equipment must be in place at the right time. The assembly line is the ultimate example of sequenced activities. Most project management and time management techniques are derived from and work well in the sequenced-assembly environment. Critical Path Method, for example, was designed for sequenced manufacture of missiles.

Knowledge work is often more scrumlike than disciplined sequences. While producing a knowledge product it is often unknown what the actual dependencies are that make individual work tasks sequential. The best way to perform knowledge product development is to converge on the result. This convergence will look like a football team's execution of a series of plays: huddle—chaotic order—huddle—chaotic order—huddle—chaotic order—touchdown. Joe Montana was asked one time how he maintained his vision of the field, and he replied, "I just watch colors, I don't focus on individuals, just on the movement of colors." However, Montana knew that at the count of 1003, Jerry Rice or another receiver would be at a sector of the field, positioned for a pass. What looks chaotic on the field is actually motion in concert according to common perceptions of the passage of seconds. It appears chaotic because all players have to adjust as the play develops. Montana, in this case, was able to project his entire team's activity for three or four seconds into the future.

So too with knowledge products. The development of a knowledge product takes numerous chaotic movements, punctuated by communication sessions that serve also as idea generation sessions. In this environment, visualization of the use of time will look like a virtual football game.

Novel knowledge technologies are occurring everywhere.

The challenges of data management and data comprehension are not limited to business. The public sector, medicine, government, and education all have similar challenges. These new approaches to displaying information show great promise in education. Indeed, two organizations, BioScope.org and digitalfrog.com, have applied computer graphics technology to the presentation of biology. Both are demonstrating advanced methods for learning and for interacting with information.[3]

BioScope.org is a collaboration of the Cytology Laboratory of Purdue University, the National Science Foundation, and the Agriculture Department of Purdue University. This web site presents high school biology in a different way by focusing on web-enabled video of the cell. The cell is the fundamental building block of biology, and much of biology is understood in terms of the cell. BioScope presents the best electron microscopy of the cell, along with interactive graphic display. To excite and engage the average teen, BioScope has developed a game, the path and perils of which seem to be like the King's Quest series of games. The viewing of the cell in three dimensions, along with the capability of rotating the view, is a fresh and unusual way to present information.

Digital Frog takes a different approach. For any high school biology student, the dissection of a frog was either the goriest or most glorious experience of high school science. Digital Frog has replaced the real frog with a virtual frog. Each student can dissect a frog digitally, without the reek of formalin and gore of cold frog parts.

These two approaches in high school biology are but harbingers of immense changes in the way we see information. Biology, the study of life, is an appropriate subject matter for the use of video, graphics, and games. After all, we transitioned from the observation of nature, to the description of nature using print, to observation and interaction with virtual reality nature.

Advances in many other display technologies are also occurring. The labs of the world are even producing digital paper.[4] This paper, likely to first appear as digital wallpaper, will be able to display images in much the same way as an LCD panel. This will lead to "experience" movies wherein you are placed within a space shuttle, within a racing car, or within a jet fighter. A chief executive could watch the simulation of her firm on one wall, financial scapes on another, newsmaps on another, and the moodscape of the firm on another. If we can simulate the world's weather, why not simulate the impact of current events on the future performance of a company? There is extensive research and development in the area of holographic display, including displays that are placed directly into the eye, visible only to the recipient. The convergence of these micro- and macrodisplay technologies with knowledge software will produce truly amazing methods of presenting knowledge to people.

We are returning to the use of information with a "natural" face. We have deconstructed information into 0's and 1's and have now the processing power to reassemble the information in a humanly digestible form. The piece-parts of the technology to perform the magic currently exist. Yet, information keeps blossoming in all directions, in hundreds of dimensions, exponentially racing ahead of the technology to process this ironic blessing of data. Information recedes away from us as a curious reverse Zeno's paradox. Zeno, a Greek philosopher of the fifth century BC, outlined the following famous paradox: Stand a short distance from a wall, then advance to the wall in successive steps by advancing each time one half the remaining distance to the wall. While you will converge toward the wall by halves, you will never reach the wall. The reverse Zeno's paradox we now face is that each time we approach the frontier of information, it recedes away from us at twice the rate of our advance.

Summary

The horizon of knowledge is always receding beyond our grasp, despite the dramatic, accelerating and incessant improvement of our reach.

As outlined in Chapter 5, information is being produced in unspeakable quantities; the amount of new information is so large that it requires the invention of new names for these quantities. This has caused the creation of metadata, which is data about data. While this metadata is crucial to processing vast troves of data, metadata by itself does not create human understanding. Even using metadata, vast troves of data remain beyond comprehension.

We have no choice but to turn to technology to assist us with producing meaningful information from these immense mountains of data. The method is to deploy technologies that front the data with a human face. Emerging technology does and will utilize sight, sound, and touch to impart truthful information. The first of these kinds of technology utilizes visual display, imparting attributes such as color and movement to data to convey factual attributes of the data.

Important advances are being made in the display of the use of time. There is no more critical attribute of productive enterprise than the concerted use of time. The organization, hierarchy, and communication protocols of organizations are the kernel of organization speed and agility.

While we have more data to work with, we still are frail. Our decision-making facility is tunneled with mental illusions, anchoring, expert bias, and myriad mental frailties that enable our day-to-day existence. However, they hobble objective decision making and prejudice our thinking.

Technology and display systems are even producing methods to capture trustworthiness and reputation within database systems that will materially improve their reliability and utility. They will also reduce time spent searching the data, or searching for an expert person.

These technologies and the color of data imparted by them can bring true competitive advantages to firms. They will increase the quality of information used for decisions, and effect this improvement in less time.

CHAPTER 11

Principled Agility

It takes three years to conceive a new automobile model, design it, and roll the first vehicle off the assembly line. By contrast, eBay created an *entirely new industry in three years:* the peer-to-peer auction/sales industry, supplanting physical flea markets with a global virtual flea market. Pierre Omidyar, the founder, did not conceive that his creation would become so big, so fast, and would be so revolutionary. I am sure that he did not call his creation "the peer-to-peer market" in 1996. It was simply a cool way to locate Pez dispensers using the Internet.[1] But eBay won this market by a combination of skill, organization, leadership, product and service quality, brilliance, and consumer demand. Moreover, eBay won fast. Very, very, very fast. Three years for a new car, compared with three years to conquer the entire world through conceiving and creating a new industry.

eBay provides one of the starkest examples that *speed overcomes almost any other attribute in knowledge and technology industries.* Microsoft, AOL, IBM, Sun Microsystems, or any of a hundred other high-tech giants were capable of making technology similar to, or even better, than eBay's. Certainly they had much more marketing muscle, presence, wealth, and talented staff in 1996 than eBay did. Yet eBay has won primarily because of lightning fast execution.

As shown in Chapter 9, the structure of a traditional, hierarchical organization prevents it from acting quickly. Many new

183

companies, including eBay, are organized differently, as their rapid growth demonstrates. Several of these companies have become sizable; yet they maintain rapid response and keep pace in their chosen markets. I call the style of organization that has emerged to sustain speed *principled agility*. This style has emerged, cultlike, by trial and error through two decades of new enterprises and start-ups. The job-changing, veteran executives of several such firms propagate the behaviors that underpin this style. This style does not preclude the need for inspired leadership, but there are recurring elements that can be contrasted with a traditional, hierarchical organization.

Hierarchical Organization	Principled Agility
Cost based.	Time based.
Instruct/obey.	Contribute/create—Assent/ dissent.
Asset optimization.	Time optimization.
Pyramidal structure.	Webbed, circular, constellar.
Decisions pulled to the center and upward.	Decisions spun to the bloody customer edge.
Sequenced activities.	Convergent huddling.
Perfect work is required.	On time is better than perfect.
Planning horizon 3–5 years or more.	Planning horizon 6 to 18 months.
Time is usually not measured. The organization produces a truth to work with. There is trust in the pyramid and in the firm. Privacy and corporate secrecy are treasured.	Overarching motivation is using less time. Truth is baked in because it is the fastest way to communicate. Workers have self-confidence and trust in each other. Speed lessens the need for secrecy.

Software provides a chronology and case study of the development of principled agility.

Software development is the barometer of the technology industry. Software development began as individual, machine-specific code. A small team would tend the code alongside the operation of the computing machine, and all development was directed to optimize the computing asset itself. This development was rigid and rule-based, with clear instruct-obey patterns of working together. Development then shadowed and silhouetted the industries served, which were hierarchical, asset-intensive industries. There was no opportunity for agility, since there were no personal computers. There was no communication mechanism with which to openly share code, ideas, and comments. Development stayed within an individual shop, closed to the outside and even closed to anyone outside the computing department.

The Internet community began as a tiny kernel of open, free-wheeling, idea-sharing scientists, engineers, and computing science professionals. Although their use of the Internet was anarchic, it was bound by codes of accepted behaviors and etiquettes that, for the most part, have survived.

The anarchy of the Internet is not chaos; it is the rule of voluntary association. The Internet demonstrates principled agility and this anarchy has engendered the stunning technological creativity of the past 20 years. All of the innovations of web, including the World Wide Web itself, were possible because of the simple anarchism of the Internet.

> **As software continued to grow in importance, the difficulty of its development increased exponentially.**

Norman Augustine, formerly the chairman of Martin-Marietta Corporation, a major aerospace and defense contractor, wrote an irreverent book dealing with the procurement of large defense contracts. In this book, *Augustine's Laws,* he outlines several laws of defense procurement, and one in particular deals with software. He introduces Law XVIII this way:

> Optimally, what is needed is something that can be added to airplanes and other systems which *weighs nothing,* yet is *very costly,* . . . it can be reported with confidence that such an ingredient has already been found. It is called software.

This introduction leads to the law:

> Software is like entropy. It is difficult to grasp, weighs nothing, and obeys the Second Law of Thermodynamics; i.e., it always increases.[2]

According to the market research and forecasting firm IDC (International Data Corporation), the worldwide software industry was valued at $157 billion in 1999 and is projected to grow 15 percent per year; this growth rate will cause the industry to double in size every five years. This growth is in addition to a decade-long spike in software investment during the 1990s. The looming threat of the year 2000 milestone motivated massive investments in enterprise resource planning (ERP). These systems are meant to manage information across the entire enterprise, and seamlessly link the disparate activities of the firm, such as order entry, accounting, production, customer service, and procurement. The estimates of ERP investment in the late 1990s, just by U.S. firms, range from $200 billion to $400 billion. The business case for this investment was motivated by fear of total shutdown of a legacy system on New Year's Eve, 1999. The sales pitch for even $100+ million projects was simple: Invest in remediating your legacy system to prepare for Y2K, which cost is $100 million, or buy a new ERP system which is already Y2K compliant for $100 million.

But installation of an ERP system has been likened to a corporate root canal. Whirlpool Corporation and Hershey experienced disastrous implementation of ERP systems in the fall of 1999.[3] In each case, the firm was unable to locate and ship orders. Hershey was required to place its chocolate products on allocation during the Halloween season, a first-ever product allocation for Hershey during the largest candy-selling season of the year.

With the turning of the calendar to the new millennium, executives now needed to address how to breathe life into these massive ERP investments. Advance planning systems (APS) seemed to be an answer, since APS is intended to optimize procurement, inventory, and order management across a firm. Now, the implementation of APS systems can be analogous to having the corporate wisdom teeth pulled. Dozens of firms that have implemented these extremely complex supply chain planning systems have failed to achieve the benefits promised, but none more publicly than Nike. In April 2001, Nike announced a dramatic reduction in quarterly earnings; Nike CEO Phillip Knight laid the blame on a supply chain planning software system recently implemented and was quoted, "This is what we get for $400 million?" As Charles Piller reported about the software system in the *Los Angeles Times* on April 8, 2001, "Too many slow selling styles went to the wrong places; the company produced 5 million pairs of shoe styles for which it had no orders. Popular models like Air Force One were in short supply and delivered late to impatient retailers."[4]

ERP became characteristic of the enterprises it was meant to serve, but often inverted the relationship: The master served the ERP system.

As Norman Augustine's law points out, software always increases. Growth in investment in software has been taken for granted among most firms, since leading practitioners of magical integration of advanced software with disciplined processes can change entire industries. The examples of disappointment and failed expectations, however, far outnumber the dramatic successes. At least 50 percent of ERP installations fail to meet expectations. Another 30 percent of all software projects never are completed. Imagine buying any other product—refrigerators, cars, clothing, restaurant meals, indeed any product—in which the product experience is disappointing half of the time. Furthermore, imagine building houses, highways, or dams or any construction project that failed to be completed 30 percent of the time.

The instruct-obey cycle and perfect work is the state of the software business.

The methods and processes for developing and implementing software have developed autocratically over five decades and can only be described as the *least-worst* method of development and deployment. The development free-for-all that has emerged with the Internet is changing the methods, process, and overall business model for the development of software. This model shows great promise for removing risk from information technology, and the style and work method of principled agility will spread across knowledge industries.

> **The software industry was constrained by the requirements of instruct-obey management methods, by computing asset optimization, and by the requirement to only process perfect code. Anything short of perfect code wouldn't work.**

The software industry arrived at the state it is in because it has been forced to follow the least-worst path. From the first computers up until the arrival of the personal computer, developing code was a daily exercise in compromise. In general, the computer's central processing unit and memory were limited, and coding efforts always had to compromise to fit one or the other resource limitation. Prior to the personal computer, writing computer code could only occur on a terminal linked to a large computer, whether it be a minicomputer or mainframe. To create code, it was necessary to adhere to rigid rules, protocols, and conventions. At the same time, it was necessary to receive permission from the authority that administered the computer's central processing unit. Mainframes were expensive, computing time on a mainframe was allocated, and the processing unit was shared among many users.

Personal computers, combined with the open, inexpensive communication of the Internet, have turned this autocratic method on its head. With personal computers, central processing power became essentially personal and free since the computing power is housed within a programmer's possession. Formerly, release of versions and version control were tightly regulated. Delegation of responsibility was carefully described and monitored with project plans, milestones, and other measures of performance against a planned outcome. Source code was rarely shared, and echelons of security and administration protected it. With the Internet, open-source code has become an accepted practice. Indeed, Microsoft has recently offered to share the source code of its Office suite of software with its top customers.

> **The seeds of principled agility were germinated with the Internet.**

Compared with the autocracy and security of an individual mainframe, anarchy reigns over the Internet. No central authority directs the Internet's development and use. No central authority commands the standards of content, conduct, or construction. Once an individual has paid access fees to an Internet service provider (ISP), there is no log-on permission step, and there is no limit on the use of the Internet resources.

The principles of the Internet are embodied in protocols, which are the instructions for moving data packets around the Internet. The principles for the Internet are very simple: The network sends data packets from one end to another, without discrimination or disturbance to the packet. There are no special priorities; there are no differing protocols for a packet. The network is simple, then, in that all it needs to know is where a packet is going. No coercive, directive, or central authority governs the Internet, only the simple principle of end-to-end. Unlike this loose, anarchic messaging, traditional bilateral EDI is centrally controlled, managed, and directed by an expert programming staff, and messages must conform to these rules. Messages can be prioritized, discriminated among, and redirected by the central processing machine. This is the classic centralized and expert management of a computer network.

Coincident with the growth of the Internet has been the growth of the open-source software development movement. The code of open-source software is openly available to anyone, usually free of charge, and is openly available to modification by anyone. Although there were examples of open-source code prior to the Internet, the free-and-easy information sharing of the Internet has radically increased open source. Unix, originally created by Bell Labs, has been subject to a handful of open-source versions that predated the World Wide Web, notably the versions created at MIT and the University of California at Berkeley. The unique characteristics of the Berkeley version of Unix figured prominently in hunting down a German hacker as described in Clifford Stoll's book, *The Cuckoo's Egg.*[5]

> **The open-source movement is a model of principled agility in action.**

Among open-source software, the most prominent and most widely implemented system is Linux. By March 2001, 35 percent of Internet servers were using Linux, and Linux was becoming the most utilized operating system for Internet servers.[6] And Linux was created by the anarchic contribution of thousands of programmers, all contributing code via e-mail. There was no project plan, no resource requirement, no user requirements definition, and no central authority dictating Linux's overall direction.

Linus Torvalds released the first Linux code in 1991, and Torvalds is now viewed as the father of open-source software development. Torvalds' three principles for developing the Linux system were(1) release early and often, (2) delegate everything you can, and (3) be open to the point of promiscuity.

These principles were directly opposite to the accepted practice of software development at the time. Linux was developed with no centralized authority and no coercive control. Thousands of individuals contributed their time and intellect to constructing Linux. The resulting product is among the most stable and robust operating systems. And it was developed according to principled agility.

The Linux community is extremely rapid in finding and fixing bugs in the software, or in the development of *hacks*. A hack is a creative software applet, bot, or sequence of code. It is to software development as a jazz riff is to a Beethoven symphony. A key to resourcing a hack, or a problem is matching the appropriate skill, knowledge, and interest to a problem or a task. When a traditional IT shop is staffing a software problem, it is limited to the resources of the shop. It is limited to the skills, experience, and interest of the programmers within the central control authority's purview. It is rare for a shop to have all the talents needed to meet every requirement.

Open-source (anarchic) development has a virtually limitless pool of talent. Anyone with access to the Internet can contribute to the development of Linux. Since the activity is voluntary, a Linux programmer will choose those problems that are interesting and fun, that provide a gnarly puzzle to solve, that add a notch on a professional belt. The volunteer knows exactly the extent of his or her talent, and exactly the amount of time available to be contributed to the Linux solution. Thus open source—with access to the entire world—has more talent available than any closed shop, and the mathematical odds predict that open source will have access to better talent than a closed shop.

It is not intuitively obvious that an anarchic method of product development could create a robust, rapidly evolving software operating system. It is also not obvious that open source—the opening of source code to anyone—is faster than the traditional, closed shop, project-managed, and supervised method of software development. However, open-source development can be much faster than the project-managed, traditional software development method because of the way time and communication are deployed.

Why principled agility saves time.

Principled agility is growing because it saves time. It is also growing because correcting errors in open-source environments will be statistically better than using traditional development methods. The reason is simply that the open-source "gauntlet" that code must pass through has more people buffing up the code. If each person brings about another standard deviation of accuracy to the code; six people can bring code within six-sigma quality.

Project management methods used in the development of software and knowledge products are designed to describe the use of time. Among the most useful tools is a Gantt chart, which has vertical lines to denote a unit of time and horizontal bars to graph activities. The amount of time an activity is planned to consume can thereby be easily seen. Typically, sequential activities appear as a series of arrows, each arrow beginning at the end of the previous one, and stepped slightly below its predecessor.

Traditional project management anoints an individual as a project manager, and this person receives information for processing from task workers. The project manager can decide on an action based on this information, pass the information up to another manager for decision, or pass decisions back down to the program staff awaiting instruction. These sequential uses of information consume time. When projects are large, say 30 or more individuals executing task packages, the time overhead of project administration can be considerable. In fact, as a project grows, the communication needed grows exponentially. If there are n people on the project, the complexity of communication relates to n-squared. However, each person only adds his own capability, thus the additional productivity can only be, at best, linear. So the complexity of management grows in proportion to n-squared, while the benefit of additional people is only a multiplier of the number of people: n. Project management, then, is doomed to become unwieldy as people are added. This math led Frederick Brooks, author of *The Mythical Man-Month* to postulate Brooks's Law: *"Adding programmers to a late project makes the project later still."*[7] This is particularly true because the project plan is divided into discrete tasks, many of which depend on the completion of preceding tasks and all information must be shared with anyone joining the effort. When someone joins a late project, there is a good deal of nonproductive time just learning and communicating status, relationship of effort to completed effort, and so forth. This effort can be depicted graphically:

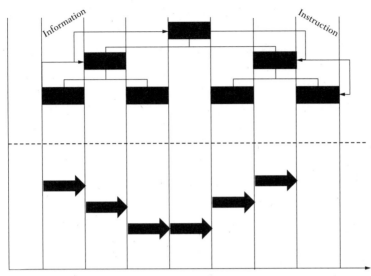

Time Consumed

An agile method of development has no project plan, no project manager who approves work and tasks, and all information is shared openly. While an individual programmer may expend much more time to comprehend enough information to contribute to an open-source project, all this time is "off-line." Then, information flow in an anarchic open-source project looks like this:

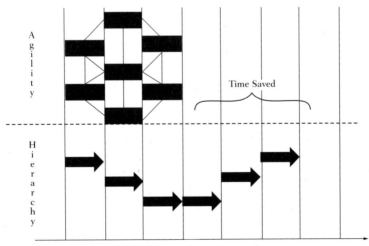

Time Consumed

Agility saves time. The instantaneous information sharing of open source can accelerate product development and enhancement because the time devoted to sequential project management does not exist.

The difficulty of development is but one challenge for the software industry. As software becomes ever more complex, the implementation of, and adaptation to, the software is a growing challenge. Again, 50 percent of ERP implementations have disappointed the buyer. In general, the simpler the product, the easier and faster its adaptation in the market. Instant Messenger is simple, easy to use, and easy to install. The simplicity of this program has facilitated a massive and quick adaptation within the market. Indeed, Instant Messenger's initials, IM, are now used as a verb, as in, "I will IM her." Contrasted with IM is an ERP system such as SAP, Baan, PeopleSoft, or numerous others. In part, this disappointment is directly related to the size and complexity of these programs, which require a good deal of training and communication regarding their use.

Adaptation is not a linear process. The rate of adaptation of any change, from new software, to the Sony Walkman, to a new hairstyle, is described by a curve. It is an "S"-shape that was first described by Henry Wallace, the agricultural seed pioneer and vice president under Franklin Roosevelt. Wallace, a biologist and founder of the Pioneer Seed Company, was intrigued by the rate of introduction of new seed hybrids among farmers in Illinois.[8] Wallace produced the first observations on the adaptation of new products and the first structured approach to new product uptake. Since his Pioneer Seed Company was based in DeKalb, Illinois, Wallace could drive amid vast cornfields in any direction from this small northern Illinois city. As he drove around the country highways, he noted the flags on the farm fences that advertised the seed brands and hybrid number. As he was looking at both his hybrids and those of competitors, he noticed that patterns emerged related to communication among the farmers as well as to the personality of the farmer. Some farmers were early adapters and enjoyed experimenting with new seeds. Others, at the other end of the spectrum, waited for nearly all neighboring farms to adapt and prove the utility of the seed. These groups of farmers, ranging from the early adapters to the very conservative late adapters formed a bell curve population; and the rate of market penetration based on this population forms an "S" curve as the percentage of the population using the innovative seed begins to increase:

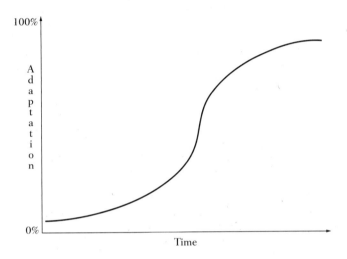

The rate of adaptation is affected by communication. The easier the communication, the faster the adoption. For some innovations, the beginning of the period can look like a flat line, and virtually nothing seems to be occurring. When the curve begins to turn, it can turn upward very quickly, and a few days of market penetration can make the difference between monopoly and misery. Since the Internet is facilitating communication and reducing the cost of communication, product introduction is accelerating. Numerous attributes of the Internet accelerate product introduction. It is possible to simulcast information to the entire world at virtually no cost. Bulletin boards and chat rooms proliferate the knowledge of new product and provide consumer review nearly instantaneously.

For technology and information products subject to the network effect, beyond a certain point of market penetration, a monopoly is virtually assured. It is assured because, for example, people do not want to use two word-processing softwares and worry about such questions as which version to save it in or which version to produce it in. For a traditional product such as an automobile, the greater the supply of product, the lower the price. For a product enjoying a network effect, the greater the supply of product, the greater the value. Demand becomes magnified.

Speed to market is amplified by the connection between the two curves. At the point when the demand curve and the penetration curve meet, a network effect product is fated to vanquish the market. And, at that point, the second player in the market is the first loser, and the biggest loser. At that inflection point, both technology products—the one leading and the one in second place—may have achieved double-digit market share. This effect has led to the common use of the term: *Game over.* For certain markets, the game is over once that inflection point is crossed. The leader enjoys a serial monopoly, and the second-place product is in the excruciating position of first loser. A first loser is likely to have invested heavily to win and thereby has lost a lot. The third, fourth, fifth, and nth losers are likely to have invested far less, and thereby have lost less.

With communication being priced so low and electronic distribution being so fast, the slope of the new product adoption curve is increasingly steep. A few weeks of adoption can be the difference in achieving the tipping point, the inflection point, and make the difference between the monopoly position and that of first loser.

Open source, and the associated principled agility that accompanies open source, has also proven to be surprisingly secure. Again, it is not intuitively obvious that a computer code openly available to anyone for inspection would be more secure than code protected deep within a corporate vault. However, because open source is open to all, every line of code is being studied and tweaked by some member of the open-source programming community. A security breach within software often resembles the cuckolding of a cuckoo (thus the title of Clifford Stoll's book), which lays its egg in the nest of another bird for nurturing. Many viruses and breach-of-security hacks work like a cuckoo's egg: They are slipped into the nest of software, unnoticed, and lay dormant until triggered.

The peer review of open-source development brings trust and privacy.

As open source and principled agility progress, there are a series of peer reviews during the creation of the product or code. Peer review assures more reliability in information processing, but it also results in a more trusted product. Open-source code, because of continuous review, is less susceptible to attack. In this way, it provides better security and better privacy protection.

The open-source process has a better chance of detecting viruses, security holes, and outright hacks. This is true because the open-source code is continually under inspection by thousands of programmers (hackers themselves, most likely) who will quickly detect changes or variations in the code. Open source, then, has better odds of detecting software incursions, simply because of the sheer numbers of eyes and minds devoted to watching the code. There is also a subtle difference in motivation for open-source coders: peer review and the egoboo (ego-boost). An individual Linux hacker who has created any sequence of lines of Linux code feels a sense of ownership for that sequence and will care for it as if it were a rare greenhouse flower. When that code was sunk into the Linux kernel, that action gained peer acclaim and egoboo from the community of Linux hackers. The individuals who specialize in certain parts of the open-source code, therefore, watch it carefully and are expert in the code's structure, use, and relationship to other sections of the code. For hacking to be accepted into the code, peer review and acceptance must occur. In this open, transparent environment, it is much more difficult to place the cuckoo's egg of malicious code.

Open source is on time, since it is a community product, and its uptake is similar to the uptake of slang language. If you give time to the Linux community, you get prestige and knowledge that can be used within the context of your applications for advantage. And Linux egoboo goes to those who crack the code and teach.

Some interesting industrial strength applications of principled agility may occur in e-market development.

Principled agility has worked well guiding the fast and robust development of the World Wide Web and open-source software such as Linux. But how far will principled agility invade current management styles in other areas? How about principled agility at General Motors? Or at Du Pont? Or at Boeing?

Each of these firms is leading or participating in the creation of Internet-enabled electronic marketplaces to provide an open community of suppliers and has focused on the procurement process to launch. The marketplace being formed by General Motors is called Covisint and includes Ford Motor, DaimlerChrysler, Renault, Oracle, Commerce One, and Fiat. The systems architecture of such a market is a Tower of Babel of differing software systems that perform individual functions, many of which have never been integrated before, and many new functions for which software, as yet, does not exist.

Should open source and principled agility be the development method for these huge endeavors? At first, this question seems far-fetched. The question of the use of open source and principled agility versus planned project-managed program approach is a question of compromises. When launched on an endeavor as large and complex as Covisint or Elemica (the market for Du Pont) or Exostar (the market for Boeing) all the companies involved, when using traditional software development are faced with certain cost versus probable benefit. Much of this certain cost occurs well before any benefit stream arrives; this often simply wears out the participants in a software development process and results in the 30 percent of projects never completed. The up-front cost also must be recouped from the benefit stream, so time to benefit is critical. The realization of benefits can be described by the adaptation S-curve, and the objective of a good implementation is to bend the slope of the S-curve upward sharply so as to capture benefit earlier.

Against this method, this certain cost and probable benefit, must be weighed the question: "What is the objective of the e-marketplace?" Presumably, it is for the participants to produce products faster, to reduce expenses of production, and to increase sales. Nothing in this objective states that creating cool software is part of the market's objective. Software is subordinate to the objective.

In this setting and context, possibly the public domain should be the participants in the marketplace, and all code related to the creation and maintenance of the e-marketplace should be open sourced among the participants. This would bring several of the benefits of open source regarding security, speed, and robustness to the market but would compromise control, individual copyright, and ownership. Markets such as Covisint, Exostar, and Elemica, however, are likely to be neutral in effect for participant companies. These electronic marketplaces are designed to become sophisticated, industrywide utilities, analogous to the electronic interbank funds transfer system. This utility is among the most secure and robust of all electronic data exchanges anywhere, yet no bank differentiates itself by its ability to wire money. Likewise, it is doubtful that any of the e-market members will be able to accrue disproportionate benefits compared with any other member. So, possibly, an open-source, principled agility approach is the best for building and maintaining the electronic nervous system of these markets.

How can a firm accelerate through principled agility?

First, principled agility is a method of choice when:

- Speed is required.
- The work is in the design-develop stage.
- There are many simultaneous tasks as opposed to sequential tasks.
- The work product is a knowledge product as opposed to a physical product.
- There is unusual complexity in the product or process.

Given these situations, there are a handful of enabling principles to consider:

- *Open Communication.* When racing toward a goal in the development of a knowledge product, it is impossible to know who will add creative insight, or where it will come from. While individuals will be added to the team based on IQ, on previous track record of creativity, puzzle-cracking, or other qualifications, there is no way to know which individual will specifically add what insights. The odds then favor exposing all information to all, and allowing curiosity to take root. Segregating and subcategorizing information also cost time.

- *Spin Decisions Out.* The process of passing information back and forth to make a decision costs time. The wait-state between transmission of information and a decision is usually the most time consuming. Adopt minimal rules regarding scope of authority for the least experienced members of the team.

- *Rules Cost Time.* A few rules save time, but constantly evaluate a minimal structure, because rules and their attendant administration can also cost time.

- *Huddle Often.* The image of rugby teams, forming shoulder-to-shoulder around the football and all pushing to move and control the ball is appropriate. A huddling meeting would push around ideas, failures, and successes, and would compare the current state of completion or progress against the objective. Huddling should occur frequently. This process will converge the group toward the objective.

- *Shorten the Horizon.* Whatever the assumptions were going in, cut the time by half. Assume that beyond two years is infinity. Usually when moving off to create a new knowledge product, no one really knows what it should look like or do anyway. Since this is the case, *on time is better than perfect.* Declare a victory, on time, release, and begin working on releases 2, 3, and so forth.

- *Assume Trust and Be Trustworthy.* Begin this endeavor with an investment in trust. Assume that everyone is trustworthy.

- *Be Humble.* Serendipity favors humility.

What about the development of physical products? Can development and production of physical products be accelerated by agile processes?

It depends.

Go back to my favorite industry, the automotive industry, for analogy. Because an automobile is a high-ticket consumer good, and a fashion good at the same time, the challenges facing the industry are possibly the most complex and difficult in the marketplace. The assembly plant cannot adopt principled agility. Once a car frame passes through the back door of the plant, and begins moving down the line, the most amazing sequential activity in modern industry occurs. Each car has about 3,000 parts that have to arrive precisely within the three to five minutes or so the car spends at a workstation.

But automobiles are now laden with electronic processing and communications gear. The vision for some manufacturers is that the car will be an infomicrocosm. The development and deployment of these knowledge products would be accelerated by adopting anarchic styles.

Principled agility and its companion, open-source development, are products of free information and massively distributed computer processing. The method—anarchy, transparency, and peer review—is perpendicular to the traditional method of development; yet, open source has created several complex, robust systems. Because of its success, and because of the checkered 40-year history of large-scale software development and implementation, there will be more principled agility. Principled agility will require a Zen-like equanimity but be motivated by individual zeal. This is an oxymoronic, but powerful outcome of the fluid movement of information, ideas, and people via pervasive communications.

Summary

Speed is the singular competitive advantage for the future. Entirely new industries have been created in the past decade. eBay provides an example of a firm's creating an industry and conquering it, within three years. This kind of pace is required for survival because many of these markets will be won by serial monopolists. In these markets, there is only fast and first.

This kind of market magnifies time and its use in an organization. As firms have been born and raced to victory or burned through their capital, a style of organization has emerged identified as principled agility. This style of working is typified by a focus on using less time; having open, shared communications; huddling frequently to converge to an objective; and pushing decisions out and down among team members. For this organization, on time is better than perfect.

There are many examples of principled agility, including the development of the Internet itself. An instructive example is the development of open-source software code. Some of the counterintuitive benefits of anarchic organization are less time used, faster communication, faster adaptation, and thereby faster to win. In the case of open source specifically, the gauntlet of contributing programmers makes open-source code less susceptible to bugs and breach of security hacking.

Because of the notable success of fleet, small companies such as eBay, because of the industrial-strength application of Linux, principled agility will increase. It is a style that must be used when faced with developing knowledge products, quickly, despite uncertainty and complexity.

CHAPTER 12

Invest in Verities

Verities are always true. Technology, no matter how magical, powerful, and pervasive, cannot change a verity. Technology does, however, affect the value of verities.

The law of supply and demand is a verity, and has not been changed by the Internet; it is the founding law of economic study. This framework provides relative values to allocate resources in a situation of scarcity. As resources become scarce, they become more valuable. As resources become more abundant, the price offered for them decreases. The future return of compound interest is another verity and cannot be changed by any technology. Compound interest is as dead certain as the results of simple addition. A lofty, but achievable investment objective is a 15 percent compound annual growth (CAGR). At this rate, $20,000 becomes $1,342,235 in 30 years. Or, alternatively, at 15 percent CAGR, an annual contribution to a 401(k) of $4,000 becomes $2,000,000 in 30 years.

The recent dot-com boom and bust has highlighted the wisdom and rewards of long-term investing. However, what will be valuable 10, 20, 30 years from now? Although the implosion of the dot-com bubble exposed the silliness of many of the "new economy" assumptions, there is a fundamental shift in the way business is executed. Much of this shift has been caused by information technology permeating industries. In the future, value will be derived from several industries that are unlike those of today.

Many industries will disappear entirely, and many new ones will rocket from nowhere to global prominence in a handful of years. For example, the typewriter industry is all but dead. The data time-share business is virtually gone. The description of value, however, will remain much the same as always. It is still necessary to become and remain profitable, or to add resaleable value over time. The four verities—time, trust, truth, and privacy—will continue to increase in value. The key to investing in verities is to understand the impact of these changes in value on industries.

It is instructive to think through the increase or decrease of these verities in terms of Warren Buffett's investment philosophies. Buffett is probably the world's most successful investor, and has been so for over 45 years. Buffett has consistently stated that he has aimed for 15 percent return per year; in the 30 years ending in 2000, he achieved 22.6 percent. Although he cloaks his investing with candor, we reliably know that he adheres to a few axioms that direct him. The following quotes from *Warren Buffett Speaks,* by Janet Lowe,[1] capture his philosophy:

- Long-term philosophy:
  "If principles can become dated, they are not principles."

- Identify value, not price, and price will generally follow.
  "If the business does well, the stock will generally follow" and "Price is what you pay, value is what you get."

- Identify growth for the future.
  "Of course the investor of today does not profit from yesterday's growth."

- Find franchises—those businesses that are surrounded by a moat and can defend attack.
  "If they say, 'I don't have a Hershey bar, but I have this unmarked chocolate bar that the owner of the place recommends.' If you'll walk across the street for a Hershey bar, or if you will pay a nickel more for a Hershey bar, that is franchise value."

- Find natural monopolies.
  "Newspapers are a marvelous business. It's one of the few businesses that tend toward a natural, limited monopoly . . . show me another business like that—there isn't one."

Invest in Verities   **205**

Buffett's philosophy is equal parts discipline and research. The discipline involves arriving at investing principles, recognizing that principles are unchanging, and staying true to your chosen principles. Then, sift through information on industries and determine which factors exist within which industries. From this research, the next step is to determine which firms are building moats around their business, which firms are tending to natural monopolies.

Examining the change in value of the verities has become a crucial step in discovering the investment quality of an industry. This has always been true, but it was formerly more obvious. Intellectual property products and services do not have the physical characteristics to examine by touch, feel, and observation. It is necessary to evaluate them more by their impact in markets. As new business concepts appear, a key question is, "Does this concept improve time, trust, truth, or privacy?" If this concept does not clearly and simply enhance any one of these four verities, it cannot survive.

Four industries exemplify the changes in value of the verities: electronic bill payment and presentment, newspapers, the packaging industry, and Internet grocers. The arrival of technology in each of these industries has been different, and the resulting change in value of the verities is different. Of these industries, two—EBPP and Internet grocers—are direct descendents of technology. Newspapers are at the ramparts, defending themselves from technology, and packaging is on the verge of adapting a powerful and revolutionary group of technologies.

The most significant change in investing is the proportionate increase in intellectual property over real property and tangible property.

When wealth was determined by land, grain, and timber, investing was much simpler. The storehouse of value represented by property was tangible, visible, and permanent. A property could be seen, inspected, and evaluated according to time-tested rules. The projection of future growth was simpler. The value of land would surely go up. The value of a forest would surely go up. Now wealth is determined by different kinds of property—intellectual property, goodwill, brand equity, and other invisible stores of value. These forms of property are ephemeral, abstract, intangible, and subject to chance.

But value is still determined by supply and demand. Land goes up in value because the supply of land is limited, and population has been growing. Timber has been increasing in value because demand is outstripping supply.

However, what is the supply of intellectual property? The price of telecommunication is tending to zero because the supply of bandwidth is expanding so rapidly. There is no limit on ideas, which implies that intellectual property will continue to expand rapidly. There will continue to be innovation, exponential increases in knowledge, leaps of technology, and dizzying change in the use of information-processing tools. These intangible forms of property will likewise increase exponentially, and the law of supply and demand dictates that increasing supply will produce falling prices. Against this background of value tending to zero, how does an investor find sustaining value? How does an investor run up a down escalator fast enough to stay even, let alone make progress?

Technology is seeping into every industry. This assault by technology causes radical reevaluations of many industries, its customers, and its suppliers. Technology can also cloud the view of an industry, as can be shown with cardboard boxes, newspapers, electronic bill payment and presentment, and groceries.

Technology now exists to enable a cardboard box to become an information appliance. This technology dramatically improves time utilization.

Examine the cardboard box industry. A cardboard box is a very simple, functional product, and would seem to be exempt from the telecommunication and computing revolution. But it is not. The corrugated container industry has continued, for 50 years, to be one of the most accurate barometers of the state of the economy. Nearly every product industry uses cardboard boxes for finished production or customer shipments. As a result, the widely followed boxboard production figures provide a close surrogate for economic activity. Cardboard boxes are a fundamental commodity spanning all industries.

It is now plausible to ask such far-out questions as "What does a cardboard box know?" with a full expectation that the technology exists to record and report exactly what a box knows. Motorola, International Paper, Procter & Gamble, and MIT are collaborating to produce an ink embedded with semiconductors that would be used to print box labels.[2] The semiconductors are activated by radio signals and report data to a radio receiver. This is the same kind of technology that triggers the alarm in bookstores, music stores, and video rental stores if you try to leave without deactivating a radio frequency tag on the book, CD, or videotape. It turns out that the box knows where it is, what time it is, what temperature the contents of the box are, and various other extremely useful supply chain facts. The question for investors is who, exactly, will benefit from talking boxes? Will the cardboard box manufacturers be able to capture this extraordinary value? Will the value accrue to consumer goods firms such as Procter & Gamble, a major investor in one form of talking box technology, or to channel master retailers such as Wal-Mart? Or will this technology be a productivity boost of unheard power for the logistic provider industry, including such major players as UPS, FedEx, and Ryder?

One of the key challenges in manufacturing and selling laundry detergent is producing precisely the correct amount that synchronizes with consumer demand. The ideal is that a box reappears on the retail shelf immediately as soon as the consumer withdraws one from sale. The ultimate supply chain goal is for products to move continuously, smoothly, with the overall principle being "sell one, replace one." When there is no laundry box on a shelf, a consumer who needs detergent will choose an alternative brand or buy the desired box from a competitive retailer. This lost sale is real, but difficult to measure. Stock-outs not only cause lost sales, but also diminish satisfaction that, over time, can erode shopper loyalty. On the other hand, too much inventory causes reduction in sales price to move product, obsolescence, and excess storage and handling costs. As a box moves from production through distribution and then through sales, there are dozens of steps. At each step, uncertainty is introduced into the chain of supply from production through to consumer. And at each step, buffering inventory or remediation processes are built in to deal with the lag in information or to adjust for imprecise information.

A laundry box that can continuously and precisely report its content, location, amount, ownership—and associate that data with a precise time—will revolutionize the extended supply chain of consumer good production and sale. Imprecision is removed, and with it immense amounts of inventory meant to buffer imprecision. Time lag for information is removed and buffering inventories created for time lag are removed. Possibly most important of all, stock-out information is now available in real time. Currently, a stock-out is noticed as a store employee walks the shelves and examines the in-stock positions and reports them. The grossest guesses about the length of time a product is out of stock would then be 24 hours, or longer, depending on the count and inspection of the store staff. With a talking box, an electronic, radio-frequency poll would be programmed to enumerate all boxes that were on the shelf, as well as to report any absences. This high-quality, accurate, and timely data can change the way retail handles in-stock, category management, and resupply.

Talking boxes likely will lead to intense collaboration between a retailer and the manufacturer, since both of these parties will be major beneficiaries of this new source of truth. And it may lead to a Win-Tel monopoly opportunity for the box manufacturer.

Retailer and manufacturer are now motivated to completely cooperate regarding the stock position at the store shelf. With perfect information and no time lag, resupply for the shelf should become the responsibility of the manufacturer. This is the least costly assignment of responsibility since the manufacturer only needs to be expert in the demand patterns, inventory, aging, manufacturing, and raw material sourcing of its handful of products occupying the shelf. A retailer would be tempted not only to retain responsibility for the shelf inventory, but also to reach for responsibility far back in the manufacturing cycle. However, there are far too many products—about 35,000 in a typical Wal-Mart or Kmart—for that assignment of responsibility to work. At the same time, it is in both parties' interest that the greatest amount of soap powder be sold, without ever stocking out, and with minimal inventory supporting the sale. Since a retailer would have to manage all the information for 35,000 products, it is more likely that the precise care needed in a precision supply chain will be provided by the manufacturer who can aggregate information about demand across numerous retailers, and thus has a better chance of precision for a dozen products than a retailer has for 35,000. The manufacturer becomes part merchant; the retailer becomes a realtor.

It is in the best interest, defined as selling the most soap at the highest margin, for a retailer to share its shelf management with the producer. The pervasive information available from a box implies both this division of responsibility and collaboration not yet practiced. Neither manufacturer nor retailer mines value from the truth provided by the box, but from the attendant reduction of time in the supply effort. The box manufacturer, however, may actually mine value directly from the data of the talking box.

The role of the box changes with this kind of technology. A box becomes an intelligent device and provides a fact package with electronic precision. This box is now telling the truth as we have defined it; it is accumulating and reporting information as polled by a radio frequency device. A box manufacturer who owns this technology will likely investigate becoming an information services company. That manufacturer will aspire to create a Win-Tel monopoly modeled after the dominance of Microsoft and Intel in personal computing. The box manufacturer can plausibly consider a role as the Intel of talking boxes, by becoming the sole supplier of semiconductors within box ink. It would further encourage the semiconductors used, and the messaging protocols associated with them, to become a companion to a software message layer for the supply chains of retailers, manufacturers, and distributors.

The following chart demonstrates the contributions to value that talking box technology will have. Such technology will dramatically increase the utilization of time, increase the accuracy and reliability of discrete item data, have little impact on the trust within the system, and potentially decrease the privacy (or corporate secrecy) of the system. From this viewpoint, talking boxes result in a net improvement of these four verities and will be implemented because of the dramatic time improvement potential:

The Verity:	Time	Truth	Trust	Privacy
Value Impact	+	+	0	—

But, will an individual firm in the talking box industry capture the lion's share of the value? Or will large sectors of the economy gain productivity in a manner similar to the improvements wrought by bar-coding? In terms of Buffett's principles, is a firm building a fortress franchise, or is a natural monopoly building in this particular new area of the packaging industry? The industry will grow, since this technology has a powerful impact on time. If there is a dramatic winner, it would be from the "natural monopoly" achieved by owning the language of talking boxes. A software language uniquely shared by all users of a box's information would be subject to the network effect and would then be likely to produce a monopoly.

The electronic bill payment and presentment market represents the effects of the changing value of the verities.

This market is being contested by numerous companies whose heritage ranges from Internet start-up, to post offices, to banks and financial firms. As noted in Chapter 6, electronic bill payment and presentment (EBPP) has gained a very small market share in the United States. As of June 2001, only 100,000 customers have signed up and are actively using this service. Two key problems hinder growth (the market is growing at a high rate, but from a very small base). The first problem is that only a few billing companies have adopted electronic presentment services. An average household processes 14 regularly recurring bills each month. It is estimated that EBPP of 6 of those bills is required for the service to be attractive.

The other, more serious problem is that a majority of Internet users do not trust Internet financial transactions. This particular service has a significant trust barrier to overcome. The changes in the verities produced by this service are:

The Verity:	Time	Truth	Trust	Privacy
Value Impact	+	+	—	—

It is acknowledged this service saves time, and it will provide accurate, comprehensive data for the customer and the financial service. On the other hand, this service faces serious trust and privacy issues.

Eventually, EBPP will overcome the trust and privacy issues, which are recurring problems in all Internet-related financial services. But the state of technology is such that these problems are not likely to be technical issues. Failure to earn trust and breaches of privacy will be process and human behavior issues. Electronic distance magnifies the challenge of achieving trust. For an EBPP service to be trusted, it must provide access by Web, phone, and face. The winning EBPP firms will endow the EBPP service with preexisting trust, and physical presence in markets. This means banks with retail networks, certainly, but also could mean Wal-Mart, Safeway, Gateway, ExxonMobil, or postal services. Any of these companies could partner with trusted financial firms such as Allstate or State Farm.

Trust and privacy issues are so important for electronic financial services that financial services firms cannot afford technical flaws or security breaches. Any breach caused by technology will cancel the goodwill and trust built by hundreds of thousands of flawless transactions. Online financial services will offer greater privacy than existing services to entice consumers to an online product. Currently, in most states, banks own financial data derived from your account and are free to sell this anywhere, or even give it away. Online financial agreements to not sell or use this data without payment or permission will likely occur. This feature would increase financial privacy and might be enough, over time, to engender trust. Because substantial market growth cannot occur without trust, online financial services *will develop* track records of trust. There is no choice or shortcut. Indeed, Epinions.com ratings of EBPP have been uniformly positive, and there have been no reports of fraud or theft of personal data based on the use of the service. Given an increase in privacy, necessary development of trust, and the convenient features of EBPP, I project healthy growth for this market. It will remain stalled, however, until privacy and trust are acknowledged to have been improved.

But who will win? What company will carve out a defensible franchise in this market? Will natural monopolies occur? The service that gains the most billers will have the best chances of winning any network effect monopoly. The current market is so small and fragmented that it is nearly impossible to forecast a franchise.

For many existing industries, new technologies are life-threatening.

There are few industries that are more threatened by the Internet than the newspaper industry. If we can receive news on our Palm Pilots, our cell phones, and our computer monitors, why do we need to read a newspaper?

Newspapers are a significant contributor to the portfolio of Berkshire Hathaway, whose chief executive, Warren Buffett, is certainly among the best-known investors of all time. His investment portfolio includes two major newspapers—the *Buffalo Evening News* and the *Washington Post*. Buffett's Berkshire Hathaway wholly owns the *Evening News* and holds 18 percent of the *Washington Post*. Nevertheless, at the Berkshire Hathaway shareholder's meeting in May 2000, Buffett cast doubt on any newspaper investments in the future due to changing technology and competitive factors.[3] Buffett essentially announced the obvious—the Internet is a major challenge to newspapers.

In the early 1980s, Buffett (as quoted earlier) thought newspapers could become natural, limited monopolies; but he has lost his appetite for newspaper investments.[4] Newspapers have not changed much since then; the overall market for media and news has changed a great deal.

Some 30 percent of revenue of American newspapers is achieved by classified advertising. This particular revenue source is very amenable to the Internet since searching classified ads on the Internet is much quicker than thumbing through pages of newspaper ads. Using the Internet, a person can browse and seek specific ads according to search criteria.

What exactly is a newspaper? At one time, its title well described its function—a paper that presented news. While many readers use a newspaper for news, Internet users find that headline scanning is often more effective and timely on such Internet media as CNN.com. My own habit is to scan the Internet periodically for news headlines, but not to actually click on the stories. I wait until the following day, and read the coverage provided by a newspaper. In part, I do not like reading extensive text on a computer screen; and in part, this is a matter of habit. For many of us, a newspaper is more about its features than its news.

A newspaper is dozens of businesses within the overall banner of the newspaper itself. A good newspaper provides community information, classified ads, sports coverage, special interest coverage, recipes, editorial opinion, and features. A newspaper is entertainment and, in this mode, competes with burgeoning uses of our leisure time. A newspaper is a communication utility and, in this mode, competes with cable television, radio, the Internet, telephony, and other print media. A newspaper is a community bulletin board and, in this mode, competes with the Internet, radio, and cable television. And, finally, a newspaper is a trusted source of fact-packages. This last role will be the sustaining identity for newspapers.

A newspaper provides two utilities: time and truth. While a newspaper may well require an investment of time, most of us who use newspapers have developed a method to minimize the time required to acquire the daily newspaper. Whether it is delivery to the door or driveway, or purchase at the box at a restaurant, train station, or building newsstand, acquiring a newspaper does not consume a noticeable amount of time. Once the newspaper is in hand, it is a stored utility. It can be used anywhere, and it is easy to re-sume a particular article or column. The stored utility of news-paper is different from and better than most of its competitive media. You cannot store a radio announcement and usually do not tape the television news for later watching (although this is a dis-tinct possibility with Tivo). Increasingly, the utility of a newspaper is that it presents compact fact-packages that save time as well as provide truth.

The truth is elusive and hard to pin down on the Internet. Matt Drudge, one of the best known of the Internet "journalists" strives only for an accuracy rate of 80 percent.[5] Indeed, he was quoted by David T. Z. Mindich in *The Wall Street Journal*, "We have entered an era vibrating with the din of small voices. I envision a future where there'll be 300 million reporters, where anyone from any-where can report for any reason." This din will not make the voices any more true than not. It is the disciplined editorial process that makes truth—the corroboration of story, fact checking, editorial review, and confirmation by more than one source. For example, re-cently on a flight from Ottawa, Canada, to Toronto, Canada, I sat beside a woman who insisted that 40 degrees below zero was not the same temperature on both the Celsius and Fahrenheit scales. When I tried to show her the math and the factual information behind that observation, she put the question to a vote of fellow passengers. Voting for factual information has no impact on its fac-tual nature. Three hundred million voices creating a din about factual material does not make the material any more factual.

Indeed, the din of 300 million voices will create more demand for fine journalism. Who could possibly have the time to assimi-late the reporting of 300 million writers, observers, or whatever we will call these voices?

Over time, technology has allowed the newspaper industry to add more and more features to its founding utility as a news chan-nel. Newsprint has become cheaper, sourcing feature material has become more economical, and consolidation and syndication have provided cost-effective means of producing the various informa-tion bundles that compose a modern newspaper. At the same time, the speed and facility of telecommunications has eroded the utility of a newspaper for being the source of breaking news. This erosion began with the widespread use of radio in the 1920s and 1930s and continues today. To the electronic immediacy of a radio report has been added the rich texture of video images. However, as shown with the Patriot missiles and other news coverage, immediacy and verisimilitude are not truth.

Newspapers survived the inception and growth of both radio and television despite prognostications of demise. Will they survive the Internet? The decline of newspaper circulation predates the inception of the Internet. Circulation has been declining in France since 1965, in Britain since 1985, and in Germany and the United States since 1990. In all cases, these dates are quite a bit earlier than the beginning of the Internet, as recognized with the creation of the Mosaic browser at the University of Illinois in 1993. The decline in circulation has more to do with the competition for time than with the efficacy of newspapers for presenting news.

The newspaper industry is being dissolved by the technology represented by the Internet weather, the abbreviation for a surrounding atmosphere of data, images, and communication. However, a newspaper, as currently organized, is one of the most important custodians of a truthful process. It is this process that provides the value for the newspaper industry, certainly not an ability to flash news spontaneously through a print media. The value realized by the newspaper industry will be in this ownership of fact-packages, and the rather slower, more deliberate, more reasoned presentation of information than electronic media. Electronic media will titillate, the newspaper will satiate. A confetti rain of data cannot be useful since assimilation takes too much time. Staccato headlines, 15-second sound bites, talking heads, and dramatic video cannot sustain our interest over the longer term—we need more information than that. The value impact for newspapers is shown in the following chart:

The Verity:	Time	Truth	Trust	Privacy
Value Impact	0	+	+	0

The verity scorecard for the newspaper industry is favorable. A well-edited newspaper will produce consistently higher quality information than most other sources. Their track record and procedures have been instituted and practiced over decades to produce this quality each day. I have rated no time improvement, and no substantial time loss for the use of the newspaper, primarily because of the portability feature of a paper. A newspaper does not compromise privacy of an individual reader, but it does not add any privacy either.

Newspapers are being dissolved and rebundled, but that is not new and did not begin with the Internet. The industry is devolving to provide verities: truth from a trusted source. As opposed to the cardboard box industry, the value of truth is clear. The competitive advantage that newspapers have is information processes that are more truthful than those of the Internet. These processes will provide sustaining value for newspapers.

The online grocery market faces difficult trust challenges.

Trust is among the most elusive of the verities because you cannot assert trust; someone must reflect it as a measure of actions, words, and authenticity. No person, no company can assert trust; the words "Trust me" automatically create suspicion. Trust is a hard-earned reflection of a history of performance, communication, and interaction.

Trust has also played a key role in the demise of Internet-enabled grocery shopping and its home delivery. The delivery of groceries to someone's home, over an extended period of time is an activity that requires the implicit trust of the delivery agent. After all, that agent often must enter the home to deliver the groceries. Home delivery of groceries is an anachronism, not a vibrant core business for the future. Home delivery occurred in small villages and in city neighborhoods when the delivery agent was usually a teenage boy well known to the grocer and many in the neighborhood. The boy was both trusted and known to the customer, or was vouched for by the grocer and other people in the community who knew him. This service was an adjunct to the core business of grocery take-with by consumers.

Now, no matter what technology is involved, the repetitive entry to someone's home requires trust. The delivery person must be well paid to value the job and to have good judgment. The recurring delivery of groceries to someone's home requires trusted behavior, time and again, for years. Just one incident of rudeness, anger, hygiene, or spoiled food can lose that trust forever. In this context, the odds are against a spotless, continuing capability for trusted delivery:

The Verity:	Time	Truth	Trust	Privacy
Value Impact	+	0	—	—

The verity scorecard for online groceries is negative. Even the core selling value of this service—time improvement—can be difficult to achieve. Depending on the shopper, a missed item can force that shopper to travel to the grocery store. Each time this occurs, that week's online groceries become more of a hassle than a convenience. There are shoppers for whom saving time spent traveling to a grocery store outweighs other possibly negative attributes of online shopping. However, I suspect this market is small, and actually changes with stages of life.

Summary

With the proportionate increase of intellectual property and intangible property in relation to real property, it has become more difficult to project future growth in value. The dot-com boom and bust demonstrated that old values such as earnings, balance sheets, and customer retention are still applicable. However, the economics of information technology can seem counterintuitive, and thereby difficult to comprehend and adhere to.

For the future, it will be necessary to assess the relative increase or decrease in the value of time, trust, truth, and privacy by a product, market, or industry. A simple means of quickly assessing this increase would be to construct a verities scorecard and think through relative increases or decreases of these four verities.

This process is most valuable to eliminate investment candidates. If a proposed concept, product, or technology does not increase any of the verities, and reduces one or more, it cannot succeed.

Like any investment screening concept, examining the value of the verities does not guarantee the success of a venture. Even a solid venture that enhances all verities cannot succeed without competent management, product, financing, and sustaining vigor of its personnel.

CHAPTER 13

Navigating the Internet Weather

A silent and near total conquest of our lives and our societies is occurring. It is the conquest by information. An atmosphere of data has silently enveloped us; we have surrendered to this conquest without even knowing it has occurred. Now, and forever in the future, we will be experiencing a gentle, incessant, and increasing pressure from knowledge.

The impact on our society and business is profound. The conquest by information—the Internet weather—has enhanced old values. This atmosphere of data has increased the value of time, trust, truth, and privacy. To navigate the Internet weather, we will change our behavior; business will continually accelerate and modify its organizations to become faster.

> Navigating the Internet weather means balancing continuous change and constant truths.

Truth, in the form of reliable information, will become more valuable. It is rare that raw data, alone, provide workable knowledge. Take, for example, the question, "How many Internet users are there?" There is no number that can be relied on, since users come and go. An accurate, reliable, and continually updated answer to this question would be almost priceless. Even more valuable would be accurate, reliable, and updated answers about new users versus users leaving the Internet. This fundamental, factual question about the number of Internet users is next to impossible to answer, despite the existence of excellent, electronic sources for data. The challenge is too many sources with too much data. Having such reliable information could have prevented the wasting of millions of dollars based on flawed information concerning Internet growth, user profiles, and user habits. There is just too much such data; the data are often contradictory and the effort to sift this data takes too much time.

For individuals, the burying of factual information beneath huge accumulations of data means adapting an informed skepticism about raw data. For example, live video, which is a form of raw data, often does not present factual events. Such slices of action can misrepresent a greater sweep of events. As the line between reality and virtual reality blurs, the challenge of assessing the factual content of video will only increase. A necessary companion to informed skepticism is the use of trusted sources that forge data into information using editing processes or peer review. Business in particular can be buried in data and must adapt new techniques for assessing data, finding truth in data, and validating that truth. Some of these new techniques involve displaying factual attributes of data in entirely different ways.

It will become common to buy privacy. This trend already exists, as evidenced by the various kinds of caller-ID and call-blocking services available from telephone companies. Well-respected financial firms such as American Express are beginning to offer "Anonymity Cards" that promise any financial transactions on the card will remain forever secret. Decrease of privacy is an inevitable outcome of pervasive communication. But the cure lies in the technology of privacy products and security. This heightened awareness and renewed value of privacy will become a key consumer concern. The current freedom that many firms have to sell personal data will decrease as consumers resign from electronic tracking and data collection. Businesses must be alert to the emergence of the sovereign consumer, who has recaptured privacy and will expect to negotiate specific uses of personal data. Those consumers who reclaim privacy will be the most affluent and savvy. Similarly, businesses face increasing privacy challenges. A business must be concerned not only about individual employee and consumer privacy, but about the privacy and secrecy of the enterprise itself. This becomes complex since any enterprise involves the interactions of numerous individuals. Business must establish what is essential to remain private, what may be tended with benign neglect, and what should be actively publicized.

Time has become the greatest common divisor of individual and business activity. All markets are at least footraces; some markets are races for the moon as shown with the race to command third generation wireless information services (3G Wireless). The reward for becoming the standard provider for 3G is hundreds of billions of dollars. There exists a race between AOL and Microsoft concerning control of the face of the Internet. The features of AOL such as Instant Messenger form networked communities on the Internet that are more difficult for a competitor such as Microsoft's MSN to penetrate. Microsoft's expanding Internet services linked to new versions of Explorer make Microsoft's services less attractive to AOL users. This race between these titans can be likened to the race between the Soviet Union and the United States to go to the moon. Microsoft and AOL are plausibly racing to command consumer access to the Internet.

For an individual, the acceleration of work means that work activities spill into all other places and times. Firms, on the other hand, must optimize the use of concerted time, and this is particularly difficult to plan, measure, and control. The concerted use of time by hundreds of individuals cannot be monitored easily. It is not obvious and it is difficult to visualize. It is therefore difficult to predesign organizations for speed. While some measures of time exist, such as labor hours per car, they have a tendency to be dated, and focus on costs rather than on the concerted use of time. What has occurred is that the fastest firms share a type of organization bound by open information sharing, decision-democracy and weblike decision-making structures. I have called this kind of organization principled agility.

Of the verities, the most difficult to possess is trust. The challenge for firms is that most technology provides electronic distance between people and decreases trust. No technology can duplicate the empathy of a person. For a business to earn trust takes time and there are no shortcuts. It is a stepwise acquisition that takes consistent, honest, authentic behavior over time. For some industries, personal touch remains critical, and can be a key differentiator.

This surrounding atmosphere of raw data and incipient knowledge is an unprecedented historical phenomenon. The control and acquisition of knowledge has been one of the key political and economic engines of the world to date. But here we are now, with knowledge tossed out like confetti at a wedding. We open our pockets and shake loose knowledge, that in past centuries nations would have warred for.

This is important because an individual can know things formerly not possible except for institutions and firms. Expertise and access to data used to be expensive and controlled. Now, with information democracy, an individual has a broad reach of capability. With electronic communication, an individual can broadcast to the entire Internet. So individuals are now better positioned to compete in tasks that formerly only larger organizations could have performed.

Because individuals can know things as never before, they can do things as never before. This is being recognized by firms by dispersing information and authority to individuals, making them both more powerful and more sovereign. This provides much greater leverage and better results for a firm.

Technology provides abundance, but abundance veils value. Technology has become a cornucopia for material goods. Food, clothing, appliances are all cheaper in real-dollar terms than 20 years ago.[1] Some appliances, such as washing machines, have average prices that are the same in nonadjusted dollar terms as 20 years ago.

This abundance pressures prices downward. The abundance of intellectual property and knowledge products confounds the value investor. However, a strategy is emerging to invest in verities: Invest in the increasing value of time, trust, truth, and privacy. If a firm is investing in capabilities, then the impact of the new capabilities should be compared with changes in relative value of time, trust, truth, and privacy. For individuals making investments in new markets or new equities, a quick check of a verity scorecard can eliminate hopeless investments. Many e-procurement ventures have not been able to overcome concerns about individual firm privacy and thereby gain the trust of the users. A good example of this was Whirlpool's investment in Brandwise.com, meant to be a trusted consumer market for appliances. The fact that Whirlpool was the major investor and founder of this site automatically compromised its consumer objectivity. Despite efforts to build Chinese walls and to make recommendations of competitive product, Brandwise.com was not able to overcome consumer suspicion and lack of trust. Whirlpool eventually wrote off a $10 million investment, as estimated by Nicholas Heymann, an analyst at Prudential Securities.[2]

This surrounding atmosphere of data has, relatively speaking, popped out of nowhere. Its birth can be dated either 1989, with the invention of the World Wide Web, or 1993, with the invention of the first Web browser. This handful of years compares to thousands of years of tiny improvements in information access and information democracy. The difference in length of time is the difference between the age of a fruit fly and the age of a giant sequoia. This phenomenon is so new that our behaviors, our society, our government, and our businesses are still adjusting. It is so new that the profound and subtle forces of advancing technology are just beginning to mold society, and there will be tectonic shifts as society adjusts.

But it is early. It is just the horizon of opportunity. Understanding the counterintuitive impacts of technology on value and on the verities will position individuals and firms to far surpass competition.

Individuals will be sovereign, but will work anytime, anyplace.

Given the disproportionate reward for being first, and the punishment for being second—the first loser—knowledge workers must produce more work than their competitors in the same fixed number of days. We are tempted, sometimes even required, to work *anytime*. Since information necessary for the execution of work is nearly ubiquitous, we actually can work *anywhere*. As information is available to us at our son's soccer tournament, our daughter's baseball tournament, we are tempted to work and gain the small advantage that use of time provides. These demands on the use of time rapidly inflate the value of the fixed supply.

Therefore, it is imperative to use this time well. Part of this use is to realize that communication demands time, but communication is not a substitute for thinking. At a certain point, there are diminishing returns. And to be effective, an individual must be able to think, but how can anyone think if that individual is turned into a marionette by the electronic strings of communication? Does anyone, no matter how busy, need a pager, cell phone, personal digital assistant with wireless e-mail, and Instant Messenger? It pays to become silent from time to time. The productivity of an hour of uninterrupted concentration cannot be achieved while being beeped, pulled, rung, flashed, and e-mailed incessantly.

Beginning with the ability to perform work at home according to individual convenience, work is being released from any single place, and from a defined and repeated schedule. This release is facilitated by technology, which increases the freedom of an individual, but also increases responsibility and risk. The release provides more sovereignty to an individual, almost regardless of desire for such sovereignty. So an individual must assess his product—the career—in terms of sustaining value. An individual must assess what he brings to a firm. At the same time, an individual must understand how her product—her reputation, her brand, her truthful information—is further developed by associating with a firm.

To be successful, an individual must position himself for productivity and sovereignty and ask these questions: Am I a trusted source of knowledge? Am I a unique source of something? Do I enhance time for others? Do I enhance privacy? Am I a trusted confidant of a customer? Does a firm increase one or more of these values for me?

Answering these questions is the first step in preparation for sovereignty. This sovereignty may or may not include becoming an independent contractor. But fast firms need their people to take information, make decisions, and keep running. Fast firms—in knowledge markets the only surviving firms are fast—cannot be as paternal as was formerly the standard practice. Fast firms must adapt Darwinism of the swift and produce work on time, rather than perfectly.

> **The increasing value of the verities will change the way firms organize, the way they make decisions, and the way they interact with their customers.**

Since firms are collections of individuals, the challenges of adapting to the Internet weather are multiplied. Each individual within a firm requires privacy. Each customer demands increasing privacy. Organizing for speed involves linking hundreds of people and motivating them to keep pace. Processing ever-increasing data and presenting it for decision is a challenge of reliability and then privacy, should the processed information provide competitive advantage. Finally, despite the increase in pace of business, there are no shortcuts in achieving trust with customers. These forces are contradictory, especially in that trust and truth consume time.

> **Time is the most important of the verities.**

Speed is the singular competitive advantage for the future. Entirely new industries have been created in the past decade. eBay provides an example of a firm's creating an industry, and conquering it, within three years. This pace is required for survival because many of these markets will be won by serial monopolists. In these markets, there is only fast and first.

In this kind of market, time and the use of time in an organization are magnified. As firms have been born and raced to victory or burned through their capital, principled agility has emerged as a style of organization. This style is typified by a focus on using less time, on sharing open communications, huddling frequently to converge to an objective, and pushing decisions out and down among team members. For this organization, on time is better than perfect.

There are many examples of principled agility, including the development of the Internet and the development of open-source software code. An agile organization uses less time. Using less time is enabled by faster communication that results in faster adaptation, that in turn results in faster wins.

Principled agility will be the organizing style for business in the future. Agility is not chaos; it is voluntary association to achieve an objective. This form of organization is gaining power within the software and information technology industry. These organizations will be more associations than employer-employee relationships.

Principled agility seems very strange, and is not comfortable for employees who have spent decades with firms. However, the trends are indisputable. The reasons for firms to have permanent employees are decreasing. Outsourcing services are increasing in breadth, spreading from information technology to accounting, to finance, to human resources functions, to logistics functions, as a few examples. Drug firms are even outsourcing basic pharmaceutical research. Alternative pension arrangements such as 401(k) plans, deferred compensation plans, and stock options have become portable. In short, services that could only be provided by an employee, are now widely available under contract. The Cunningham Motor company is an example of a start-up car manufacturer that intends to never have more than a few dozen employees. All other functions will be partnered for, allied with, or contracted out.

There is decreasing need for a physical place of work, and technology makes it possible to work anywhere. It is increasingly difficult for a skill to survive for a generation, and that means reskilling, but also usually means contracting the skills. Software skills have lasted only a short time, such as ability in COBOL, Ashton-Tate's DB2, even the original Microsoft DOS. Auto mechanics rarely need to know carburetion or know how to adjust timing—technology has replaced these formerly fundamental repair skills. The certainty associated with being an employee cannot endure and has not endured. The average person already changes employers 11 times throughout a worklife.

Is principled agility good? That is the same as asking whether the weather is good. We cannot control the weather; we must adjust to whatever the weather brings us. No individual or firm can control the forces that are causing principled agility. These forces are not good or bad; they are neutral. It is imperative for every firm to recognize these forces and organize for speed.

How does truth affect decisions?

The past decade has seen an explosion of information. As data become free, voluminous, and ubiquitous, what becomes scarce? When we have data free, in any volume, anywhere, what is crowded out? The answer is that truth is crowded out; it is truth that becomes scarce.

What is truth? In this book, I am not talking about the eternal verity: Truth. I am focusing on truthful processes—that produce reliable, reproducible observations or that submit statements, based on data, to verification. Two time-tested processes produce the truthful process I am referring to: journalism and the scientific process. These processes produce more truthful, reliable assemblies of data into information. However, both processes consume precious time. Thus a conflict: The cost of time is increasing and the volume of data to be refined is also increasing. These combine to increase the scarcity and value of truthful information, and such information is the keystone of knowledge.

A key challenge is that electronic data wear the clothing of electronic authenticity. In many cases, data are nothing more than factoids—observations wearing the clothing of fact. Raw data and fleeting images are not truth. They are to truth what a pixel is to a painting. Given the sheer volume of electronic information and images, we will begin to treasure the "true" sources such as *The Wall Street Journal*—the only newspaper able to charge for its on-line edition. We will hoard these sources, and return to them first for the truthful information we need.

Making good decisions requires sound, reliable, consistent information that is free from bias. Technology can help us attain bias-free information by distilling fact-packages. This will require relying on metadata and visual display techniques that will allow us to comprehend data faster and more reliably.

Each firm should also institute a form of peer review to debate the most important data. When the CIA and the intelligence community prepare the National Intelligence Estimates, two viewpoints are always presented and defended prior to approval of what subsequently becomes the final document. A sound debate in this instance exposes flaws in data, in logic, and possibly in conclusion. This kind of debate, say a red team and a green team assigned opposing viewpoints, would make the transformation of data into knowledge more reliable. This is particularly true of data used for market projections, new products, and competitive intelligence. Such information should be actively debated. These are areas subject to expert bias and other illusions of the mind and are too important to rely on semiprocessed or unprocessed information.

Trust is the most difficult to achieve.

Truthful processes are necessary, but are not sufficient for trust.

Of all the verities, the most difficult to achieve is trust. Truth, time, and privacy can be purchased and managed by individual effort. Trust, on the other hand, cannot be purchased, asserted, borrowed, or improved by individual effort. Trust is perceived and is a measure of numerous interactions over time. Two Chicago-based retailers, Sears and Montgomery Ward provide cases in point. Both firms were founded before 1890, and both survived two world wars and the depression. Sears has built trust through such products as Kenmore, the DieHard (the only branded battery with consumer recognition), and Craftsman tools. Despite more than a century of retail revolutions, Sears still owns a reservoir of consumer trust. Montgomery Ward lost this trust and finally liquidated in 2000, after two decades of gradual demise.

Many Internet-enabled ventures, such as Value America.com, have underestimated the difficulty of achieving consumer trust. Trust is the "touch" part of customer relationships, and no amount of software, technology, data mining, or algorithms can replace a person's empathy. In particular, online grocers have been faced with a double trust challenge—that of selecting perishables for someone else, and of consistently and courteously entering someone's home. Online bill presentment and payment, which powerfully increases convenience and lowers costs, has stalled because many consumers do not trust electronic intermediary services despite a truly admirable record of online security.

To achieve trust, even in our technological industries, there are no shortcuts. Trust requires time; consistent, honest information; authenticity; and intimacy. These things have not changed—their execution has. It is tempting to abbreviate these disciplined and perpetual behaviors, but beware of electronic distance from customers. Electronic distance may cause current customers to divorce you rather than embrace you and may cause prospective customers just to click on by.

Privacy is the emerging key issue.

Privacy is emerging as the key consumer and individual issue when dealing with Internet transactions. Communication is a form of intrusion, and there will be a perpetual leapfrog of communication intrusion technology followed closely by the technology of increasing privacy. The correlation of data will continue and only become faster. So, privacy, its loss and recovery, will forevermore be a key consumer issue. Privacy as a feature will rank with security, reliability, proximity, ease of use, and utility.

As evidence of this, privacy products are rapidly emerging, and they will change consumer marketing. Ponoi, Inc., a New York City start-up, is offering software that will allow anonymous access to a firm's Internet services.[3] A consumer may browse and buy without any information link, but can choose what information can be shared or purchased—one of the first steps to the sovereign consumer. RSA Security Systems is collaborating with Microsoft in the creation of a smart card linked to MS Passport in which all information is encrypted and stored on the smart card. Access to this information can only occur by the user, and no information is stored on a server or PC. This is yet another building block for private use of the Internet. As these products gain market share—beginning with the savvy and the affluent—a truly empowered consumer will emerge. This kind of consumer will negotiate terms of communication with companies, and demand value in return for the use of data, identity, or relationship. These consumers will be served by agents of privacy and will present new challenges when approaching and enticing them to use a company's products or services.

Empowered consumers are active rather than passive consumers. This kind of consumer permits and pursues, and thereby becomes a much more productive customer. An active consumer is a motivated buyer. It is critical for firms to develop and promote privacy to entice this group of savvy affluent customers.

In the Internet weather, the only safe assumption for a firm is that any and all electronic information is accessible by the public. While this is draconian, this assumption launches a pursuit of privacy, and frames the value of privacy itself. Privacy technologies and privacy procedures that can be instituted, but to protect the privacy, or secrecy, of any and all electronic information is cost prohibitive. Technology has taken away privacy in a wholesale manner, and technology can give privacy back piecemeal. Privacy products and procedures add cost and time to information flow. The technology of privacy, based on strong encryption, is excellent. Breaches of privacy are usually associated with breaches of process or laxity of process, rather than breaches of technology. The expense of instituting privacy technology and process means such processes must be instituted carefully and selectively. A strategy for privacy then, revolves around three kinds of activities:

- A vaultlike secrecy surrounding certain precious information, art, and practice.
- Benign neglect of certain classes of information.
- Active publicity and promotion of certain classes of information. This can also be termed preemptive publicity.

Vaultlike secrecy and security of records must be enforced in any transactions with individuals, whether these transactions be for sales or personnel purposes. Privacy and security are the key barriers for financial services firms to overcome prior to their propagation of web-based services. Certain classes of innovation and intellectual property are worthy of privacy protection and the pursuit of patent. Trade secrets can range from recipes, to procedures, to the superior practice of craft, to highly advanced mathematical formulas. Ironically, both patentable innovation and trade secrets are often best protected by preemptive publicity. Innovative intellectual property surrounding patents should be publicized as prior art to protect the patentable innovation or the trade secret. This is a strategy of scorching the earth around innovation so that a competitor cannot patent away a process already in use.

Making the Choices: Investing

With the proportionate increase of intellectual property and intangible property in relation to real property, it has become increasingly difficult to project future growth in value. The dot-com boom and bust demonstrated that old values such as earnings, balance sheets, and customer retention are still applicable. However, the economics of information technology can seem counterintuitive, and thereby difficult to comprehend and adhere to. It is counterintuitive that electronic data would become valueless. Electronic data wears the clothing of authenticity; the problem of overwhelming volume is not, at first, understood.

For the future, it is necessary to assess the relative increase or decrease in the values of time, trust, truth, and privacy in regard to a product, market, or industry. As shown in Chapter 12, constructing a verities scorecard is a simple way to quickly assess and think through relative increases or decreases of these four verities. This process is most valuable to eliminate investment candidates and to assist arriving at sound business decisions. If a proposed concept, product, or technology does not increase any of the verities, and reduces one or more, it cannot succeed.

Like any investment screening concept, examining the value of the verities does not guarantee the success of a venture. Even a solid venture that enhances all verities cannot succeed without competent management, product, financing, and the sustaining vigor of its personnel.

Navigating the Internet weather, then, means examining the changing values of time, trust, truth, and privacy. Sustaining value can only come by examining future business, technology, and markets and increasing these verities in products, services, and individual careers.

As we become surrounded by an atmosphere of data, communications, and technology, the sustaining value will be found, not in those changing technologies, but in those things that do not change. Our desire for privacy will not change. Our finite amount of time given for each day, week, month, or year cannot change. Our desire for truthful and trusted interaction will not change. In fact, given the surrounding surfeit of data, images, and the intrusion of technology into our daily lives, each of these verities—time, truth, trust, and privacy—will greatly increase in value. These verities are becoming scarce, and scarcity creates value.

Notes

Chapter 1

1. Neil Gross, The Earth Will Don an Electronic Skin, *Business Week,* August 30, 1999.
2. Joseph Coleman, Matsushita Exhibits House of Future, *Chicago Tribune,* May 8, 1999.
3. *Data Does Not Exist to Conclusively Say How Well Patriot Performed*—Report by General Accounting Office, September 1992, B-250335.
4. Stan Liebowitz and Stephen E. Margolis, *Winners, Losers and Microsoft,* The Independence Institute, Oakland, CA, 1999.
5. Christa Degnan, Novell's Schmidt Outlines "Digital Me" Technology, *PC Week Online,* March 22, 1999.
6. Daniel J. Boorstin, *The Discoverers,* Random House, New York, 1983.

Chapter 2

1. Carl Shapiro and Hal Varian, *Information Rules,* Harvard Business School Press, Boston, 1999.
2. Carl Shapiro and Hal Varian, *Information Rules,* Harvard Business School Press, Boston, 1999.
3. Larry Downes and Chunka Mui, *Unleashing the Killer App: Digital Strategies for Market Dominance,* Harvard Business School Press, 1998.
4. Carl Shapiro and Hal Varian, *Information Rules,* Harvard Business School Press, Boston, 1999.
5. Stan Liebowitz and Stephen E. Margolis, *Winners, Losers and Microsoft,* The Independence Institute, Oakland, CA, 1999.

Chapter 3

1. Lou Dolinar, *The Automated Home,* www.future.Newsday.com.
2. Daniel Poole, *What Jane Austen Ate and Charles Dickens Knew,* Simon & Shuster, New York, 1993.
3. John Markoff, FCC Mulls Wider Commercial Use of Radical Radio Technology, *New York Times,* December 21, 1998.

4. Don Clark, Secrecy Service for the Internet Is to Go Online, *Wall Street Journal*, December 13, 1999.

5. James Evans, American Express Launches New Online Security, IDG News Service, reported in *PC World*, September 7, 2000.

6. Seybold Report on Publishing Sytems, Vol 25, No 21; and IBM.com /products/security.

7. Hewlett Packard web site: HP.com.

8. Christa Degnan, Novell's Schmidt Outlines "Digital Me" Technology, *PC Week Online*, March 22, 1999.

Chapter 4

1. Keith Alexander, Study: Jet Lag May Cause Memory Loss, *The Washington Post*, June 24, 2001.

2. Larry Downes and Chunka Mui, *Unleashing the Killer App: Digital Strategies for Market Dominance*, Harvard Business School Press, 1998.

3. *Actuality Systems to Demonstrate "Walk-Around" Prototype Volumetric 3-D Display at SID 2001;* Business Wire, June 4, 2001, as reported http://biz.yahoo.com.

Chapter 5

1. *How Much Information?* Research project at the School of Information Management and Systems at the University of California at Berkeley. Principal Researchers Peter Lyman and Hal Varian; Research Assistants James Dunn, Aleksey Strygin, Kirsten Swearingen. First release October 18, 2000, http://www.sims.berkeley.edu/how-much-info.

2. Household Goods Carrier Bureau of the American Movers Conference, 1611 Duke Street, Alexandria, Virginia.

3. John Boddie, *Waste Management*, Software Development, July 1999.

4. Baruch Fischhoff, Paul Slovic, and Sarah Lichtenstein, Knowing with Certainty: The Appropriateness of Extreme Confidence, *Journal of Experimental Psychology: Human Perception and Performance*, 3, 552–564 (1977).

5. Clayton M. Christensen, *The Innovators Dilemma*, HarperCollins, 1997.

6. http://www.urbanlegends.com/driving-barefoot.

7. Massimo Piattelli-Palmarini, *Inevitable Illusions,* John Wiley & Sons, New York, 1994.

8. Thomas C. Greene, Feds Use biometrics against Super Bowl fans, *The Register*.co.uk, February 1, 2001 and Viisage.com web site.

9. Robert Hercz, Mega-Network: Strength in Numbers, *New York Times*, September 28, 2000.

10. Hacker Journalism, *The Economist*, December 4, 1999.

11. Alfred North Whitehead and Bertrand Russell, *Principia Mathematica*, Cambridge University Press, London, 1910, 1927, 1962, and 1997.

12. Douglas R. Hofstadter, *Godel, Escher, Bach: An Eternal Golden Braid,* Basic Books, New York, 1979.

Chapter 6

1. Jakob Nielsen's Alertbox, *Reputation Managers are Happening,* Useit.com, September 5, 1999.
2. Debra Sparks, The Global Rush to Find Partners, *Business Week,* October 25, 1999.
3. *About London Taxis,* londontaxi.co.uk.
4. *Examinations of Broker-Dealer Offering Online Trading: Summary of Findings and Recommendations.* Staff Report, Office Compliance and Examinations, U.S. Securities and Exchange Commission, January 25, 2001.
5. Mindy Charski, Online Bill Paying Is Still Waiting for the Big Payoff, *US News Online,* March 6, 2000.
6. James Van Dyke, *Overhyped and Misunderstood: The Fraud of Online Fraud,* Jupiter Research Service, April 10, 2001.
7. Mindy Charski, Online Bill Paying Is Still Waiting for the Big Payoff, *US News Online,* March 6, 2000.
8. Natasha Haubold, *USPS Puts Stamp on Online Billing,* CNN.com, April 10, 2000.
9. ePost.com web site.
10. Rick Brooks, Postal Service Defends Talks with FedEx, Insisting Antitrust Worry Is Unfounded, *Wall Street Journal,* September 20, 2000.
11. Susan Solomon, *Just Like a Woman to Want Better Content,* Clickz.com, March 13, 2001.

Chapter 7

1. Peter Drucker, Managing Knowledge Means Managing Oneself, *Leader to Leader,* Spring 2000.
2. Contingent and Alternative Employment Arrangements, Report 900, U.S. Department of Labor, Bureau of Labor Statistics, February 1999.
3. Sloan Wilson, *The Man in the Gray Flannel Suit,* Simon & Shuster, New York, 1955.
4. Robert Manor, Accenture's IPO Estimated Value Near $1.8 Billion, *Chicago Tribune,* June 12, 2001.
5. Ken Gross, An American Racer Comes Back, *Forbes,* April 30, 2001.

Chapter 8

1. Sam Walton and John Huey, *Sam Walton: Made in America: My Story,* Bantam Books, 1993.
2. Troy Wolverton, eBay to receive $1.2 million in dispute settlement, CNET News.com, July 27, 2000.

3. John Wilke, Justice Department Probes eBay's Ban on "Bots," *Wall Street Journal,* February 4, 2001.

4. Dan Goodin, Microsoft e-mails focus on DR-DOS threat, CNET News.com, April 28, 1999.

5. Richard Dawkins, *The Selfish Gene,* second edition, Oxford University Press, Oxford, 1989.

6. Mark Pendergrast, *For God, Country & Coca-Cola,* second edition, Basic Books, 2000.

7. Hau Lee, *New Supply Chain Business Models—The Opportunities and Challenges,* Achieving Supply Chain Excellence Through Technology, Ascet vol. 3, May 1, 2001, Montgomery Research.

Chapter 9

1. Robert L. Simison, Toyota Develops Way to Make a Car within Five Days of Customer Order, *Wall Street Journal,* August 8, 1999.

2. Brian Milligan, Push Is on to Shorten Leadtimes for Custom Car Orders, *Purchasing,* October 7, 1999.

3. *Renault Aims to Cut Delivery Times to Two Weeks by 2001 Through Reorganization of Its Distribution System* reported in Automotive Intelligence, April 25, 1999.

4. Jim Mateja, Choice—If Perhaps Unlikely—Ideas, *Chicago Tribune,* November 20, 1999.

5. Fara Warner and Rick Brooks, Ford Is Hiring UPS to Track Vehicles As They Move from Factories to Dealers, *Wall Street Journal,* February 2, 2000.

Chapter 10

1. Massimo Piattelli-Palmarini, *Inevitable Illusions,* John Wiley & Sons, New York, 1994.

2. Jeremy Wagstaff, New Services Search for a More Visual Way to Navigate the Web, *Wall Street Journal,* March 5, 2001.

3. http://www.Bioscope.org; http://www.Digitalfrog.com.

4. Robert Lemos, *Digital Paper Turns a New Page,* ZDNET News, October 12, 1999.

Chapter 11

1. http:/www.eBay.com.

2. Norman Augustine, *Augustine's Laws,* 6th Edition, American Institute of Aeronautics, June 1997.

3. Stacy Collett, SAP: Whirlpool's Rush to Go Live Led to Shipping Snafus, *Computerworld,* November 4, 1999.

4. Charles Piller, Complexity, Bugs converge to upset supply software, *The Los Angeles Times,* April 9, 2001.

5. Clifford Stoll, *The Cuckoo's Egg,* Doubleday, New York, 1989.

6. Survey of Software, *The Economist,* April 14, 2001.

7. Frederick P. Brooks Jr., *The Mythical Man Month,* Addison Wesley, New York, 1995.

8. *Wallace, Henry A.,* Encyclopedia Britannica.

Chapter 12

1. Janet Lowe, *Warren Buffett Speaks,* John Wiley & Sons, New York, 1997.

2. International Paper and Motorola Introduce "Smart Packaging" press release of Motorola, Inc. and International Paper, April 13, 2000.

3. "Newspapers are a category that is very threatened by the Internet." Warren Buffett addressing Berkshire Hathaway annual meeting, as quoted in the *Wall Street Journal, Heard on the Street—Newspapers Find it Difficult to Click with the New Economy* by Suzanne McGee and Matthew Rose, July 11, 2000.

4. Newspapers and the Internet, *The Economist,* July 17, 1999.

5. David T. Z. Mindich, The New New Journalism, *Wall Street Journal,* July 15, 1999.

Chapter 13

1. Stephen Moore and Julian L. Simon, *The Greatest Century That Ever Was: 25 Miraculous Trends of the Past 100 Years,* Policy Analysis No. 364, December 15, 1999, The Cato Institute.

2. Amy Kover, Why Brandwise Was Foolish: Whirlpool thought it had a great e-commerce idea. It just didn't expect the execution to be so hard. And now the site is toast, *Fortune,* November 13, 2000.

3. Christina Lourosa-Ricardo, Privacy. Technology Has Taken Away Privacy. Now it promises to give it back, *Wall Street Journal,* June 25, 2001.

Index